Fire Under
the Snow
Palden Gyatso

THE DALAI LAMA

FOREWORD

I am happy to learn that Vanessa Walker has written a book on the Tibetans in exile. It is my hope that her book will inform more people about the issues and challenges that confront the Tibetan community in exile. I also hope that through her book a greater number of people will come to appreciate the consistent efforts by the Tibetans in exile to preserve Tibet's spiritual and cultural heritage.

I believe this book constitutes a fresh look at the Tibetan community. She explores traditional Tibetan institutions like the Nechung state oracle based in Dharamsala, which was relocated to South India ever since we came into exile in 1959. The author revisits our efforts to democratize our administration, and the debate generated in our community by my Middle Way Approach of not seeking independence for Tibet but for Tibet to operate within the overall framework of a confident, stable and prosperous People's Republic of China.

However, the main merit of this book is its narrative on the concern of the generation of young Tibetans who were either born in exile or who recently fled Tibet. I believe a frank and open discussion of the problems and challenges faced by this new generation of Tibetan exiles is critical in our common attempt to help this generation of Tibetans to live fulfilled and productive lives.

This book also highlights the lives of many young Tibetans who have dedicated themselves to the cause of Tibet, and on whose shoulders will fall the responsibility of ensuring the happiness of the Tibetan people and the preservation and promotion of Tibet's rich spiritual heritage and its distinct culture.

The Dalai Lama
October 3, 2005

Vanessa Walker worked as a journalist at *The Australian* newspaper, as their social affairs, film and, most recently, religious affairs writer. For the past decade she has studied Tibetan Buddhism, undertaking various retreats in Asia. She is a frequent traveller to India.

In 2004 Vanessa resigned from her position at *The Australian* to live in the small Indian town of McLeod Ganj, the epicentre of Tibetan Buddhism and the home of the Dalai Lama. She now lives and works between Sydney, Australia and her hometown of Auckland, New Zealand, where she and her Tibetan husband are raising their newborn baby.

MANTRAS &
MISDEMEANOURS

An accidental love story

Vanessa Walker

ALLEN&UNWIN

Some of the people in this book have had their names changed and their stories merged or separated to protect their identities.

The phonetic and most common
spellings of Tibetan words have been used

First published in 2006

Allen & Unwin
83 Alexander Street
Crows Nest NSW 2065
Australia
Phone: (61 2) 8425 0100
Fax: (61 2) 9906 2218
Email: info@allenandunwin.com
Web: www.allenandunwin.com

National Library of Australia
Cataloguing-in-Publication entry:

Walker, Vanessa.
    Mantras and misdemeanours: an accidental love story.

    ISBN 1 74114 583 X.

    1. Walker, Vanessa—Travel—India—Himachal Pradesh.
    2. Himachal Pradesh (India)—Description and travel.
    3. Himachal Pradesh (India)—Biography. I. Title.

954.52053092

Text design by Zöe Sadokierski
Set in 11.5/16 pt Fournier MT by Bookhouse, Sydney
Printed in Australia by McPherson's Printing Group

10 9 8 7 6 5 4 3 2 1

To the Tibetan people, whose freedom will benefit us all.
To my husband, whom I love.
And to our precious child.

CONTENTS

Preface: Ants Across the World *ix*

1   My Himalayan Obsession *1*

2   Moving On Up *22*

3   When First We Meet *42*

4   Choying's Escape *71*

5   The Devil in the Detail *80*

6   Divine Governance *100*

7   Of Marriage and Money *107*

8   A Belly Full *125*

9   Mela Madness *146*

10 Beauty and the Brutality *157*

11 Realised Women *175*

12 Buddha Air *196*

13 Respite in a Maroon-Coloured World *211*

14 The Looming End *238*

15 The Reluctant Rinpoche and Long Goodbyes *260*

Epilogue *288*

Acknowledgments *292*

References *294*

PREFACE

ANTS ACROSS
THE WORLD

There I was, stuck in a dank hotel in Boudhanath, in Nepal's Kathmandu Valley, simultaneously getting changed and brushing my teeth, when I looked out the window and saw a bank of moon-faced boys in monk's maroon, their arms casually wrapped around each other, staring back at me. They were unabashedly curious, not at my semi-nakedness—that didn't seem to occur to them. No, nine pairs of dark, slanted almond eyes were glued to the electric toothbrush vibrating in my mouth. Realising they were caught, they turned and ran away, all gangly legs and flying robes, back into the colourful concrete building from whence they came. I was twenty-four, newly aware of the catastrophe that had befallen Tibet. This country, whose very name is resonant with a quality both magical and tragic, was split open for the world to see after the brutal invasion by communist China in the 1950s. Thousands of Tibetans poured out into India, following their leader, the person who means everything to them, His Holiness the Fourteenth Dalai Lama.

During that first trip I went to the famous stupa at Boudhanath, a magnet for newly escaped Tibetans. Circling round and round the stupa, the stringed beads known as *malas* in hand, whispering mantras under their breath, I was taken by the way Tibetans appeared strong-minded yet kind and calm. I was intrigued at how they preserved this demeanour in the face of the horrors that had been perpetrated against them. That is what led me to Tibetan Buddhism.

Back in Australia, I fell in to the Buddhist world, going to my local centre, doing retreats and taking initiations. I found my lama and travelled to Tibet on pilgrimage, a trip that only increased my fascination with the Tibetan people. In Lhasa I joined great streams of Tibetans circumambulating the sacred Jokhang Temple, falling in next to an ambling elderly nomad who had taken his best friend—a goat on a leash, its snout covered with a pink-crocheted mouthguard—on the circumambulation in an attempt to rid it of its bad karma so it could climb higher up the species ladder to be reborn a human.

Like many western Buddhists I also gravitated to India. In Bodhgaya, where Buddha gained enlightenment under the Bodhi tree, I did as my lama asked and finished tens of thousands of prostrations. My neighbour was a skinny smiling monk who had spent the previous three years prostrating his way across Tibet, down through Nepal and into India. Using broken English and sign language he told me he planned to prostrate all the way to America in the name of world peace.

Like thousands of Buddhists I was drawn time and time again to the Himalayan hometown of the fourteenth Dalai Lama, McLeod Ganj. It is a modern-day frontier town filled with indigenous Gaddi Indians, entrepreneurial Kashmiris, exiled

Tibetans, and Buddhists from around the globe, all of whom have come to seek the special wisdom of the Tibetan people. With its lamas and stupas and pilgrims, McLeod Ganj is the epicentre of Tibetan Buddhism. And it was there, over successive visits, that I had my Buddhist coming of age. I was able to be absorbed in an overtly spiritual world; I met and got advice from some of the wonderful old-time lamas who had made the place their home, and I had the privilege of joining thousands of people from around the world absorbing the enlightening teachings of the Dalai Lama. If there is one certainty in my life it is what Buddhism and my teachers have taught, and continue to teach, me. It is my guiding principle and has benefited me enormously. I have found a certain freedom in realising that it is not external circumstances that really shape me, but my response to them. I realise I have no control over the former, but every opportunity to grow mentally and spiritually through the latter.

However, somewhere along the way I also got the blinkers ripped off. Maybe it was an experience with a monk during one of my early visits to McLeod Ganj. I thought his keenness to get to know me was all about friendship and a shared interest in Buddhism—but was disabused of this in an embarrassing denouement that included an expensive piece of jewellery and a declaration of love. Looking back I can see his desperation to leave the poverty of India and make a life for himself in the west—a desire shared by a large number of young Tibetans in robes and lay clothes alike. The episode made me realise my own naivety and how important it was to understand who Tibetans were, not who I wanted them to be.

As a perennially curious person, I also couldn't fail to notice over the years the extraordinary number of western women, with all the accoutrements of sanity—careers, social lives, beliefs, intelligence—who would take the trip to McLeod Ganj and return with a Tibetan husband, sometimes within weeks. What was it about this place and these people? My own close friend wrenched herself away from a happy, secure relationship in Australia to learn Tibetan for a year and by the time I caught up with her in McLeod Ganj ten months later had succumbed to the charms of a former monk with dodgy English. I heard of a Canadian lawyer who visited for a week, met a Tibetan man and had her nuptials just days later. Was there something in the water?

When I wasn't visiting India, I had a parallel life in Sydney as a news journalist for the *Australian* newspaper. During my final year at the paper I was religious affairs correspondent and it was during this time that Buddhism became the fastest growing religion in Australia. In what were to be my last months on the newspaper we ran a front-page story about a rogue National Australia Bank foreign-exchange dealer who was being blamed for recklessly losing more than three million dollars in unauthorised transactions. Pursued by the media and facing a possible jail sentence, he told anybody who would listen that he was a Buddhist and would welcome the chance of being incarcerated so that he could teach other prisoners about Buddhism. He pointed people towards a website he ambitiously called 'Enlightened Buddha'. Yet in news reports at least, he seemed to have no insight into his own actions—just the bright face of a new convert. No wonder people have a mixed-up idea of just what Buddhism is.

I have found that because Buddhism focuses on personal transformation, in fact is more a psychology than a religion, it is hard for the public to grasp what exactly it involves—and even harder to know what people mean when they call themselves Buddhist. Are they really practising a 2500-year-old tradition of training the mind in altruism, or are they subscribing to the kind of catch-all lite Buddhism that simply pieces together some feel-good beliefs?

All these complexities were swirling around in my mind when I first had the idea of writing a book about what lies at the heart of Tibetan Buddhism and how its beliefs play out in the lives of its most devoted adherents. Daubed in mysticism because of their history, Tibetans have the benefit and the burden of being an especially loved people—a people who hail from the mythical Shangri-la. Did their wholesale adoption of Buddhism truly make them more pious, or was that simply what the world wanted to believe?

I knew I would have to be honest about whatever I found in McLeod Ganj. This is difficult when you believe in the doctrine and is made more treacherous because of the delicate situation the Tibetan people in exile are in politically, culturally and spiritually. But in this my guide has been the Dalai Lama himself, who never, in my opinion, shies away from the truth.

Tibetans have now been in exile for forty-five years. The Tibetan diaspora originates in Nepal and India and reaches into America, Europe and the Pacific. It is as the revered monk

Padmasambhava foretold back in the days of Tibet's isolation in the eighth century: 'When the iron bird flies and horses run on wheels, the Tibetan people will be scattered like ants across the world, and the dharma will come to the land of the red man.'

In exile Tibetan society has been forced to come to terms with more wildly divergent ways of living than they chose in their years of seclusion. For the first time they have a secular media, democracy, materialism, degeneration of their spiritual beliefs and thriving differences about which direction their society should take. But in the face of rapid modernisation, they have also resolutely kept their most unique traditions. The democratic government consults a divine oracle for matters of the utmost state importance and, against all the odds, pursues a nonviolent Buddhist agenda. Their parliament reserves seats for representatives of the four main schools of Buddhism, their monasteries flourish, the majority of people believe wholeheartedly in the truth of miracles, and the Dalai Lama remains the central figure in their daily life.

Given their history, today's Tibetans in exile have inherited a unique and rich culture yet one that is now at a crossroads. Despite severe psychological trauma and great poverty from China's occupation, during which 1.2 million Tibetans are believed to have perished, the government-in-exile germinated; orphanages, schools, monasteries and businesses were established. Through sheer hard work and determination the second generation helped build one of the most productive and successful exile communities in the world. They developed universal free education for Tibetans in exile, healthcare systems and thriving astro-medical institutes.

Now the third generation of Tibetans are growing up torn between their rich culture and the seductions of the west. There is a growing debate about whether nonviolence is working, or whether their country as they know it is lost to them forever. It would be an untold tragedy for both Tibetans and the rest of the world if they lost not only their homeland, but the spirituality which has sustained them so strongly in their trials, for they are at heart a wonderful and unique people with much to offer us all.

What I have written is of course in no way definitive or universal, it is only my perception of events and my musings on what I found. It is simply the true story of what happened to me. I went to McLeod Ganj and I drank that special water. This is what happened...

1

MY HIMALAYAN
OBSESSION

If I wasn't so self-conscious, and if the jeep I am travelling in wasn't hurtling so fast along the rutted, twisting mountain road that I have to constantly swallow the bile rising in my throat, I would purr the name out loud. *Dharamsala.*

I am a little bit in love with Dharamsala on the craggy spine of the Dhauladar mountain range in northern India, but I am totally smitten with the smaller town that hangs just above it and goes by the name of McLeod Ganj. Before each visit, and this would be my fourth, I spend hours and hours recollecting the scene at the dusty bus station that doubles as McLeod Ganj's town square. I can see the languid Tibetan boys appraising new arrivals as they step down from the buses that make the twelve-hour stomach-churning trip from Delhi, the canny stall owners surveying the passing throng for monied tourists, beeping buses blindly reversing as three-wheeled tuk-tuks whip past their rear, all watched over by crusty chai-shop patrons. Groups of unsure maroon-clad monks huddle together like private-school boarders on day passes and western women, their sunburned shoulders revealing idle bra straps, remain deep in conversation oblivious to the need for modesty. A venerable old lama quietly strolls through the square and a frisson of acknowledgment passes through the crowd. For an instant all activity pauses. The same look flitters across the faces of the monks, the traders, the backpackers and the ardent Buddhist students. It is as if everyone is suddenly reminded why we have ended up in this strange, distant, Himalayan town.

My fascination with McLeod Ganj began about nine years ago. Soon after I became interested in Tibetan Buddhism I heard of a place in India so filled with Tibetan exiles it was known as Little Lhasa. However, for much of their history the Tibetan people, through a unique geography and their own wilful disposition, lived in virtual isolation on the world's highest plateau. Dwarfed by a majestic landscape of snowy mountains, raging icy rivers and endless plains, they were, until the introduction of Buddhism in the late seventh century, a race of nomads and subsistence farmers with a reputation as formidable people with an appetite for war.

Buddhism was introduced into the country during the reign of King Songtsen Gampo and is traced to the influence of his two Buddhist wives, Wen Chang, a Chinese princess, and Bhrikuti, a Nepalese aristocrat. It is no small indication of the Tibetan people's ensuing passion for the teachings of Buddha that, after coming into contact with his philosophy, they sent emissaries to India to invite their neighbour's most renowned teachers, including Atisha and Padmasambhava, to come and foster this religion in their homeland.

Their determination was profound. They collected the vast canon of the Buddha's teachings and throughout the next centuries studied, cultivated and integrated virtually every facet of its wisdom into the fabric of their society. By the time the world came to hear of them—through the writings of explorers like Hsien-Tsang, Alexandra David-Neel and Lama Anagarika Govinda—Buddhism had long since been superseded by Islam and Hinduism in India, its land of origin.

But in the Land of Snows, Tibetans had incubated a unique, highly refined style of Buddhism and produced an exceptional number of spiritually accomplished beings. There were reports of alchemy, of flying tantric yogis, of lamas—or teachers—who manifested in multiple bodies, of naked ascetics who could melt snow through the power of their minds, of people who could forgo food and live off the essence of air, and of deceased beings whose bodies did not decompose. Great monastic universities were built to study Buddha's teachings and whole social and financial systems evolved to support spiritual practitioners.

Tibetan lamas wrote detailed treatises on subjects such as how to develop altruistic qualities, the process by which faculties dissolve during the death process, what happens during the *bardo*—the state between death and a new life. They also elucidated the matrix of karma—what actions led to what result in future lifetimes. It was Tibetans who reignited the practice of tantra, the secret fast-track route to enlightenment. Rumor had it that some of Buddhism's most renowned lamas, those trusted and experienced enough to pass on the Buddha's teachings, chose to live in McLeod Ganj. On the rare occasions they came to

Australia, their visits required months of preparation by dozens of volunteers. Students would take time off work, put their lives on hold and join crowds in big auditoriums to hear them speak. In McLeod Ganj it was possible to simply pop in for a visit with a lama. Ask for some advice. Their existence was woven into daily life; one even baked cakes for a local restaurant. They had all chosen to live in McLeod Ganj because it was the home of the most important figure in Tibetan Buddhism, Tenzin Gyatso, the Dalai Lama, whose consciousness Tibetans trace back through thirteen previous lifetimes. I soon deduced that because there are only seven roads in McLeod Ganj, all of which splay out from the bus station, no matter where you stood you could say, 'The Dalai Lama lives just down the road.' I decided that was just what I wanted to do.

I was hardly alone in my ambition. Since 1959, when the Dalai Lama first sought refuge in India after the Chinese invaded Tibet, more than 100 000 Tibetans have followed in his footsteps. At first it was an assortment of nomads, aristocrats, serfs and farmers who decamped with the Dalai Lama, then—as Red Guards rampaged through Tibet's 10 000 monasteries—came great floods of monks and nuns. In the 1970s, as the Chinese Communist Party's Cultural Revolution slowly died, newly free political prisoners picked their way over the Himalayas, the very idea of McLeod Ganj pushing their battered limbs through treacherous snowy passes. The monk Palden Gyatso, a Chinese political prisoner for more than thirty years, wrote in his memoir *Fire Under the Snow*: 'In prison we had uttered the name Dharamsala in hushed tones, developing a sense of reverence and awe for the place.' It takes up to a month of walking from Tibet to the freedom of neighbouring Nepal and from there refugees must get to India. Over forty-five years came the fierce warriors of Kham in the southeast, the nomads of Amdo in the northeast, and the people of U-Tsang including the traders, the Lhasa sophisticates and the inhabitants of western Tibet's most remote plains. Each refugee arrived with one precious wish—to meet the Dalai Lama. For Christians, the nearest equivalent would be a pilgrimage across continents to see the second coming of Jesus Christ.

Afterwards, the new refugees dispersed to camps or settlements around the subcontinent. Some went overseas. But over the years a number from each region chose to stay, forming a Himalayan microcosm of the country they had left behind, albeit the 2.5 million square kilometres of Tibet squeezed into a town the size of a single Sydney suburb, home to around 9000 people.

The jeep begins its steep ascent into the narrow clay roads that lead to the centre of town. It is close to 6 a.m. and the driver turns off the headlights, leaving the dawn light to show the way. Small, hunched-over figures start to emerge from the alleyways and houses that line the road. As we come closer, the single figures meet up, merging into small groups, while still others silently spill out of the maze of steps that interlace the terraced houses. I realise they are the old people of Tibet, the ones who lived the first part of their lives on the isolated plains of the world's highest plateau with the Dalai Lama in the Potala Palace and then travelled across the Himalayas, spending their last years in longing for their homeland.

As their creased faces slide past my window, I see their mouths repeating the mantra *Om Mani Padme Hum*, at once a praise to Buddha and a plea to be released from suffering. By their sides, fingers are slowly clicking off bead after bead on their *malas*. They are patiently observing one of Tibet's most enduring customs: the dawn circumambulation of the local monastery. To walk clockwise in a *kora* around the perimeter of a monastery, with all its Buddhist texts and statues inside, is believed to bring blessings. It is considered one of the greatest compensations of life in exile that these old people have the privilege of circling the *Tsuglag Khang* or Central Cathedral. Attached to the Central Cathedral is the Dalai Lama's residence—and inside, His Holiness, a living buddha, might be home.

Sensing we are about to come into the most built-up part of town, the driver, naturally, puts his foot down. We fly through the vegetable market. A cow chewing a plastic bag pauses to look up. An Indian man shakes his head behind a carefully arranged display of emaciated cauliflowers and wizened grapes. I notice one of the town bakeries is already open. Outside, a hungry traveller with a huge backpack is about to bite into a cream-covered jam donut. This must be his first visit. I turn my head just in time to catch his look of horror as the taste of bicarbonate of soda explodes in his mouth. Throughout India, I've learned, every donut looks good and tastes bad. We drive past the jumble of concrete and wooden shops that slope into one another. There are bulk-food shops, their entrances clogged with sacks of grain, beans, flour and butter; postcard stands with colourful pictures of almost every lama and deity known to Buddhists; gaudy money-change vendors, and a multitude of higgledy-piggledy shops featuring hanging bundles of chips, chewing tobacco and one-rupee sachets of shampoo. A tangle of electrical wires cascade in between each dwelling, connecting them up to the leaning wooden power lines on which families of monkeys sit and pick their lice.

As we pull into the bus station, which at this time of the morning is locked in a jumble of shouting Indians and manoeu-vring buses, I see my two friends, Kate and Tenzin, anxiously scanning the vehicles. I am so pleased to see them. I met Kate, an Australian, on a three-month retreat in Kathmandu, and over the years we have travelled through Nepal, India and once to Tibet on a five-week pilgrimage we dubbed 'the great unwashed' because neither of us saw soap or a shower for the entire journey. She and Tenzin are not only my good friends, they also represent a side of my life that often doesn't get much of an airing back in Sydney. At home much of my life is shaped around my job as a newspaper journalist. That means long hours, lots of fun, but lately a tendency to judge quickly and speak harshly. Although I visit my local Buddhist centre every week, I have to be content with my beliefs bubbling away below the surface—or sometimes completely submerged—while I get on with the business of chasing and shaping news. With Kate our beliefs are the foundation of our friendship. Here, half a world away from Sydney, seeing her feels like coming home. There is a great relief in spending time with like-minded people. Kate has spent many years in Asia and laughs off the frustrations and peculiarities of living in India while finding herself increasingly disconcerted by her visits back home—at designer clothes, silicone breasts and $100 haircuts.

Kate has just started working as a program coordinator at Tushita Meditation Centre, which is nestled in the deodar forests above McLeod Ganj. Tenzin, a nomad from the Amdo region of Tibet, arrived in India in 1996 to seek better opportunities. Like many Tibetans, he is good-looking with beautiful tapered eyes set in a broad face; unusually, though, he has a great dark mop of barely controllable long, ringleted hair. His body is smooth, brown and compact, while Kate is freckly and statuesque. She literally looks twice his size. They have been together for three years and are soon to be married; Tenzin, who has never seen a plane and whose mother has never laid eyes on a foreigner, is to fly with Kate to Australia to start a new life. There he expects to quickly become a millionaire.

'Nessie-la,' Tenzin says, *la* being a term of endearment in Tibetan. We are now sitting in one of the rooftop restaurants, the majestic Himalayas surrounding us, with a big plate of juicy steamed *momos* in front of us. I am in a one-person race to devour the small dumplings before the milky juice from the cheese and potato stuffing dribbles down my chin.

'I know of a man who once wrote a book.'

I smile, ready for a nice tale. I've just told them I'm on a two-week reconnaissance mission to see whether I should come and live here and try to write a book. Four previous visits have taught me this is a story waiting to be told: McLeod Ganj is a town at the centre of a flourishing religion, a place where east meets west; it is full of vice and virtue, true eccentrics and strong faith mixed up with breathtaking scams. On the other hand, I could simply come to study Buddhist philosophy. Tenzin's memory has, however, been sparked by the book idea.

'He thought it was really good so he printed it himself. Then he gave everyone a free copy. He would walk around town handing it out to anyone he met.'

Very nice, these Tibetans, I think to myself.

'Oh it was terrible. So embarrassing. It didn't make any sense. I don't think a lot of it was true. Oooh Nessie, many mistakes.'

I sense doom.

'One day he came down to the square and one of those mangy dogs ran up to him, really excited, jumping around.'

Kate, I notice, has a big oblivious smile on her face.

'Nessie, someone had tied the book to the dog's tail. Even worse it had been wandering all over town. Everybody knew. Now he can't go out because he is so embarrassed. His wife was so ashamed she left him. Now no one ever sees him around.'

I'm mortified. I'm used to the niceties of literary criticism. But Tenzin is just warming to his theme. He tells us about a foreigner who wrote a book on the sexual practices of Tibetans. Since then she has been alternately shunned and pelted with stones when she appears in public.

I reassure myself that Tenzin is something of a rogue storyteller. Encouraged by Kate and me to tell us about his old life as a nomad, he once told us that a man who lived in his village was so humiliated when he farted in public that he committed suicide.

The next morning I decide to join the old people on their circumambulation. I pass a big crowd gathered around a sheet on the ground covered with shoes. An Indian stallholder is trying to control a flock of Tibetans, as a mass of hands pick through his stock and voices try to bargain with him for what look like an assortment of used velcro sandals and trekking boots. The shoes look suspiciously like they have been divested from a shipment of aid.

I pass a man who has been sleeping in a corrugated-iron and tarpaulin humpy on the edge of the marketplace for twenty years. Sometimes, according to local gossip, he grows his hair long and wild and then simply shaves it all off again. He used to sleep on a rubbish heap but years ago someone made him a bed and put some sheet iron over his head. People say that he goes to the toilet at the same times each day, once at 11 a.m. and once in the evening. The rest of the time he sits on his rotten mattress not talking to anyone, putting up with the two stray dogs who consider the end of his bed their territory. All day he watches the world go by through slit eyes while raising a rolled-up cigarette to his mouth, puffing mechanically. Apart from his ablutions, the up, down, in, out of smoking is his only activity. No one knows if he is a holy man or a crazy man.

I have made it out of town and am heading into the open space of Dalai Lama-Gi Road, taking in the wide-open green plains of the Kangra Valley. 'Good. Morning. Madam,' a voice calls out. It's delivered in the kind of breathless staccato one speed walker would use overtaking another. I look around. Then down. It's a beggar perched on a makeshift skateboard on the side of the road. He's got a torso but his legs are stumps that end above the knee. He's not going anywhere; I am the only one speeding past. That, I take it, is the point. 'OK, all right,' I say under my breath as I bend to drop some rupees on his plate. Payment for the social commentary on his disadvantage. He nods at me approvingly as I head off at a much slower pace.

My eyes are staring down at the road as I puff up the hill. Suddenly I stop. Two feet are planted in front of me. My eyes travel up spindly legs, a dirty dress and layers of filth-encrusted rags. A snotty baby is attached to the hip. There is an outstretched palm. A grimy neck and on top a face, matted hair, sly eyes and a big white smile. I'm caught. It's Sunita, and we are a dysfunctional couple. 'You are back,' she says, registering immense satisfaction. I met Sunita the first time I came to McLeod Ganj. She is one of the thirty or so Indian beggars who have made the place their home. She must have taken me for a soft touch straight away. Not only did I give her an extraordinary amount of rupees and fetch some old clothes for her, but I also asked her about an earlier small snotty baby in her arms. Thereafter whenever I see her—and I soon realised McLeod Ganj is a very small town—she positively beams with delight. Each time I dig into my pocket because now we have a connection. Sometimes she makes a cursory effort to ask how I am but we both know she doesn't care. I am a human ATM. Once, I decided I was giving money to her out of guilt and I would stop until I could do it out of generosity. But she followed me all around town pointing at the child, mimicking bringing food to her mouth, whining, 'Didi, Didi,'—sister, sister. She waited while I ducked into shops, followed two steps behind me wherever I went and lurked around anyone I stopped to say hello to on the street. Finally, for all the wrong reasons, I gave up. 'Hello Sunita,' I say and in an instant work out how I'll approach it this time. I reach into my pocket and pay up. I'm beginning to remember India's particular brand of charm and frustration.

Walking the *kora* clears my head and I decide that if I am going to risk being stoned or shunned by writing a book it may as well be with one of my teachers—Tenzin Palmo's—blessing. In the 1960s Tenzin Palmo became one of the first foreign women— she is British—to take robes in the Tibetan tradition, shaving her head and changing her name from Diane Perry. She is also famous for spending twelve years of her life undertaking the spiritual challenge of a solitary retreat in a cave in Dalhousie, India, as told in Vicki MacKenzie's book *Cave in the Snow*. When I first met her about ten years ago she was touring Australia teaching, and while I was impressed by her words, at that stage I wanted all teachers to be like the Tibetan lamas I knew, full of warmth and personal magnetism. I found her forthrightness slightly confronting, her manner a bit aloof.

Over the years unexpected opportunities to get to know her kept cropping up. I was invited to a small dinner with her at an acquaintance's house; I interviewed her for a story I wrote for the *Australian*; and I kept encountering her whenever I was in India. I slowly came to see that there is something more important in a teacher than blinding charisma. Like many people whose focus is to benefit others, she has the ability to pull off the seemingly impossible. For many years she has been living in, and working from, a modest office and residence in the Kangra Valley below McLeod Ganj, at Tashi Jong Monastery. There she is trying to address one of the greatest imbalances in Tibetan Buddhism, namely the place of nuns. In old Tibet, monasteries were the most important institutions in society. Tibetans embraced Buddhism so strongly that, before the Chinese arrived, one in ten people was a monk or a nun. One of the first things Tibetans did when they went into exile was to rebuild their three largest monasteries so monks could immediately continue their study. But they took old habits with them. The nuns were forgotten. Many faded into obscurity and poverty, their traditions dying with them. Tenzin Palmo hasn't recoiled from pointing this out to the Tibetan hierarchy, including the Dalai Lama. Despite her pennilessness she has gathered sponsors from all around the world to build a nunnery, called Dongyu Gatsal Ling, for the new generation of young nuns living in exile. There she is resurrecting a lineage of female *togden-mas*, or yoginis, that has almost been lost. Only one elderly male practitioner who knows the secret teachings is still alive and he is passing on the knowledge to the nuns before he dies.

A few days later I make the bone-chattering ride down the mountain to Tenzin Palmo's residence. Tashi Jong Monastery is set in a verdant valley and is a testament to the Tibetan love of colour. Backed by green hills, dotted with women in saris scything the swaying grass, the *gompa*, or temple, is carefully painted in delicate yellow, red, blue, white and green with a gold pagoda roof. Flowering bushes in intense reds and greens bloom in small perfect patches of grass.

Below the *gompa* are plain workrooms where artisans make traditional woodprints for prayer flags, trinkets and handwoven rugs. Out of their windows they look down on Tenzin Palmo's modest office.

Tenzin Palmo has always reminded me of a little sparrow. She is slight, with a tiny shaved head, intense eyes and a stoop. You can't fail to notice that she has oversized hands that she loves to gesticulate with. What I once thought was coolness I now see as a kind of pragmatic passion to achieve her tasks. Over the years she has been generous when I have needed advice, wrathful when I've been remiss and warm when I've needed encouragement. We spend half an hour discussing my idea and I am relieved when she says writing a book sounds like a constructive and fun project, especially if it avoids the pitfalls of being too cynical or too rosy-eyed in its view of Tibetans and Buddhism. She also suggests a back-up to check whether I have the karma to pull it off. Why don't I visit Kamtrul Rinpoche? Rinpoche is the honorific title given to reincarnates of accomplished spiritual masters known as *Bodhisattvas*. Tibetan Buddhists believe that within the range of humanity there exist people who have made such significant progress on the spiritual path that they have enough mastery over the death process to choose their next incarnation. *Bodhisattvas* are propelled through their reincarnations by the singular wish to benefit other people and show them how to be liberated from suffering.

In old Tibet, and more surreptitiously today, Tibetans specialise in sending out envoys to locate the reincarnation of a *Bodhisattva*. Typically, within a couple of years of their passing, search parties made up of teachers, students and close associates would set out from the place the person died, disguised as travelling peasants. Using auspicious signs, such as reading visions in the waters of the sacred lake Lhamo Lhatso, and in some cases directions from the previous incarnation, these groups would scour the Tibetan plateau looking for children who seemed specially gifted or unusual, or whose birth was accompanied by miraculous signs such as rainbows or spontaneous melodies playing out across the valley. Visiting the homes of each candidate's family, they would present themselves as wandering peasants and clandestinely perform memory tests to see if the child could pick out any of their previous incarnation's possessions or recognise those in the search party they had been close to in their former life. Usually, once the search party ascertained they had the right child, he or she would be installed in a monastery to continue their education so they could fulfil their mission of helping humanity. These people, like Kamtrul Rinpoche, are given the honorific title and, like the days of old, they are still held in the highest esteem in Tibetan society. Kamtrul Rinpoche is also renowned for his ability to divine the future using a system of throwing dice, called *mos*. *Mos* work by making clear to those able to read them what obstacles or bad karma, if any, an individual has in their way. Most often the advice given to remove the obstacles consists of performing offerings, prayers or commissioning a *thangka* of a deity in order to elicit their attention and assistance. The Dalai Lama is said to consult this lama—he also happens to be Hollywood action man Steven Seagal's teacher.

Back in McLeod Ganj I realise that if I am to visit Kamtrul Rinpoche I will need a translator. I put the word out, and my request spreads in great ripples, mouth to ear, through the maze of personal connections around town, until it alights on Thuten. He is fluent in English, Tibetan and, most importantly, lama protocol. Someone gives me his phone number and I invite him over to discuss my plan. I also want to find out what an educated man makes of Tibet's predicament.

That night he comes to my room and, over chai—cardamom tea—on my balcony, he tells me the time has come to get Tibet back by force. Like many Tibetans he has wearied of perpetual life in exile, the dream of a free Tibet receding like the tide. But, unusually among Tibetans, he has decided that if it takes violence to get Tibet back then so be it. In the darkness Thuten's intensity reminds me that although most Tibetans are nonviolent, they have a fire that rages deep in their bellies. They are, after all, a people who before Buddhism concentrated all their energy into creating formidable armies in a country that was on an almost permanent war footing.

That night, as I lie in my bed in my rented concrete box, the sounds of my neighbour's family—children laughing, adults talking in that particular Tibetan cadence, the clang of cheap metal cooking pans—filter into my silent dark room. All the noise makes me feel inexplicably lonely. All the audits I usually do to count my good fortune—my beliefs, career, good friends, freedom to travel—suddenly feel empty compared to the clatter of family life. I fall asleep and dream of chasing naughty children round and round a playground.

The next morning I meet a different Thuten. Despite the heat he looks as though he has just stepped out from under a cool shower. He ushers me judiciously along the uneven streets. As we approach Kamtrul Rinpoche's house, a large concrete two-storey maroon building that Tibetans refer to as a palace, he begins to hunch his shoulders, dropping his voice to a whisper. By the time we come to the large wooden door, perspiration is leaking off his forehead and he is leaning over in a semi-bow. Any lingering revolutionary zeal has gone, he is the ultimate disciple. He knocks to no avail. Then his eyes fall on the electric bell. He presses it gently then almost jumps of out his skin when it lets out a loud, assertive buzz. The door opens and in the darkness I can just make out the robes of a monk. As he steps into the light a serene face and soft fluid movements come into focus. He beckons us inside and there, waiting patiently, is Kamtrul Rinpoche.

Rinpoche looks about sixty. It isn't until I glance at him shuffling away after our visit that I realise he is perhaps eighty or ninety years old. Grey bristles sprout through his shaven head and ancient thick-rimmed glasses take up much of his face. One lens is so thick, there appears to be only a brown blob floating behind it. After prostrating and offering the traditional white scarf known as a *kharta*, which symbolises purity, we settle on the ground in front of Rinpoche and Thuten translates my first question. As Thuten tells Rinpoche I am contemplating two things, the first being moving to India to study Buddhist philosophy, Rinpoche slowly picks up two *mo*, or die, in a small metal container and shakes them, studying the way they fall.

Then Thuten translates. 'For you, it is too early. You must be careful not to mimic others. You need to develop real faith, from your heart, in the dharma. You will know when the time is right.' Rinpoche waits patiently, the monk who opened the door downstairs looks away. My heart sinks, I feel laid bare. Exposed. I am a spiritual fraud. Worse, I may have to slouch back to Sydney and resume ordinary life.

'Rinpoche, Vanessa would like to come to India to write a book about McLeod Ganj and Tibetans in exile. Is this possible?' Rinpoche throws the *mo*, peering through his glasses at the combination of symbols. This time he speaks quickly in Tibetan. The monk leans forward. 'Come. You are educated, you can write, you can tell the story of the Tibetan people. This will be beneficial. There are no obstacles, this you can start at any time. For you, to come and write this book will be the real practice of dharma.'

Dharma is the name for the entire range of Buddha's teachings. It implies the thoughts and actions one must cultivate in order to advance along the spiritual path. Difficulties and challenges are considered the very best conditions in which to apply dharma because it's then that you get to confront your own self-interest. Only, right now I don't think of that. I hear only the welcome of the word 'Come'.

Emboldened by his answer I slot in an extra question, borne of my thoughts from last night. I am thirty-four and have been single for many years. This has given me the freedom to travel and explore at will yet, I wonder, if this continues, will I ever have children? As Thuten translates I am struck by the enormity of the question and the burden of knowing the answer. Rinpoche throws the *mo* and then looks directly at me. Thuten translates: 'If you want children it is beneficial to commission a *thangka*'—a fabric painting—of Green Tara.' Then he says he must go—he is meeting the Dalai Lama. I thank him, push forward my offering of green grapes and back out the door, bowing behind Thuten.

Tara is among the most loved of the Buddhist deities and is said to be the mother of all the Buddhas. She was born from a tear that fell down the cheek of Chenrezig, the God of Compassion, after his realisation that sentient beings were locked into a cycle of suffering. Her image represents enlightened activity. I am vaguely mindful that Tara has a reputation for fast action. Most Buddhas are shown in the lotus position; Green Tara, however, is depicted with her right leg outstretched. So eager is she to help sentient beings, she is already moving in the direction of her supplicants. Commissioning a *thangka* is said to bring merit to a person as it brings another image of a buddha into the world, and the mere act of looking at an enlightened being brings benefits—not the least of which is a sense of calm and the impetus to consider the meaning of life—to the onlooker. I email a friend who is a *thangka* painter in Nepal. She is busy but happily agrees to paint an image of Green Tara. It may take a year, she says.

I am a Buddhist but also a newspaper journalist. I commission her anyway but take it with a grain of salt, then promptly file away Kamtrul Rinpoche's divination in the back of my mind. I'm almost resolved, though, to write the book. I figure that I can sell my car and use the money to fund a one-year stay in

McLeod Ganj, during which time I could write the manuscript and try to find a publisher.

Two weeks later I am in my editor-in-chief's office trying to explain why I want to resign to go and live in India. He is an avowed atheist. He doesn't seem to hear that I want to write. Instead he is convinced that I'm throwing in my hard-won career at a national newspaper to go and gaze at my belly button. Worse still, he suspects I am one of an ever greater number of people who are deserting real life for the great black void of mumbo jumbo. What began as a straightforward resignation conversation quickly turns into him pitting spirituality, a word he clearly feels uncomfortable uttering, against newspaper journalism. His point is that journalism is the higher calling.

'Mate, I'll tell you, there is no life after death. It's newspapers that make a real difference. We're better than politicians and lawyers, because we change the world, we expose the crooks.'

Years ago I would have rallied to the call. But I feel weary of the ethical compromises I find myself making in the course of a day. I've come to realise that it's a rare story that changes things for the better and a fortunate news journalist who gets to spend their time concerned with what is in the public good. Like me, most spend their days breathlessly caught up in the chase, often doing questionable things to please their masters. I don't want to contribute to the machine any more.

He declares, with a dash of irony, that he will 'save me from the lamas' and tells me to reconsider things over the weekend. He makes vague promises of a promotion, an overseas posting.

In a moment of weakness I waver. It is then that I have my own little Chairman Mao epiphany.

In 1954 the Dalai Lama embarked on a last-ditch diplomatic mission to avert the annexation of Tibet by China, by meeting Chairman Mao in Beijing. By all accounts the two had a cordial discussion but when the Chairman felt certain he had the Dalai Lama's confidence he leaned over and breathed in the Dalai Lama's ear: 'You know, religion is poison.' It was then, the Dalai Lama later wrote, that he understood the dire threat Tibet faced.

In an attempt to convince my editor about the scientists, physicists and psychologists who are investigating the many aspects of Buddhism—from meditation to its theory of the interdependence of all things—I inadvertently call the Dalai Lama 'His Holiness.' He leaps on it. 'You're not that involved, are you?' Then, leaning back in his chair as though inspired to speak the truth, 'The Dalai Lama's just a materialistic old monk.'

That's it. The decision has been made: I am going to live in McLeod Ganj. Two weeks later I discover an author friend has talked to a publisher about my trip. By the time I leave Australia I have a book contract in hand and a feeling my life is about to take a strange new turn.

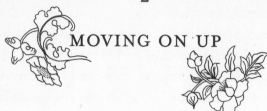

2

MOVING ON UP

I arrive back at Delhi's Indira Gandhi International Airport in the small hours of the morning and, after a seventeen-hour flight, find myself staring, enamoured, at the Laura Ashley green and pink flowered wallpaper pasted onto the customs partition walls. It lends an air of bathroom intimacy to the hollow utilitarian building. In front of me is a line of travellers waiting patiently for Indian customs officers who seem to consider it a matter of national pride to keep up their cross-counter banter, pausing only to frown disapprovingly at each new arrival's travel documents. Their demeanour—officious, cantankerous and with an air of willingness to be compromised all at the same time—is touchingly familiar. Like a somnambulist I follow the flow of arrivals past customs to the luggage rotunda and then to the doors of the world outside where a wall of 42°C heat hits me in the face.

This time I hoist myself onto the dreaded night bus for McLeod Ganj. At 7 p.m. each night a convoy, packed with cheap goods, contraband dried beef, ragged travellers and Tibetans, leaves from Majnukatilla, a settlement in North Delhi. It is the place that Tibetans fled to when police forcibly removed them from their previous tent city outside Delhi's main bus terminal a kilometre down the road. Being largely from nomad stock, they decided the dumping ground was as good a place as any to put down their roots and proceeded to build a haphazard Tibetan enclave that now thrives with restaurants, shops and hotels.

A porter, who is all sweetness and light, carts my bags fifty metres in his rickshaw to the bus, but when he sets it down demands a hundred rupees, probably his average daily wage. When I refuse, his anger turns to insistent whinging; his eyes roam over his lower body until they alight on his perfectly healthy foot. He points and hops like a madman. When I finally fob him off, two angel-faced Indian boys step forward to help me load my bags onto the back of the bus—then demand twenty rupees each for the one-metre lift. A Tibetan man with the swank stride of a police officer comes over and indicates with a flick of the wrist that I should pay the boys. He is skinny, wears a pith helmet and carries a big stick. His ear lobes are dragged down by a pair of ornate turquoise and coral earrings. I'm momentarily flummoxed by India. He looks like a demented amateur theatre enthusiast but quite possibly he's an official. That he is in cahoots with the boys is a given; that he is an impostor is revealed only when I notice his 'uniform'. Under a police jacket is a 'Free Tibet' T-shirt with a scrawled handwritten message, 'Give me Pussy'. I am too tired to put up a fight and the two boys grin delightedly when I pay up.

I have come to McLeod Ganj immediately after serving out my notice at work, but it is July and reports of the ceaseless rains that fall until September have left me apprehensive. The rumours say it doesn't stop raining for weeks on end; that the air is so thick with moisture, and the concrete rooms that have sprung up all over the town such perfect incubators, that if you set a book down and leave the room for a few hours, it will grow a skin of furry marbled mould. Long-time residents hoard plastic bags and stuff everything into them for the duration of the monsoon. The roads, which in the dry season are compressed clay with a thin crust of asphalt, become rivers of filth, huge swirling seas of rubbish and cow faeces. People get around town in knee-high gumboots and waterproof ponchos.

Yet as the bus pulls into McLeod Ganj at 6.30 a.m. I am greeted not with a deluge but a gentle summer's day. Wiry porters stand around swinging the two straps they use to secure luggage on their heads; bread sellers crouch behind low wooden tables, and a bevy of Indian spectators' eyes roam while their hands crotch-scratch. As the bus shudders to a stop I scramble off and turn to see who has been caught. First-time visitors, who don't realise they have only seconds to escape, are immediately surrounded by a swarm of Indian touts waving business cards in their faces, speaking rapidly in sing-song Hinglish—English spiced up with Hindi—about the virtues of their hotel's hot-water showers.

It is the morning of the sixth of July, the Dalai Lama's sixty-ninth birthday. McLeod Ganj has woken up early. In Tibetan settlements all over India it is a national holiday. A man with a loudspeaker roams the streets shouting commands as though he is rounding up convicts, but he is in fact informing the town about the timetable of celebrations at the Tsuglag Khang. The

Dalai Lama's birthday is the only birthday Tibetans really celebrate. They rejoice that the Dalai Lama, who they believe to be the human embodiment of Chenrezig, has chosen to stay with humanity for another year. Often the Dalai Lama appears at the celebrations, although his presence is not guaranteed. But this year everyone is in for a shock. Scheduled to visit Barcelona as part of his intense international schedule, the Dalai Lama has fallen ill and is marooned at Apollo Hospital in Delhi. A press release is issued; the Dalai Lama is suffering from exhaustion brought on by a long-term cold. Doctors have ordered him to cancel public engagements for six weeks and to cut down on all obligations in the future. I expect a pall of worry over the celebrations.

Ask a Tibetan their birthday and most will shyly nominate an animal that corresponds to the twelve-year astrological cycle commonly used in Asia, simply to give you the courtesy of an answer. Most ordinary Tibetans don't celebrate, or often know, the date of their birth. There is an ingrained belief that a birthday is only another reminder that life is ticking by and one has still not reached enlightenment. To celebrate such a lack would be like whooping it up at the pearly gates before St Peter has directed you to either enter heaven or depart for hell.

Instead, every Tibetan adds another year to their age at *Losar*—the start of the astrological Tibetan New Year that usually falls in February. To add to this there is another anomaly that makes it difficult to extract a Tibetan's age. For Buddhists, all sentient beings continually reincarnate until they reach enlightenment. The moment a woman conceives, a being has taken a human rebirth. So by the time a baby is born it has already aged. In a mathematical flick-flack the child is considered to be one year old immediately upon delivery. The next time *Losar* falls, the child celebrates their second birthday regardless of whether *Losar* is a day or a year later. Curiously, I've found the lack of standardisation in this process has the liberating effect of loosening the attachment to age. In my social milieu, knowing someone's age is a way to subtly measure their achievements in life. This kind of reckoning is refreshingly absent in Tibetan culture.

I check into my hotel and wash away the night's accumulation of grime, then get ready to join the colourful parade heading down Temple Road, or Dalai Lama-Gi Road as it is known by the Indians—*Gi* being the word Indians add to the name of those people they respect. At the bottom of the road is the Tsuglag Khang and behind that the entrance to the Dalai Lama's home. Everyone everywhere is dressed in their best finery. Tibetan woman have painstakingly divided their long black hair into 108 auspicious plaits. Some have woven coral and turquoise chunks through their braids or attached large clumps of amber to their forehead and wear long, heavy gold earrings. Nearly all the women are dressed in their brightest brocade *chubas*, the sleeveless full-length oriental style dresses that cross over in the front and wrap around the back. Combined with the richly hued silk blouses worn underneath, the clothes are of such ornate finery that each woman looks like a stately court princess. Many men are wearing the male *chuba*, a heavy, woollen long-sleeved dress worn over trousers, with one of the arms released to hang down by the side.

Some have threaded red cotton through their long dark hair in the style worn by Khampas. I notice a sprinkling of western women dressed in *chubas*, walking beside Tibetan men.

Outside the monastery two queues snake their way back up the hill. One is for men, the other for women. Tibetan snack-food hawkers, it seems, know the routine. They have set up so the plumes of aroma from steaming *momos*, fried bread and butter tea waft over the crowd. I join the ladies' queue. Being a Buddhist, with a clean slate in McLeod Ganj—and in the vicinity of the Dalai Lama's home—I approach the human traffic snarl feeling a sense of equanimity. All adverse conditions are considered prime opportunities to practise virtue; in this instance I can cultivate patience. But as I settle in I notice invaders in the queue. A toothless old *momo-la*, or grandmother, strolls up to a Tibetan she obviously doesn't know and wordlessly squeezes in; raising her shoulders and sticking her tongue between her teeth she turns around to smile benignly at the people behind. In front of me the modus operandi is repeated every couple of minutes. Groups of Tibetan women call their friends from further back and shuffle forward to make room, avoiding the indignant gaze of westerners behind them.

I catch another westerner's eyes. We are outraged, but too ashamed to know what to do as all the foreigners helplessly flow further and further back in the queue swelling with smirking Tibetans. Should we be Buddhists about it or tell off these pushy old queue-jumpers? No one utters a word.

Eventually I inch forward, past some foul-smelling toilets that mark the start of the security area where a team of beefy Tibetan security guards with short back and sides and dressed in cotton safari suits direct people past a shoddy old metal detector. I've never heard it beep, only wheeze and rattle when someone brushes against its poles. Men rifle through my bag and I get pushed on to a female security guard who frisks me. As I make my way up the courtyard, I can see it is already packed with thousands of pilgrims sitting waiting for the festivities to begin. Harried, defrauded westerners seek distraction, talking to friends, reaching into their bags for food, or readjust their thin cushions after the cold of the concrete seeps through to their bottoms. Cross-legged Tibetans, now assured of prime positions, sit waiting patiently for the entertainment to begin.

On the stage is an empty throne. Below the throne is a line of chairs towards which members of the *Kashag*, the Tibetan government-in-exile's cabinet, and various short, heavy-bodied dignitaries are making their way. Most are dressed in plain brown woollen *chubas*, the political equivalent of a navy blue suit. Suddenly the crash of cymbals rings out. Tibetans straighten up; westerners make their final adjustments. The show is about to begin.

A procession of dancers comes into the forecourt dressed in the most exquisite leopard-skin-lined *chubas* and tall fur hats. The red silk blouses underneath the *chubas* have extra long arms that fall graciously about a metre past the dancers' hands. A band strikes up and the dancers, now in a circle, begin to wave their arms to the side, above their heads and in slow arcs around their bodies. They are deliberate and graceful, the overall effect is mesmerising in its simplicity, its tribute to a singular movement.

Suddenly the crowd goes up in a raucous bellow of laughter. Disconcerted westerners look around, unable to make out the cause of mirth. Again the crowd erupts. Gold-toothed *momo-las* fall against one another snorting; monks hit each other and point at the performers. One of the dancers has taken a misstep and is now struggling to keep in time. Tibetans start shouting out at him. Indignant looks pass over the western faces in the crowd but there is no rescuing the hapless dancer. The mockery makes his discomfort worse, he waves his arms like a maniac trying to find the rhythm he has lost. His are up while others are down. The anarchy spreads to his feet and he starts to bump into the other dancers as they gracefully sway side to side. Watched gleefully by Tibetans who clearly feel they are getting their money's worth, he becomes a rogue element, destroying the carefully crafted synchronicity. Mercifully, the band winds it up and the dancers stumble off stage, humiliated.

The Tibetans clap appreciatively, having had their fill of the kind of public spectacle they evidently enjoy. They break out bags of *kabsay*, fried Tibetan bread, and twist open Chinese thermoses full of butter tea, passing them around to anyone in the vicinity, inordinately pleased with the day's entertainment. I wonder what would have happened if the Dalai Lama had been present.

Despite such a fine start, that night, staring at the ceiling, I have an attack of nerves. What on earth have I done, moving to McLeod Ganj to write a book? I realise the longest story I have written is a two-page feature, yet my contract says the manuscript must be 80 000 words—that's 75 000 words outside my comfort zone. Anyway, how do you write a book for goodness sake? Other people are sensible enough to fulfil their dreams on two-week holidays, but no, I've jumped in the deep end. I feel embarrassed about my enthusiasm and wonder how I can dampen down expectations and slowly recede from view.

In the morning I remember to take one day at a time and decide to put down some roots by moving from my hotel into a two-roomed apartment in a building high up on one of the hills that overlook McLeod Ganj. I soon discover it is a cross-cultural haven. In each of its seven rooms live a western woman and her Tibetan boyfriend. Thankfully I am used to being a single amongst couples. Kate and Tenzin live next door and beside them is a forest that is home to a raggedy team of monkeys. My room has a single gas ring for cooking and some pots and pans. There is no telephone, oven or fridge, and hot water comes only after a geyser has been switched on for an hour and a half. Signs are everywhere warning residents to turn it off after use in case it explodes. Great. My new home is lacking many of the things I would take as necessities in the west. But as no one else has them, or expects to have them, they never become something I think I need. I decide to forget the full range of appliances and implements I once possessed and start to unpack my bags, reminding myself that a certain amount of deprivation is part of the deal of living in India.

The next morning I diligently tend to the huge pile of washing that has accumulated since I left Australia, soaping it up in my bucket and rinsing it in the freezing tap water. I hang a heap of white shirts and Cottontail underpants on my balcony and then decide to do some shopping for the house. In town I bump into Tenzin, who spends his days *chum-chumming*, in Tibetan literally 'going around without a distinct purpose'. I give him the present I brought for him from Australia, a Wiltshire stay-sharp kitchen knife. He immediately feels through the wrapping that it's a blade and his eyes light up. Straight after he opens it a crowd of jealous-looking long-haired boys gather around him, fingering it and plunging it into invisible opponents. Tenzin inserts it in the side pants of his trousers for a street knife, although later he reports it was good for cutting salad.

In a country where there is little standardisation and information is the sole preserve of the person lucky enough to stumble across it, finding even basic necessities is a major undertaking. It's even harder in a town like McLeod Ganj, which has an abundance of Buddhist books, dharma bags, incense and statue shops but lacks daily provisions like knives and forks. The best bet is always Shop Number Five, one of a row of small dark holes that line Dalai Lama-Gi Road. Shop Number Five is also known as the Magic Shop and not without reason. It is the size of a changing room but, like an expanding cube, seems to have endless supplies of both useful and arcane goods. The dour-faced shop assistants almost hiss when customers request an item, but then reach into a shadowy corner and fish it out. Numberless times their elbows have dug into deep recesses of the shop to emerge with miraculous goods: cheese graters, needle and thread, gas igniters, sanitary pads, baking soda.

If by some misfortune the Magic Shop doesn't have what you want, the only option is to traipse down to Kotwali Bazaar in

Dharamsala. Kotwali Bazaar is a proper Indian market town, with narrow back alleys, *dhaba* wallahs (the Indian equivalent of fast food merchants), shops brimming with plastic bangles, ball-breakingly tight men's jeans, and that peculiar Indian stench of rotting vegetables mixed with kerosene. Rattling buses ply the fifteen-kilometre route down the mountain from McLeod Ganj but the quickest way is by jeep. Each jeep has an emaciated, chain-smoking Indian driver with a death wish. So keen are they to squeeze in as many bodies—and fares—as possible, the driver sits squashed up against his door, from where he reaches over to steer. Always off-centre, he veers away from oncoming vehicles and the steep cliffs only when he knows certain death is coming. The lamas, forever trying to instil in students the knowledge that death is ever-present and unpredictable so one must take full advantage of living, need only to recommend regular jeep rides to Kotwali Bazaar to remind people the end is likely to be just around the corner.

I make it through the day's shopping alive. Exhausted and laden with kitchen utensils, a bed cover and fresh vegetables, I decide to catch a local bus back up to McLeod Ganj. Unfortunately there is only one seat left, next to a teenage Punjabi tourist. I smell trouble. Literally. He stinks. Emanating from his body is an unholy combination of fetid fruit, dank socks and BO. Still, I sit. His Sikh friends, spread out around the bus, almost dissolve into hysterics they are so excited their friend is in close proximity to a western woman. Fed a steady diet of B-grade western films, their minds almost burst with the knowledge that western women have sex before marriage. Reportedly they even enjoy it. They call out and joke and giggle and squeal out no doubt lewd comments to him in Hindi. A western woman in the front looks around sympathetically. My neighbour twists in embarrassment at the commotion his friends are causing. But then, as though programmed, he asks the inevitable questions. 'Madam, what is your good name?' swiftly followed up by 'Madam, are you married?' I answer catatonically, but his posse are beside themselves, ready to wet their pants. The bus lurches from side to side. I can't resist. 'Your friends are really immature,' I say pompously. Under his turban his face goes bright red. I still haven't finished the ice-cream I bought in Kotwali. It is starting to melt. I lick it furiously, unsettled by a sudden vision of myself as an unlikely porno actress in a Bollywood film licking an ice-cream in front of a gaggle of sex-starved pubescent Indian boys.

The notion of karma is that every thought or action has a result—usually experienced in a future lifetime. This time, though, mine is instant. As I heave myself and my booty up the winding stairs that lead to my house I see Tenzin waving at me excitedly. He has been smoking on his balcony, watching the world go by, and can't wait to tell me about that afternoon's entertainment. In my absence monkeys rampaged along the balcony that rings our building, collecting an assortment of washing on their way. They were particularly keen on my Cottontails. Two baby monkeys had amused themselves—and the entire house who had gathered on their balconies for the spectacle—by playing tug of war with a pair of my underpants. The victor then put it around his neck and swung from tree to tree parading his winnings in front of an admiring crowd.

Some clothes have been salvaged but my underpant stock has fallen dangerously low. I enlist the help of Rajeesh, our Bihari houseboy, to help me search for them. One of many sons born to a peasant family in the most cursed state in India, Rajeesh has been indentured to the Tibetan family who own our building since he was a child. Now fifteen and showing the first wisp of a moustache, we all know his days are numbered. With facial hair comes the knowledge that he is man enough for (an arranged) marriage and the responsibilities of a family. But for now his wide smile and shy questions show a glimpse of the young boy he is still allowed to be. Together we set out into the monkey-infested forest to search for the culprits. A gaggle of mothers and their babies hang around picking lice out of each other's hair. They hiss when we walk past as though we are the thieves. But after hours of searching we both return empty-handed.

Later that day, before the sun sets, Rajeesh calls me up to the roof so we can survey the forest. Suddenly he starts and points. There hanging off one of the top branches of a tree, like a limp flag, is a pair of huge, stretched dirty underpants. The enlarged bottom catches the intermittent wind, making them billow out like a pair of fat woman's thighs. Rajesh is mortified. His eyes bright with horror, he hurries downstairs. There is no way I can rescue my pants or my dignity. The bloomers remain like a mocking sentry—sometimes deflated, sometimes bulging with wind—for the first week in my new home.

The next day I open my bedroom door to see one small monkey has squeezed through the bars of the dining room-cum-study-cum kitchen and is feasting upon a ripe plum. We both get a shock: it drops the plum, which explodes on the floor, and runs for the window. The last I see is an inflamed red bum surrounded by fur as the monkey squeals in alarm, trying to push its posterior back through the barred window. I buy a slingshot and tie it up to the rail on my balcony, hoping its fluorescent colour will remind the monkeys of being stung with stones. They scatter at the sight of it. But one morning there is more than the usual clatter of monkeys playing up and I yank open the door to see they have undone it and are perched a couple of metres away, trying to gnaw on it.

Each morning I am lulled out of my sleep by the muffled sound of bells, then the slow rhythm of chanting. It takes me weeks to realise that the tiny shed made from flattened cooking-oil cans below my room is a monastery. The ancient stooped men in faded layers of worn clothing I have often seen fossicking around in the forest are monks who belong to this tiny, disguised, evidently toiletless hermitage. One day I also catch sight of an equally ancient woman with a thick waist, long grey plaited hair and dressed in maroon and white robes. I realise she is a *Kang drolma*, a female yogini. A spiritual practitioner in her own right, she is a tantric consort to equally accomplished spiritual masters.

I walk around McLeod Ganj with one eye peeled for my friend Elizabeth, who I know is in town. Both New Zealanders, we flatted together there in our early twenties and then again in Sydney in our early thirties. We have been through thick and thin: the death of close friends, relationship peaks and troughs, career angst, an interest in Buddhism and some of the best times of our lives. Elizabeth is a double-degree kind of woman—

literature and film design—the type who straightens up the bedcovers and never runs out of toilet paper. She has a classic kind of beauty, perfectly balanced green eyes in a broad brown face, her thick brown hair parted down the middle. Constant diarrhoea and a fussy approach to Indian food have reduced her ample curves somewhat. She is newly svelte and loving the fact that she can now eat chocolate with impunity. Eighteen months ago she gave up struggling in the film industry in Sydney to come to India and study Tibetan. She wants to become a translator for the lamas, many of whom do not teach in English. It's a particularly hard job. Since the Tibetan language was developed in the seventh century it has had one dialect for everyday use and an entirely different honorific vocabulary used when speaking to those of higher standing than yourself, including lamas. There are horror stories about nomad people who do not know the polite language and who are forced, when speaking to lamas, to employ the rough language of laypeople to communicate. To Tibetans this is the equivalent of Tourette Syndrome, like unwillingly shouting profanities at a vicar when all you want him to do is pass you the scones. A translator needs to know both vocabularies to master the Tibetan language.

One day last year Elizabeth surprised us all by writing to say that while on a break in Nepal she had married Lobsang, a former monk we both met years ago when we were on retreat at a monastery in Nepal. She had been partly sponsoring his study, convinced he was going to become a leading scholar who could come out to the west to teach, but when he decided to disrobe they got married. She described the wedding as the strangest event of her life. Stuck at the front of a silent room, they sat for hours as monks solemnly walked by draping *khartas* around their necks. In front of them was a table laden with food, which they couldn't touch until all the formalities were over. Guests filled offering envelopes with donations or stepped forward proudly with the most coveted of wedding gifts: Chinese velour blankets featuring tigers in jungle scenes.

I haven't yet bumped into Elizabeth, so I decide to pass the time by walking the *kora*. As I am spinning the prayer wheels a man on a motorbike streaks past, heading in the opposite direction. As he passes the spot of the Dalai Lama's private residence further up the hill, he raises his hand gently off the handle and places it on his heart. Halfway up the hill I notice a bush on the edge of the path begin to shake. Somebody emerges from the foliage. My world momentarily stops; synapses spark into life but then fizzle. I recognise the face but not the context. Then I realise. It is Elizabeth and she's just been to the bush toilet. We laugh at meeting in such 'reduced' circumstances and race up the hill to find her Khampa husband.

Although the outside world understands Tibet as one country, it is mainly in exile that Tibetans have come to appreciate the idea of statehood. Prior to the Chinese invasion, of the three provinces, Amdo, Kham and U-Tsang, the government in Lhasa had effective political authority only in U-Tsang. As activist Tenzin Tsundue says in his book *Kora*, before the Chinese invaded Tibet individual lives were so taken up with spiritual aspirations that the politics of the capital Lhasa seemed a lifetime away. Tibetan Prime Minister Samdhong Rinpoche even refers to 'the

Tibetan nationalities', the people from each place being so distinct. In exile, geographical loyalties are strong and people from different regions sometimes cannot understand each other's language. The street scene in McLeod Ganj is dominated by the long-haired, charismatic Amdo boys who break into beautiful song at the slightest provocation and see the world as artists do. Khampa people tend to be the most direct and toughest of all Tibetans; their reputation as people who, once riled, will fight to the death frightens even other Tibetans. It was the Khampas, *pa* meaning people or person, who escorted the Dalai Lama to exile in 1959 and who, in those early years, formed the CIA-trained Four Rivers Six Ranges, the guerrilla group that was the backbone of armed resistance to the Chinese occupation. Those from U-Tsang or Central Tibet tend to be worldlier. Unlike Amdos they don't need a singing voice that will carry across distant valleys and they have long since filed down the rough edges of the Khampas. Other Tibetans will secretly whisper that Lhasa people smile at you, uttering soft words as they poison your drink.

Despite her happiness at our reunion I can see all is not well with Elizabeth. She develops a scowl as we get closer to the cafe where Lobsang is waiting. She tells me she has given him a (quasi) affectionate nickname: Nasty. Despite their love, the few months of their marriage have been marked by difficult adjustments on both sides. Lobsang has perfect skin, long, narrow black eyes and a tiny tuft of hair on his chin. Since he stopped being a monk he does everything with unbridled enthusiasm. He is charming and kind and uses his shady contacts in a second to help out his friends. His newly grown hair shines with a kilo of gel. He longs for a mobile phone. His English is wild and indiscriminate. Elizabeth tells me that when he discovered flares were cool he took all his trousers to the tailor and demanded 'flys'. The bewildered tailor had no idea what he meant. 'Flys, flys, flys,' intoned Lobsang. 'Big problem' is interchangeable with 'big party'. Unable to cleanly finish words ending in soft letters, he refers to McLeod Ganj as 'McLeod Ganj-ee'. She has also discovered he helped finance his monastic studies by manufacturing false Nepalese passports between *pujas* and prayers.

Lobsang, it seems, loves the new-found freedom of life outside the monastery, save for the one thing that riles him. His wife will not obey him. Lobsang has spent half of his life in a traditional Tibetan village and the other half in a monastery with 500 monks. He is slowly learning that marriage to a westerner is not quite as straightforward as he had imagined. Women, especially Elizabeth, have opinions. And in a culture where in public wives are seen and not heard, her oft-voiced opinions are a constant source of friction.

After hugs and a catch-up he edges closer to me. Finally he pulls me aside and confides 'We always farting.' I believe he means fighting. He thrusts a finger in Elizabeth's direction, saying plaintively, 'She very unique-ee one.'

Tibetans have never experienced women's liberation. Society is essentially conservative. Wives still honour and obey their husbands. A wife's behaviour reflects tenfold on her husband. In this world the best thing a wife can do for a harmonious relationship is to be observant of traditions, subdued and shy in public and accommodating in private, although with access to free education this is slowly starting to change. None of this is likely with a western wife. This is a cautionary tale, I think to myself; relationships with former monks are difficult and Khampas are notoriously single-minded. I determine to be careful around handsome Khampa former monks.

Elizabeth, however, has come to an entirely different understanding of the origin of their problems. 'It's because someone has put a spell on us, trying to destroy our relationship,' she tells me. She has the pent-up look of someone who has seen the dark underbelly of a small town. I wonder what has happened to her in India. She was a rational human being when she left Australia.

She tells me that sometimes she wished she didn't understand Tibetan. She said that the day before, she and Lobsang were sitting on a bench next to two elderly Tibetan men who were both serenely reciting prayers, counting off the beads on their *malas*. She smiled shyly at them when Lobsang got up to talk to a friend. As soon as he moved, one old man turned to the other: 'That woman is old, her husband is young. I think he got a bad deal.' She sat there with a frozen smile, mortified at what she had heard.

She explains that they have been staying in a tiny two-bedroom apartment with Jamphel, a friend of Lobsang's from Lhasa. Jamphel is surrounded by Tibetan men with western girlfriends and wants one for himself. Despite the Buddhist statutes in his house and his professions of faith, Jamphel has tired of karma taking its course and has employed the services of a Hindu magic man, a *baba*, who specialises in putting spells on his clients' enemies. Elizabeth suspects Jamphel has put a hex on her marriage, his aim being that once it is destroyed he will simply come along and pick her up like a spare part. She has found their photos with their names and those of their parents printed on the back. Strange talismans have also been turning up in their personal things. Recently Jamphel offered her a chocolate bar with one segment removed. Lobsang immediately threw it away. They are caught between fear at what he might do and sadness that he is willing to go to such lengths to satisfy himself.

I've only been in McLeod Ganj a week and already I'm throughly confused about who, and what, to believe. It dawns on me that there may be no easy answers to the questions I have set out with. I also have a sneaking suspicion that I can't remain a mere onlooker to other people's dramas, that this town is about to draw me into its web.

3

WHEN FIRST
WE MEET

It is Wednesday and the rains have finally started. I feel a cold coming on but submerge it beneath a precious store of Codral tablets brought from Australia. Elizabeth has invited Kate, Tenzin and I to dinner. A friend of Lobsang's will also be coming. I groan—that means, inevitably, he will be a Khampa and most likely a bolshie one at that. I reason that even if he is insufferable, the more people I know in McLeod Ganj the better. Connections make this town and he might know some useful people. I also detect in Elizabeth's tone that he might have her judiously dispensed respect. She tells me that once he sided with her over Lobsang in a debate about some complicated aspect of Buddhist philosophy, much to Lobsang's consternation. Lobsang couldn't decide whether to be proud or ashamed his western wife might have a better understanding of the complexities of the teachings than he did. The combination is enough to get me down the hill to the dinner.

It is early evening and the rain has eased, leaving a luminous dusk. Elizabeth and Lobsang have moved into a room they are house sitting. Already they seem more harmonious. When we arrive Elizabeth is alone, slaving over her single gas ring, stirring a large pot of noodle soup or *thukpa*. She points outside where candles surround a rug on the balcony. Lobsang arrives half an hour later, passing outside the windows. He waves to us and stops, turning around to beckon someone to follow him. There is a short pause, as though their guest might have changed his mind. Then a man walks past the windows and stops at the door, his head down.

He's not the swaggering Khampa I expect, in fact his shyness seems to be contagious. I'm suddenly too timid to look up, but can feel an unusually peaceful and relaxed presence. I register from the bottom up: sneakers, wide loose-cut jeans and a white T-shirt fitting perfectly over smooth brown arms. The seconds tick by. I can feel Lobsang's palpable excitement; he is almost squirming with anticipation that he is responsible for an introduction. Finally, I force myself to look up. We smile.

The guest steps into the room and sits on the bed. He is compact, with short black hair and long dark eyes that taper off finely. His name is Choying and his face is broad with some of the highest cheekbones I have ever seen.

I offer him some *kabsay* then find my voice. 'Where are you from?' I ask. His voice is quiet and deep. He says he is from a village in eastern Tibet. He spies a map of Tibet on the wall and points at his home. He then describes, with great attention to detail, the escape route he took from his monastery in the east, across the width of the country, to the sacred mountain of Kang Rinpoche in the west, and into Nepal. I notice white teeth, a face that easily creases into happiness when he smiles. Then it dawns on me, a Khampa and a former monk—exactly the combination I had resolved to avoid.

He is muscly for a Tibetan and his body has a peculiar posture, as though he is halfway out of his shell but could fold back into it at any moment. Later I understand that what for me was a relaxed dinner with friends was an entirely alien experience for him. Being invited to eat with people his age, with women as well as men, for the pleasure of it, is not how things are done where he is from. He was raised in a small village then went into a monastery at fifteen. After he escaped from Tibet he went to the largest Buddhist university, Sera Monastery, in South India. It is a city of some 4500 monks and is renowned for producing students well versed in the complex philosophy of Tibetan Buddhism. Yet somehow he has ended up with a crew cut and hip-hop jeans in McLeod Ganj.

The moonlight is gentle. Tenzin is telling us another story, this time about a bird in Tibet that gives birth to a dog. He describes an eagle-like creature that lives in the highest mountains. Each year it lays three eggs, the second of which is a tiny being with canine features. Tibetans who live in these regions sometimes hear its mournful bark and they rush towards the sound to save the dog from its mother, who will refuse to feed it or will kill it before it eats her chicks. Tenzin says the dog usually lives for only ten days, so the people scurry all over the mountains to find it, led only by its occasional bark. If rescued these dogs are considered amongst the most precious and rare responsibilities a family can have, and are often given as a gift to the village's lama.

We continue to eat, Choying wanting to make sure that all the bowls of salad and chilli are passed around. We are seated next to each other but he doesn't talk much, just listens as conversation swirls around him. Then he leans over to get a plate of food, resting his elbow heavily on my leg. I bristle. What a strange person. Too shy to talk but happy to be overly familiar.

Soon after dinner is finished, Tenzin and Lobsang decide to go dancing at McLeod Ganj's one and only disco, Rock n' Roll. Tenzin can, and often does save up all his unspent daytime energy to dance all night. Choying looks hesitant. Another entirely unfamiliar crossroad. Does one go with the men to a—by India's standards—notorious pleasure-seeking bar or stay back with the women? I try to help, saying to Lobsang, 'Go and have a good time.' Choying's face lights up. I suppose he's used to orders. Obviously dancing is a new experience for him as well, as monks are forbidden from dancing for pleasure as opposed to culture. The boys take off up the hill. As soon as they are safely out of earshot, Kate, Elizabeth and I fall about giggling at how handsome Choying is.

The next morning I get a phone call from Lobsang and Elizabeth. Choying had knocked on their door at first light, ostensibly to thank them for dinner. And, he wondered, who was the woman sitting next to him? In a typically Tibetan manner, he wanted to know, 'Does she have a good heart?' In my experience one of the most refreshing things about Tibetan men is their attitude to female beauty. While it is given the highest currency in the western world, in Tibet it is simply not that relevant. It is a person's heart, and their mind that count.

After a few days my cold is full-blown. My nose is like Niagara Falls; my throat is itchy and dry. I feel like death warmed up. I call Pema, a Tibetan woman who has agreed to start teaching me Tibetan, to tell her I am sick, I have a bad cold. It is better she comes another day. She is alarmed. She convinces a friend with a moped that there is a medical emergency and roars pillion up the hill.

She bursts into my home, unloading a backpack of Cornflakes, milk, orange juice and mineral water. Then she sits down. 'Are you all right?' she huffs, her face in a deep furrow.

'Yes thanks,' I whimper. 'It's just a cold.'

When Tibetans are sick they like company. Pema settles in on the couch and we chat about how she escaped from Tibet. She tells me that both her parents died young and that her sister and her sister's husband wanted her to work out in the fields rather than go to school. Pema wanted to be educated so she ran away to Lhasa with a friend.

'I was such a stupid village girl,' she said. 'I had never been away from home, never seen tall buildings or highways.'

In Lhasa she found work as a waitress and eventually saved enough money to pay a guide to take her over the Himalayas. It took two weeks of the most arduous journey over snow, wading through icy rivers, and hiding in forests lest the Chinese police come upon them. Eventually Pema made it to Nepal and the Tibetan Reception Centre in Kathmandu, which is set up as the first point of call for those who have made it over the Himalayas. They helped her to enrol in the Transit School in the valley below Dharamsala, a free school for new adult exiles. Their history of isolation, coupled with the years of oppression by the Chinese government, has denied many Tibetans the basic knowledge we take for granted. Thus it takes five years to graduate. Since then she has been scraping together a living as a sometime tailor and Tibetan language tutor.

Pema has a western boyfriend and I know this has made things difficult for her. While single Tibetan men seem to accumulate western women at great speed, there is a taboo when it comes to Tibetan women with foreign men. Many older Tibetans believe that when a couple have children the bones, or real identity of the child, are provided by the father and the flesh and blood, or personality, by the mother. A child of a western woman and Tibetan man is thus Tibetan, but the child of a western man and Tibetan woman is not. Some silently frown on this kind of union.

When we have loosened up with each other Pema pauses. 'Actually,' she begins shyly, 'a cold is not considered a sickness in Tibet. Parents tell their children it goes away faster if you keep working through it. When you said you were sick I thought that maybe you needed to go to hospital. But now I see it's nothing.'

I am mortified. I have always considered myself a sturdy type, always avoided any show of sickness; it was one of my hallmarks, for goodness sake. Now I am being painted as a hypochondriac.

My mobile phone rings. The line is fuzzy and the voice booming. 'I am Choying.' I immediately feel nervy. I think I like this man. 'Hello,' I say.

He shouts at me, 'I heard you have a cold. If you need anything I will bring it. What do you need?' It is delivered without pause as though he is in a race against time to finish the sentence.

Oh God, I realise, he probably thinks I'm fatally ill too. 'It's nothing,' I say. 'How are you?' But the slight divergence from the script throws him. He runs out of words. I can sense he desperately wants to get off the line. 'Good. Bye.' The phone clicks dead.

I'm exhausted by this weird culture.

Elizabeth calls my mobile to tell me she saw Lobsang, through a crack in the bathroom door, squatting on top of the toilet seat. It is a western toilet. She asked him what on earth he was doing. Eventually he confessed he couldn't 'go' with his feet on the ground he was so used to squat toilets. 'How long have you been doing this?' she asked. He told her since they met. She extracted a promise—borne by fear he will fall off the toilet seat and damage himself, or worse, be caught doing it in Australia where they hope to emigrate—that he will practise with his feet planted on the ground. She is already a veteran of the Underpant Campaign. It took her more than a month to convince him it was unnecessary for married men to shower in their underpants, that was only what happened in the monastery.

Soon afterwards, Lobsang and Elizabeth arrange for Choying and I to join them in a walk to the famous pizza restaurant in the nearby village of Dharamkot. It is sunny when we all meet up at the bus station but soon the clouds gather. Lobsang is exuberant but I can see Choying is nervous. While we stand and talk he seems to have no idea where to put his arms. After dropping them by his side and placing them on his hips, he settles on folding them across his chest, looking entirely ill at ease. As we set off, Elizabeth and I walk ahead, Lobsang and Choying following. Soon it is bucketing down and Choying runs up to us, attempting to deflect with his umbrella the splatterings of mud that flick from passing tuk-tuks. Fighting a losing battle we decide to risk the wet and squelch on until we reach the restaurant. Just as we are looking longingly at the outside table, the sun reappears. We spend a long afternoon, drinking the Indian version of spicy lemonade, Limca, eating pizza with our fingers, laughing and chatting about life in McLeod Ganj.

That week I get news my grandmother has died. She was sitting outside with my uncle and aunt having a cup of tea when she muttered, 'It's so nice to be sitting outside in the sun,' then simply dropped her head and was gone.

Although the finality of death is always sad, I can't say I feel bereaved in the usual woeful sense. Before I became interested in the dharma, I fully accepted that it was unwise to think about death, lest it make you dark and morbid. When people I knew died, I always thought it was an unjust catastrophe. Death was unfair, a kind of blight on life, to which I thought each person was entitled to about eighty years. Over the years Buddhism's emphasis on death has lessened its power over me. Lamas are always reminding students to contemplate that death—the gateway to reincarnation—can come at any time. They also teach what actually happens during the death process—the order of the disintegration of the physical and mental faculties. Death is used as a constant reminder both to value life and to be vigilant about one's thoughts and actions because their results come to fruition in possibly imminent future lifetimes.

I have never doubted the truth of reincarnation because it has seemed to me to make scientific sense. It is a law of physics that there must be a cause to have an effect. A life must precede a life, an event must have an origin. In contrast, I always considered the idea of a literal heaven and hell to be a well-intentioned moral invention. In some ways this is the root of my faith in Buddhism, that I trust its analysis.

At the risk of sounding cold, I try not to dwell on my sadness—after all, death is inevitable. In fact, as a Buddhist, it is necessary now to be practical. This is a pivotal time in my grandmother's transition through this life and on to another, so instead I take comfort in the thought that I know what I can do to help. Meanwhile, Lobsang has called Choying to tell him the news and he offers to help arrange prayers. As a former monk it is his area of expertise. There is a tiny voice inside my head telling me that Choying and I would like to get to know one another. To my mind our karma has bought us together, and even though these are unusual circumstances for a third meeting, it's somehow right that this isn't another frivolous dinner date.

Together we walk down to the Tsuglag Khang and ask the monks to hold a *puja*, or series of prayers, for my grandmother. The prayers are thought to reach her consciousness as it wanders in the *bardo*, the intermediate state between death and a new life, waiting for her karma to draw her towards a new birth.

Choying and I quietly walk the *kora*. It is full of Tibetans muttering mantras and spinning prayer wheels. It is a wheel-turning day, the anniversary of the time when Buddha started his second round of teaching 2500 years ago, when he taught on the true nature of reality, or emptiness. Later I join the group of people making tea-light candle offerings around the stupa in the sunset. I pray that in the next forty-nine days—the longest time it can take for a person's consciousness to pass through the *bardo*—my grandmother will have a good rebirth. Later I speak to my mother in New Zealand. The most nominal of Christians, she is keen to find a way through her grief. She wants to hear about how Buddhism deals with death. When I cry, I cry for her and all of our inherited confusion over death.

A week crawls by before another torturous, scratchy phone call. I have been wondering if my instinct about our connection was wrong, but Choying wants to invite me to his house for dinner. Tonight. Of course I want to go, but explain that I am having some friends over. He repeats his invitation word for word as though I have a problem comprehending. I repeat that friends are coming over. The phone clicks dead. Ten minutes later he rings back. Would I like to come tomorrow night instead?

Choying lives in an area of McLeod Ganj where the rent is cheapest. He comes around to collect me and we set out on the winding concrete path that heads down into the valley at the back of the town. It is spitting lightly. We leave the chai and statute shops behind, squeeze past tiny shepherds controlling lumbering cows with a twitch of vine and a whistle, wade through water gushing from a broken pipe, and pass Indian compounds where goats live in open-air quarters below the first-floor rooms of their owners. By the time he points out his building in the distance we are caught in a torrential downpour. We scamper through the blinding rain for ten minutes until we come to a damp, concrete two-storey building with several separate apartments. Water rushes out of open pipes on the roof, joining the missile-like rain hurtling down on us. I wonder why we have stopped when Choying steps through the door of a small concrete bunker and turns around, inordinately proud. This is his home.

Inside it's simply four concrete walls and a floor, a low roof and posters of Bollywood stars on the walls. There are two single beds and a small colourful altar at the far end. I notice mould creeping down one wall. Near the door, where I stand dumbly, there is a makeshift kitchen with two gas elements, a bucket of water and a knee-high shelf carefully stacked with dishes. In one corner is a large old-fashioned tape deck. His home is the size of a photographic darkroom, but inside, his flatmate, Tashi, with whom he escaped from Tibet, is also beaming with pride. On a wooden board in the 'kitchen' vegetables are chopped and waiting, next to a large green plastic bottle of Limca.

Tashi and Choying immediately start debriefing in Tibetan. They interact like two *nammas*—wives—diligently weaving around each other as they cut and dice, collect water and wash the rice and make sure that I have plenty of drink and conversation.

Choying is attentive and thrilled to have me there and, handing over the tasks to Tashi, starts to bring out his entire wardrobe for inspection: more wide jeans, a fake Dolce and Gabbana shirt, sensible black pleated pants that remind me of Chinese salarymen, and a couple of jumpers he shares with his friends.

After half an hour Tashi manages to come up with a vegetable buffet, placing it neatly on a low table in front of me, while I sit cross-legged on the bed. Choying takes advantage of the lull to show me his photos from Tibet. There are only about ten and I ask if there are any more. He explains that some friends of his took the rest, they were so homesick for pictures of a Tibetan family. There is one in particular that stands out to me. It shows a middle-aged Tibetan woman crouching down in a full *chuba* with two young men and a monk standing in a field of tall grass. I recognise the monk as a well-fed Choying, his high cheekbones filled out, his arms crossed in front of him, his gaze somewhere in the middle distance.

I ask Tashi what he did after he arrived in India. Did he also go to the monastery with Choying? 'I was there for a little time until I was put into jail...' It is spoken so casually, and without the self-conscious honesty that accompanies personal revelations in the west, that it slides effortlessly into my mind. Then I stop. Jail. 'What were you in jail for?' I croak.

'I did nothing wrong,' he says simply. 'I didn't hurt or kill anybody. I was arrested with nine other Tibetans in Nepal. The police said we didn't have the right documents. They sentenced us all to ten years.' Imagine the anger at being behind bars when your only crime is to be a refugee without proper documents.

The way Tashi delivers the information, just recounting the facts with no anger or machismo, intrigues me. Mind you, I stop myself, time does heal most wounds. He's probably talking about something that happened years ago. 'How long ago were you released?' I ask.

'Eight months ago,' he replies.

There is nowhere else to go, no need to delve into the subject as I would as a journalist, leaping on someone else's misfortune with barely concealed hunger. It was as it was: the suffering is stated but without attachment. I ask him what happened.

'After I escaped to India I went to Sera Monastery with Choying. When I first came I studied really hard. I would get up at four o'clock but then some monks told me don't study hard like this because you can get a kind of mental sickness. They said it's good to study but you must take time. For one year I studied hard then I became a little lazy. I helped my teacher build a house for one and a half months. I thought I would go to Nepal then come back and study and it would be good. So with one of my friends we went to Nepal. I thought I would study English. One day I was with one of my friends at a restaurant he was working in. I told him about a really bad dream I had the night before. He said, "Oh that's a really big problem, that's a really bad dream. If your family don't have a problem maybe you are going to."

'Maybe five minutes later the police came to the restaurant and asked my friend if he had a passport or not. I waited for my friend. I had a refugee certificate so I was not afraid. Then the police said, "Do you have a passport?" I don't have a passport so I said no. They checked my body and said, "Do you have money?" and I said no. Then they caught us and sent us to the police station. They put us in jail for three days. On the forth day they put handcuffs on us, put us in a police car and sent us to immigration. At immigration they asked us some questions then said US$2250 fine or ten years in prison. My friend and I were there, then came four other men and four other women. In the afternoon they sent us to jail. I was in jail for two-and-half years. A long time.

'Many times the Tibetan Reception Centre and the United Nations tried to help us. Our lawyer took the case to the Supreme Court, with documents and everything, but nothing happened. After two and a half years a Tibetan Reception Centre worker came one day and said please sign here. He was with a man from the UN. He said the Tibetan Reception Centre had found a sponsor to pay the fine. It was a secret, they wouldn't tell us who had helped us. Also when we were released from jail the Tibetan Reception Centre said please keep this a secret. Because there were many Chinese and they didn't want them to know. So we kept the secret.

'For one week it was not in the newspaper. They said if we were still in Nepal and it was in a Nepalese newspaper then the government could still catch us. That would be a problem. After jail we had one week to leave Nepal. It took a week to make documents. Usually for new Tibetans it takes three months but we were prisoners so we couldn't wait. They gave us a visa for India from the Indian embassy.

'The Tibetan government told us they could have paid the fine but they thought if they helped us, when new Tibetans came they would have to pay more and more because the police would start catching more and more people. If they paid for us and then not the next people, the new people would never be released from jail. So this is good thinking. I can accept that.

'I didn't tell my family I was in jail so I didn't talk to them for two and a half years. I called them from McLeod Ganj two or three months after I was released when I found out a friend of mine returned to Tibet and talked to my family about me. They were all crying.'

Soon after he was released Tashi asked his teacher at Sera Monastery if he could disrobe. He felt as though he had seen too much to remain a monk. He moved to McLeod Ganj to be with Choying, whom he had known since birth, and to start life as a layperson.

After dinner Tashi disappears without a word. Choying and I talk into the evening about Tibet, about the monastery and about life in McLeod Ganj. As the hours creep by I realise it is still thunderous and raining outside. By midnight I wonder whether I should brave the hard rain and run up the long dark path home or accept Choying's hesitant offer to stay the night.

I have always been cautious about relationships, aware that just below the surface many men are uncertain about who they are and how they want to be. I feel sympathetic to them but have rarely wanted to get involved in their journey of discovery, at least as a girlfriend. As a result I have often felt one step removed from my few-and-far-between boyfriends, spending a good portion of the time doubtful about whether I really want to be in the relationship at all. I have often wondered whether I should simply accept things as less than perfect. Perhaps that's what other people do. Perhaps that's life.

With Choying it is different. I know what I am attracted to is partly cultural and partly personal. The difficulties he has experienced would be enough to throw most western people into despair. It seems to be a Tibetan trait to be perceptive yet angst-free. Unlike many of us raised in the west it would never occur to Choying that his self-esteem would go up and down according to his fortunes or that he should judge himself by comparing to others. His deep acceptance of the law of karma, that whatever happens to him in this life is the result of his past actions, gives him an ease of being that I find refreshing.

I am also drawn to his combination of unaffected masculinity and kindness. At some deep level I know that this excruciating shyness between us, this newness, is simply something we have to pass through until we can be natural with each other and get on with being together. It is as though our outward dealings belie the honest confidence that already exists between us, the un-questionable connection.

I decide to stay the night. We squash onto Choying's single bed fully clothed, trying to give each other most of the single blanket, lying next to each other as though we both have rigor mortis. When I finally fall asleep I dream I am in a concrete car park, trying to get someone's attention by doing gymnastic manoeuvres on the parallel bars.

In the morning Choying wakes up early. But then a look of worry passes over his face: there is only a cold shower for me. But, he says, it is all right, only nine people share the bathroom. Choying guards the door when I shower, then escorts me back to the room, has several changes of clothes before he decides what to wear, applies Fair and Lovely bleaching face cream, a smattering of hair gel and is ready to leave.

Outside the rain is still bucketing down. Choying asks me if people in the west know how to control the weather. I start to explain about cloud seeding, but it's a bit complicated so I say, 'No, not really.' He is surprised we westerners haven't figured it out yet. 'In Tibet, monks know how to make rain with prayers and *puja*. It's really easy.'

Choying has to go to his English class so we part ways at the end of the path. On my way home I stop to buy a drink. As I open the fridge door I hear appreciative slurping noises behind me. I turn to see a wide middle-aged nun, with a three-sided cap on her head that resembles an upside-down shovel, shuffling towards me. Her eyes gleaming, she points at a bottle of Coke. I reach for it and hand it back to her, happy to oblige. By the time I have shut the door she has disappeared, ambling down the street, lugging great gulps from the bottle. The shop man tells me I must pay for both. I am used to making offerings to monks and nuns, so I don't think twice. It is considered a pleasure to help provide for people who have renounced much of the advantages of worldly life to dedicate themselves to a life of contemplation.

A while later I am passing the main prayer wheels in town when I see her again. She is waiting expectantly beside a woman who is fishing around in her purse. After the money is handed over she shambles away happily. I begin to see her everywhere. One day she comes into a *dhaba*, sits down and orders a big lunch, smiling one by one at the patrons. She polishes it off quickly then pats the knee of the man next to her as she gets up to leave. He is left to pay for two. I wonder if she is a poor old nun with a good heart or a schemer who has discovered the best way to extract a decent lifestyle.

Lobsang and I arrange to meet Elizabeth at an outdoor cafe after her class at the Buddhist School of Dialetics, where she is studying the intricacies of Buddhist philosophy in Tibetan. Up trundles the nun, all hot and sweaty after doing the *kora*. She sits down heavily and beckons the waiter to get her a Coke. Her eyes alight on us. A smile creeps across her face and she nods hello in our direction. Oh no, I think, not again. After her repose she signals to the waiter that we will pay. Lobsang isn't happy and tells us he's going to stop her. 'No, you had the drink, you pay,' he says in Tibetan. I look at her. Will she reassure me of her good heart? Will she apologise and come back with ten rupees in her hand? She rises up, stares at him menacingly, spits out some rapid Tibetan, then turns on her heel and walks off. I ask Lobsang what she said. He looks at me wide-eyed. 'She told me to piss off.'

When I get home the path to the house is painted with white auspicious symbols shining in the dark. There have been lamas for lunch. The guest of honour is an eleven-year-old Rinpoche who has taken to teaching Rajeesh the joy of soccer.

The population of McLeod Ganj has swelled to twice its usual size. The streets are filled with groups of giggling shy nuns delicately bargaining over sacks of *tsampa* flour and butter, strolling monks and an international assortment of foreigners—from dreadlocked hippies to neat Bermuda-short-wearing academics. It is the Dalai Lama's annual monsoonal teachings and he will teach for ten days on the classical Buddhist poem written by a much-loved eighth-century teacher called Shantideva. Called 'A Guide to the Bodhisattva's Way of Life', each stanza is an in-depth step-by-step poetic instruction to how to train one's mind in altruism.

The beggars, acutely aware of the calendar of Buddhist holy days, teaching dates and the Dalai Lama's schedule, arrive from all over Himachal Pradesh by the busload. Buddhists consider that the merit one gains from acts of generosity are multiplied on these special days and always dig deep into their pockets— for the beggars it's like getting paid triple time. By the start of the first day Dalai Lama-Gi Road looks like a carnival of the bizarre. Lepers, polio victims, drunks, the insane, undernourished and mutilated, their Jaipur prosthetics sitting beside them—as well as some industrious enough to have smeared masala paste on their legs to look like festering wounds—line the streets, their dark hands outstretched towards the flood of people who pass by heading to the Tsuglag Khang.

By 7 a.m. the concrete forecourt and terraces are packed to capacity with Tibetans and westerners, although the teachings don't start until 9 a.m. The Dalai Lama is usually early so those people who want to catch a glimpse of him walking past get their seats by dawn. Because the Dalai Lama is still in fragile health, his bureau has warned everyone that he will teach only half the day. The Tibetans, I notice, are reverent and subdued, in sharp contrast to the birthday celebrations. They silently click their *malas* while waiting for him.

The Dalai Lama emerges from the gates of his residence and walks across the forecourt preceded by a retinue of incense-bearing monks and smiling officials, following a path cleared of people only moments earlier. At the sight of him thousands of people rise and, in one flow, prostrate towards him. He makes his way past slowly, checking out who is present, stopping, squinting into the crowd, pointing and waving at people, never in a rush. He climbs the stairs to the middle level of the *gompa* and makes his way towards a small throne covered in gold fabric, with all the ritual implements—including a bell whose ring symbolises emptiness, a *dorje* or *vajra* to represent cutting through illusions, and a *damaru* or hand drum—laid in front of him. He sits down and immediately folds his hands to begin a deep sonorous prayer, while still perusing the crowd over the top of his glasses.

Despite the Dalai Lama's reputation the teachings are still, like many things Tibetan, only just twentieth century. Paper signs taped to rope with bitten-off sticky tape tell people where to sit to pick up the radio frequency that transmits simultaneous broadcasts in a variety of languages. People walk around frowning, staring at small radios and swaying their antennae this way and that to get reception. Indian families labour up the steps and wander through the attentive crowd, staring unabashedly at the faithful. There is little organisation or demarcation about where to sit so whispered disputes frequently break out. Despite a ban on mobiles, mine gets through security. Kate puts it down to me wearing a *chuba* because she heard the security guards cluck with approval when we passed by. Tibetans, it seems, have little possessiveness over their culture or religion.

I met the Dalai Lama once about five years ago when, during a holiday in Delhi, I helped organise a one-day teaching he gave in the city. The handful of workers were rewarded with an audience the morning he arrived at his hotel. There we were, the sweaty and nervous Indian sponsor, the wife of a famous BBC journalist, an Irish lawyer, a Malay–Chinese accountant, a troupe of invigorated Australian women fresh from a tour of famous Buddhist sites, some Indian Buddhists and me, all seated in a tiny anteroom, having been frisked by the security team. The Dalai Lama strode purposefully into the room. He slipped off his sandals, reached for his bare feet and folded them up underneath, clapped his hands together and said, 'OK, questions?' I am embarrassed to say that he was met with stunned silence until an Indian Buddhist launched into a complicated esoteric question with all the minute concentration of a forensic pathologist. I don't remember the Dalai Lama's answer other than noticing it was more precise and accurate than the question.

I feel now as I felt then: that in front of me is a person who is living up to the full potential of human goodness, someone with fully developed intelligence and compassion. Given all these qualities it is irrelevant whether he is labelled 'a living buddha' or not. I would follow his human example anyway. I didn't say anything to His Holiness that day and was pushed back in the almighty shuffle to stand next to him when we all posed for a group photo. Still, I left the hotel a happy woman and I feel that way again today, looking at his face.

Despite their respectful silence, the Tibetans near us take to throwing small grains of rice, supposedly set aside for use as a symbolic offering during the opening prayers, at each other. As the Dalai Lama extols the virtues of generosity, patience and perseverance, a Tibetan husband and wife team take turns to wake each other up when they nod off. They instantaneously perk up when a troupe of young monks head out with giant kettles of butter tea to distribute.

I take time in the slurping break to look around me, noting with alarm the way the armed Indian police contingent who guard the Dalai Lama look ready to shoot their feet off, leaning lazily on the butts of their old rifles. I am dying to stare at three beautiful, strong-looking nuns with an air of absolute serenity sitting directly behind me. They are in their twenties and dressed in traditional maroon robes but have kept their long thick luscious hair. I later find out they are yoginis—mystic tantric practitioners—who live in a nunnery in Dehra Dun and have probably just come out of a three-year retreat, hence their manes. I am, I admit, totally enamoured of them. The combination of their restful equanimity with the strength of their femininity is magnetic, totally different from the other nuns who reflect their renunciation with shaven heads.

The only sign that the Dalai Lama is about to wrap up for the day is the arrival of the person I come to call the Flap Man. About fifteen minutes before the day's teachings finish, he sweeps the path the Dalai Lama will walk on back to his residence. The Flap Man, a tall, thin-faced, immaculately groomed Tibetan with long hair, then quietly unfurls a flap of narrow yellow material and wraps it around the handrail of the stairs the Dalai Lama will walk down, securing it with a quick press of velcro on velcro.

But today at the appointed time, as the Flap Man stands back after executing his task, a jolt of horror pulsates through the crowd. An unsuspecting family of Indian tourists are walking down the steps, idly running their hands down the covering. The Tibetans can't bear it. Several elderly men heave themselves up from their cross-legged position ready to scold and remove the unwitting offenders. But the Flap Man spies the indiscretion and urgently beckons to the family to remove their hands from the sacred cloth. Minutes later the Dalai Lama is up and walking past the crowd, smiling, his eyes gliding over those gathered. He sees an old man propped up in a chair and stops to touch him on the head. The rest of the crowd look on in happiness as the man utters mantras looking both proud and blissful. His eyes glisten with tears as the Dalai Lama continues on down the stairs. The handrail cover remains pristine.

Slowly over the course of the teachings, a pile of neatly folded men's underpants rise in my wardrobe. Choying stands at the sink doing the dishes as soon as dinner is over, and I never again have to do laborious hand-washing. I slowly come to realise that Choying and I are living together. He is entirely at ease with the transition—in Tibetan culture there is little notion of dating and once a couple are in a relationship they are automatically referred to as husband and wife. In the past I've had to struggle with relationships because of my fear of losing my independence. It's different this time: despite some residue worry, I feel instead that we are so fortunate to have found each other there is no time to waste.

One morning my mobile starts to screech. It is 5.40 a.m. and still dark. Elizabeth is on the line in a panic. Lobsang has had some kind of fit. He looked like he was in a dream but his body convulsed and his eyes rolled back in his head. She slapped him and tried to get him to drink some water but he leapt up from their bed and ran into the bathroom. She said she could see his heart almost jumping out of his chest. Then he said he was scared of her, so he jumped out of the window and ran up the road, completely naked.

Choying and I leap out of bed and pull some clothes on, running down to the vegetable market. The early morning bread sellers we pass are talking, astonished, about the lunatic who just ran by. We split up. Five minutes later Choying calls my mobile. He has found Lobsang on the street, obviously just coming out of his dream, staring down in shock at his naked body. Choying put his jacket around him and they went to Jamphel's house where Elizabeth and I meet them.

Lobsang is spaced out and has a throbbing headache. He looks so vulnerable... our little ball of energy stopped in his tracks. Elizabeth says she heard some Tibetans talking about a naked man, horrified he was not a drug-crazed western hippie but a Tibetan. Choying is sure it is a bad dream and wants to take him to a lama for a divination to determine what bad influences are at play. Like Lobsang he thinks a doctor is superfluous. They run off to consult a lama who reassures Lobsang it won't happen again but advises him to make daily recitations of a special protection mantra.

Back at Jamphel's Choying says that many people talk about Elizabeth and Lobsang and don't wish their relationship well. He says quietly that sometimes Tibetans are strange, always talking about other people. Apparently a lot of people have witnessed their arguments on the street and disapprove of them. Jamphel weighs in, shaking his head, saying the gossipers have small minds.

After the next day's teachings I call in on Elizabeth and Lobsang. Elizabeth takes me aside and whispers that the day before Lobsang's naked dash Jamphel had been showing off that his *baba* had a new spell that could make western women want to take their clothes off and run through the streets. Is it a coincidence that Lobsang ended up doing exactly this and that the lama said he should recite protector practices? Apparently Jamphel's motorbike is outside the *baba*'s more and more as he conjures up new ways of securing a western girlfriend. I am usually the most sceptical about such conspiracies but what has occurred seems very strange.

We all become a little weary of Jamphel, his wan smile and his Hindu conjurer. Elizabeth and Lobsang decide it is a good time to go to Delhi to lodge their visa application for Lobsang to move to Australia. Soon Elizabeth's visa will run out and she will return home to earn some money. As is the custom in McLeod Ganj, we pack our *khartas* and see them off at the bus stand.

This is the stomping ground of Balu, the town drunk. Black from never washing, he looks as though he lives down a coal mine; with long gnarled rotten nails and a thicket of hair so matted it looks like a twisted black rope. He is a sight to behold.

But Balu is no fool. Rumour has it that many years ago he was in the Indian army but became a victim of their policy of dispensing cheap and nasty alcohol at low cost to its soldiers. It is also said he used to be enormously wealthy and owned McLeod Ganj's first motorbike before things turned sour. Balu worked out long ago the western habit of kissing friends goodbye, now he slips in at the end the line of farewelling friends, his eyes closed and his lips puckered, waiting for moist lips to brush his dirt-encrusted cheeks. For an illicit second he can be swathed in the clean, loving arms of a stranger.

The rains don't cease. I wake up to waterlogged faces staring through my window. Often they are mother monkeys with babies suckling at their breasts. In the rain their fur turns spiky, making them look like forlorn punks. If the window is open—the monsoon may be wet but it's also humid—and I scare them away, they casually swing over to the clothesline hanging on my balcony and unclasp a peg to run away with.

Outside, the roads are like rivers running with dirty water. At the teachings the accompanying mist hovers like a ghost over the heads of all the gathered people, who together emanate the smell of soggy clothes. The Dalai Lama teaches on suffering and how if someone hurts you it is your karma that has combined to produce the situation you now find adverse. It is important not to blame your enemy for causing you pain because it is your responsibility.

I think of Jamphel and suddenly am not so excited by the drama—after all, his actions are just the result of a suffering mind.

On the final day of the teachings a large *puja* is performed. When it comes time for the small monks to distribute the food and red cotton strings that have been blessed by the Dalai Lama, there is a major scrum as Tibetans of all shapes and sizes rush forward to grab what they can. The old people scold the younger ones, then push in front to grab the goods. I think this an unbecoming huddle of greed until I see Tibetans emerging, grinning whether they've secured the booty or not. It is the teenage serving-monks who look stressed. They surface dishevelled and distraught, having defended themselves against an army of grasping hands and elbows. Choying gets lost in the melee but manages to get three blessed *tsampa* balls to send to his family back in Tibet.

We finish the teachings with sore bodies but I feel a renewed freshness in my approach to life. Just hearing about the importance of kindness and compassion is a welcome break from my everyday mundane mind full of writing worries, grocery lists and mental notes about whom to email. It reminds me of the bigger picture.

As we leave the Tsuglag Khang Choying and I realise we need to go to Kotwali Bazaar for supplies. On the way back to McLeod Ganj a fierce rainstorm starts to rumble across the sky. Within seconds the weather is in a fury, spewing down water, thunder, lightening and whipping winds. The jeep driver kindly says he will drive us right up to the bus station next to a shop. But there are two Israeli girls in the jeep, one next to a window that won't seem to roll up. As it starts belting down she begins to get wet. She sighs and wriggles and harrumphs and sticks her umbrella out the window to try to get some shelter, nursing her anger into quite a state. By the time we pull up to the bus station she is saturated and incandescent with rage.

When people fumble to get their purses, extract their fares and pay the driver, holding up her exit in the process, she becomes livid, muttering that she is going to get pneumonia. This rude attitude always makes everyone in India adopt a go-slow attitude and as she sits there boiling, people do their business in an unhurried manner. She shouts, 'Hurry up will you. I'm getting wet.' Her friend pulls out a hundred-rupee note to pay the fifteen-rupee fare. It takes more time to find the change. Finally, drenched, she grumps off into the deluge. The driver silently turns around and winds up the window.

We get a call from Lobsang and Elizabeth in Delhi. Lobsang went to McDonald's and was so impressed he wanted to report that he was bringing a paper cup back to us as a special gift and souvenir. Never in his life has he been in a mass-manufactured environment. He tells Elizabeth that he will probably own a McDonald's once he's settled in Australia.

One day as we are heading into the rain, with Choying holding an umbrella over us as we stumble down the disintegrating road, another couple emerge from a guesthouse and begin walking ahead of us. She is a westerner, my height and shape. He is similar to Choying. She puts on her backpack and pulls him and the umbrella close. He puts his hand on her back and escorts her through the dislodged stones. Choying and I silently walk behind. It's like seeing a carbon copy of us. For a moment I step out of our private relationship and see us as a cultural phenomenon;

after all, I am one of seemingly hundreds of western women in this town who have a Tibetan boyfriend.

Part of me is embarrassed that I might be seen as just another western woman who's picked up a Tibetan man along with Buddhism and a packet of prayer flags. But there is absolutely nothing I can do about other people's perceptions, although I have to admit it has all the symmetry of a comeback—because that's how I've judged other people in the past.

While it leaves me disconcerted, Choying is unconcerned. In fact, his primary fixation is what will happen the night Lobsang takes Elizabeth to the airport when she leaves for Australia. I interpret this as Choying being scared of the airport by proxy and mock him, saying I can't believe a Khampa guy is scared to go there but a western woman—ie, me—has been five times alone at night.

Choying looks at me with his black eyes then says, 'But you have passport. If you get in trouble your embassy is powerful, it will help. If we are in trouble the Tibetan government cannot help.'

No nation recognises the Tibetan government-in-exile. Tibetans stay in India through the kindness of its leaders. They are at everyone's mercy.

I am silent. Ashamed at the thoughtlessness of my taunt.

4

CHOYING'S ESCAPE

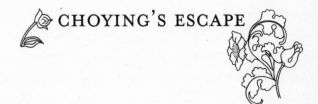

It begins to fascinate me how the choices that Choying made in a centuries-old monastery in Tibet, and I made thousands of miles away in a newspaper office in Australia, led to our meeting over dinner in India. If that isn't karma, I don't know what is. One quiet night in our home I ask Choying if he could tell me about his journey to McLeod Ganj. It takes some persuading to get around his natural reticence to talk about himself, but just as he agrees I make a mistake by pulling out my tape recorder. He looks at it, then at me, and tells me it is better we talk only the two of us. I realise how deep the scars go—it would be hard to shake off the memory that in Tibet it was mortally dangerous to have your conversations recorded.

Choying tells me that he grew up in the green grasslands of Kham, the fourth of five children. His father was a carpenter greatly respected in their village, who, he tells me with a hint of pride, took little Choying with him everywhere he went. Like most sturdy Tibetan women, his mother stayed at home to tend the family's fields and their herds of horses and yaks. Choying was sent to the local school where he became fluent in Chinese.

Despite heavy government taxes and a frugal lifestyle, the family had a happy existence centred around the traditional arts of animal husbandry and crop rotation.

Then, with no change of tone, Choying tells me that when he was eleven years old he came home from school one day to find his mother distraught. A drunk Chinese policeman had veered onto the wrong side of the road and crashed into Choying's father who was riding his bicycle home from work. He was killed instantly.

Like most Tibetans, Choying's father had a sky burial—a testament to the impermanence of the body. His body was taken to the top of a mountain where, as his corpse was fed to the vultures, a specially qualified lama prayed that he be given a good rebirth.

The family struggled on until four years later Choying asked his mother if he could become a monk. She readily agreed—having a least one monk or nun in the family is a matter of pride for most Tibetans. Soon afterwards he moved into a monastery in the next village. He tells me this was the turning point in his life.

'When I was at school I didn't know Tibet and China were different. When I was a child the Chinese government showed many movies about China so I thought Tibet and China were one country. The movies were often about China fighting other countries and China always won so I really loved her. We were never allowed to read any books on Tibetan history as it was labelled "political" and politics can get you into trouble in Tibet. So when I went into the monastery and the monks talked to me,

I came to understand that historically China and Tibet were separate countries. People's faces, their clothing, how we live, even what we believe in, it's all different.

'Before the Cultural Revolution my monastery had two hundred and fifty monks, but when I was there only forty were allowed to study. If you want to learn Buddhist philosophy it is best to have many monks to debate against, so it was difficult to learn. We also had little time for study because we had to do so much work. I was in my monastery for three years before I decided to do some political actions. I put posters up around the monastery and our village. Afterwards I became afraid. If the Chinese found out I did this they would put me in jail. For a long time I had also wanted to meet the Dalai Lama. I thought about going to a monastery in South India to learn Buddhist philosophy. So I decided to escape. I couldn't tell anyone because if the Chinese government came looking for me it would be very difficult for them. Also they would have been scared for me going such a long way, to India. So I didn't tell my mother or brothers or sisters or my lama.

'I escaped with two of my monk friends, Tashi and Gelek. We had studied how to get from our monastery to Nagchu, the nearest big town, and then to Lhasa. First we caught a truck to Nagchu. It was full of trees and freezing. We arrived at a guesthouse and stayed there for one night. The next day we caught a bus to Lhasa. In Tibet if you don't have a passport you can't rent a room at a guesthouse. We have no passports so there is nowhere safe to stay. If the Chinese catch us they can put us in jail. I remembered a friend of my sisters who runs a hotel, so we stayed there.

'We went from Lhasa to Shigatse. That's the home of the Panchen Lama. There we met three people who were also from Nagchu. They had passports so we stayed with them. They asked us where we were going but we couldn't tell them. They said, "Maybe you want to escape to India. You must be careful."

'The next day we paid a truck driver to take us to Latse. The truck was full of clothes so the Chinese thought there was nobody inside. But when we got near Latse the driver told us to get out because there were many police checks. We got off the truck and hid outside Latse for maybe three hours. We were really scared. Latse has a big river with a bridge. In the daytime they have police at the start of the bridge. If the police were there we would have to jump into the river and try to get across. It was winter and full of ice. But that night there were no police.

'The bridge was long so we ran as fast as we could across it. There was a village at the other side and a dog was barking. We were scared the police would hear so we kept running for hours. We stopped in the woods. We were so tired and cold and hungry but there was no food so we just tried to sleep. In the morning our blankets had turned to ice. We put the blankets in a bag and ran and walked for two days.

'One morning we climbed a really high hill. At the top we saw a village below. A farmer stopped and said not to go to the village because they had a lot of police checkpoints. We were really scared that if they saw us they would shoot us.

'We ran to the next village and found a truck that was going to Ngari in western Tibet. It was full of big buckets of salt and cloth. We travelled in it for three days. One morning we were dropped off outside Ngari. That night we couldn't get water or wood for the fire so we all felt faint. We took some snow and put it in the pot and found some grass to make a small fire. We melted the snow to make tea. The place was strange. Nobody lived there. We thought we might die there and no one would know, so we decided to go into Ngari. We found a factory with lots of empty rooms. An old man who was guarding it let us stay there for three days. But then our money ran out.

'Tashi became really sick. Blood was coming from his mouth and penis. I thought he would die. I was afraid but decided to go to the hospital and ask for some medicine. One injection was fifteen yuan and the doctor said Tashi had to take this medicine every day. So we needed money. We decided that I would go out to work and Gelek would look after Tashi. We met some old people who collected and sold wood for fires because it was so cold. I told one woman that I wanted to work, that our money was finished. I said, "Please help us." She lent me a boat. At four o'clock in the morning we went out onto the river. It took three hours to get to the other side because we had to row the boat through ice. I collected one bucket of wood a day. When we returned in the afternoon the river was water. The boat leaked so everything got wet.

'We are poor like beggars and Tashi is still sick because we don't have enough food. I am afraid he will die. Some days I help him to go to hospital. Then the man comes and tells us we must leave the factory. His friend lent us a tent. Then comes *Losar*. We have nothing to eat...really. Tashi is so sick he cannot move. I have to go and beg. I am so ashamed; at home I would rather die than beg. But at that time we have a problem so I do it.

'One day I went and sat outside the tent with a Buddhist book and prayed to Buddha. A man who was passing by asked if we were monks—since we left the monastery we had taken off our robes. He said he needed monks to pray. The next day he paid us twenty yuan to do a *puja*. Afterwards he was so happy he asked us to do a week-long *puja* for three people. He pays us 1000 yuan. Then another woman and her daughter also asked for prayers so we made a lot of money. We stay for three months. Tashi gets better.

'One day we meet a man who says he is a guide and can take us out of Tibet. But he tells us there is so much snow we need to wait for another two months. Eventually he takes us to the most sacred mountain in Tibet, Mt Kailash, or in Tibetan, Kang Rinpoche, to do *kora*. When we are halfway around I meet someone from my village. He tells me the police are waiting for me in Darchen, the nearest town. They are telling people they have money from my brother they want to give to me, so to come quickly. But I know they want to arrest me. We hide in Darchen and then go to Lake Manosarovar—in Tibetan, Tso Mipham—the most sacred lake in Tibet, to do *kora* before we leave. It is the last time we will be in Tibet.

'Eleven people were in our group. We set out but when we were walking the police caught us. They suspected we wanted to go to India but we told them we were pilgrims. They take all our money and jewellery and say that when we have finished the *kora* we can come back and get it. We walk for days but the women and children get sick. We go back to the police to get our money. That night we sat there and got all the money and then we escaped from Tibet.'

The place where they escaped is a mountainous area on the southwest of Tibet that is close to the border of Nepal. It is the quickest but also the most dangerous route so is not used as much as the Nangpa-La pass. That journey often takes between twenty and thirty days depending on weather and how often people must hide from Chinese police patrols.

'We walk all night and all day until we come to a village that maybe was once part of Tibet. The people look like us and speak Tibetan but they tell us we are in Nepal. They tell us the Chinese police are looking for us. So we keep running for four or five hours. We sleep in the woods. In the morning we can't find firewood so we dry some yak dung and make a fire to cook some food. For three hours we walk and then we meet some Mombas.'

I have heard this word before and realise it is the name that Tibetans use for people who live inside Nepal but who are ethnically Tibetan.

'They tell us the Chinese police were there the day before looking for people who had escaped. They say they will shoot us if they see us. So we walk for maybe another six hours. Our feet are bleeding. It is difficult to walk. Then we hide in a Momba village for the night. In the morning our guide takes us up a mountain like this.' He holds his hand vertically. 'He has to punch a hole in the snow so he can put his foot in it to lift himself up. We get to the top of the mountain then walk for two or three days. We are so tired, when we see the Nepalese police they catch us easily. We are scared but it is better to be caught by the Nepalese than the Chinese. For two or three days they hold us in a village. Then they take us to an airport. They say if you have money you have the chance to use an aeroplane but they need 1200 Nepalese rupees.'

Choying tells me that one man sells his gZi, a highly desirable bead whose origins are shrouded in mystery. Black with white patterns, these beads are said to have been dropped from the heavens to benefit those who have the good karma to find them. Some gZi beads are thought to be thousands of years old and can fetch enormous sums but few people would ever consider selling such a precious gem.

'So we all take aeroplane and come to Nepal. We arrive in a big city. It is so hot it is like fire. Then the police put us on a bus to Kathmandu. When we are there they call immigration and take us to the Tibetan Transit Centre. We are free.'

It is, of course, a limited freedom, and turns out to be reliant on the fickle kindness of Tibet's neighbours. Since 1989 the Nepalese government has allowed fleeing Tibetans to be handed over to the UN High Commission for Refugees in Kathmandu where they are designated 'persons of concern'. Under a gentlemen's agreement they are sheltered in large, cold, barn-like dormitories at the Tibetan Refugee Transit Centre in a suburb of Kathmandu until the Dalai Lama's office arranges the periodic buses that ferry refugees to India.

It is a rare Tibetan who has a passport, so the government-in-exile is reliant upon the Indian embassy in Kathmandu to issue permits to enter India. The arrangement, however, is inherently unstable. Maoist activity, pressure from China and the slaying of the Nepalese royal family have recently seen the Nepalese turn over escapees to the Chinese border police and arrest others on immigration violations. Choying was fortunate enough to slip through. In early 2005 the Nepalese shut down the Tibetan Refugee Transit Centre altogether. Tibetans must now fend for themselves.

'After some time in India,' Choying finishes, 'the Dalai Lama's office said I should go and study at Sera Monastery in South India. I stayed there for four years before I decided that I wanted to see more of the world. I decided I wanted to be near His Holiness so I came to McLeod Ganj.'

And the path that led to McLeod Ganj also led to me.

5

THE DEVIL
IN THE DETAIL

If the Dalai Lama is a god for many Tibetans, the devil is Lhasang Tsering. On a good day, ask Lhasang Tsering how he is and his deadpan response is 'still alive'. It is a reference to the fact that he believes many Tibetans would rather he wasn't. He is one of a group of former CIA-trained guerrilla fighters who were, and are, prepared to wage war for Tibetan freedom. Forced to hand over their weapons some thirty years ago, Lhasang is one of several now middle-aged men—many of whom were educated in exile in Christian schools in India—who have formed a nucleus of Tibetan intelligentsia bitterly opposed to the government's policy of nonviolence.

In a town that has built its reputation as the home in exile of the most spiritual and peaceful people in the world, Lhasang sticks out like a cactus. I decide that I will seek him out, but not before I go on a brief sojourn to Tashi Jong for a two-day writing retreat.

I'm trying to reassert my purpose for being here, having realised that being in McLeod Ganj has lulled me into a bliss-induced domestic stupor. In the west I had honed any chores into a fraction of my time. I would bung my clothes into the washing machine before work and hang them out to dry for an hour in the warm Sydney evening. I'd grab a coffee from the barista specially planted in the foyer of the News Ltd building and later wolf down a bought lunch at my desk. Dinner was often as thoughtful as dialling the local Thai takeaway. However it is becoming apparent that in McLeod Ganj my life has taken a distinctly different turn.

The shortage of hot water, the lack of whitegoods, the intermittent electricity and endless rain conspire so the entire day is dedicated to simply getting the most routine tasks achieved. With no fridge, vegetables must be bought fresh each day, while water is constantly boiling on our gas ring for dishes and laundry. Drying our clothes is an endless struggle against thieving monkeys and incessant rain. Some days it's all I can do to get fed, clothed and make a few frustrating phone calls to indolent government offices before the sun goes down. Alone it would be frustrating, but for Choying and I it's developing into a bubble of happiness.

Our day begins when the *doot* wallah, a tiny Hindu boy with enormous wet brown eyes, knocks on our door to deliver milk freshly squeezed from his family's cow. Choying then runs down to the shops to collect freshly baked *kabsay* from the women who crouch behind wooden crates selling steaming bread wrapped in newspaper. Back at home I juggle a pot of boiling water for tea, a frying pan for an omelette, and an open flame to toast the bread, all on a single gas ring.

Under Choying's influence, we have acquired the Asian habit of leisurely eating each meal, our idyll punctuated only by me jumping up and down to twist the radio dial, trying to trace the plumy voices of BBC radio commentators who seem to leap frequency every couple of minutes. Water must then be boiled for the dishes and laundry, the floors swept and the bed made. By then it's lunchtime and the cycle begins again, with Choying running down the hill to buy some vegetables. I, meanwhile, try to write in the small time I seem to have left.

Choying washes all our laundry, including my long ago salvaged bloomers. While I count my blessings at having, in the Tibetan parlance, 'caught' a man who does the shopping, cooking and running to get any small sweet treat I might fancy, Choying has discovered how much he enjoys being a nurturer—although he makes me swear that I will never mention his undie-washing to anyone. With baffled wonder he tells me that when he was a monk in Tibet he would never even have considered washing his own robes—and his mother forbade anyone but her to launder them, they were considered so sacred. Now, more often than not, he is up to his elbows in soap suds, scrubbing and wringing women's intimates.

The writing retreat is meant to focus my attention on the book. At Tashi Jong, Tenzin Palmo is away, so I book a room in the monastery's deserted hotel and spend days staring at my screen, flipping through my notes and thinking about nothing but Choying.

On the day I return the sun is beating down on McLeod Ganj. The mountains that surround the town are without their usual shroud of gloom, revealing a panorama of green. An enormous grandfatherly monkey is perched high up on a deodar tree taking in the scene, his back against the trunk and legs stretched out before him on a branch. The resident family of mongoose has emerged from the wood stack and are tumbling around on the small patch of grass play-fighting in front of our building.

Throughout McLeod Ganj, washing has been flung on bushes, pegged to makeshift washing lines and laid out on flat rooftops. The sound of wet clothes slapping against hot concrete seems to come from all directions.

When I come home I ask Choying if he thought about our relationship while I was away. He looks shy and then tries twice to express himself. He says that before, when he lived in the monastery, he was happy. But over the past two days without me, he felt unhappiness because 'one thing wasn't there'. It reminds me of a poem I have just read by the sixth Dalai Lama, a renowned libertine who swapped his cloistered life in the Potala for the bawdy back streets of Lhasa. In it he talks about his longing for his lover. Stanza after stanza recounts his need for her but the last two lament that his desire has replaced his wish for spiritual liberation. It is the classic tale of *samsara*: that grasping at sensory pleasures only prolongs our suffering.

The break has reasserted my need to get under the skin of McLeod Ganj and I put out feelers about how to contact the man they call the devil. I am told to seek out Lhasang Tsering in a bookshop he owns and runs called Bookworm. It is a small, jam-packed shop with an eclectic range of literary titles: from Thoreau to birdwatching to an analysis of the synergy between Christianity and Buddhism. It is wedged between shops selling Buddha statues and crystals on Rich Ingie Road, a short street that spikes off from Dalai Lama-Gi Road and is opposite McLeod Ganj's handful of questionably upper-range hotels. Four steps above street level, Bookworm allows Lhasang a good look at who is approaching from his perch at the counter.

I have been warned repeatedly that Lhasang is a volatile character at ease with creating enemies. So, I confess, I lurk around the bookshop for weeks posing as a customer, trying to get the courage to ask for an interview. One day, when all the other customers have left, he finally looks at me directly. There is a challenge in his gaze; am I making a pathetic attempt to shoplift? Cornered, I swallow my fear and step forward. Behind the counter Lhasang looks oversized, like a primate who has lived too long in a tiny zoo enclosure. He can't pace so he huddles.

He is swarthy, with salt and pepper hair and a small wiry goatee unattached to a carefully nourished but nonetheless down-turned moustache. He is handsome in a soft way, with brown eyes that are deep with sadness. He has, I am surprised—and relieved—to discover, a shy and courteous manner, his intensity evidently sparked only by the issue of Tibetan freedom. To understand his rancour it helps to understand a little bit about Tibetan history.

In 1949 China's People's Liberation Army marched into Amdo and Kham. By October 1950 the 8000-man Tibetan army was defeated after just 12 days of direct combat. Ten years later the Dalai Lama fled his home in Lhasa as his fellow Tibetans started to rise up against the Chinese and their collaborators within the Tibetan community. In 1960 the International Commission of

Jurists warned the world of China's 'wanton killing of Tibetans'. Just months later they issued another urgent report saying 'acts of genocide have been committed in Tibet in an attempt to destroy the Tibetans as a religious group'.

By 1962 ninety-seven per cent of monasteries and nunneries in the area designated by China the Tibet Autonomous Region (and up to ninety-nine per cent in areas outside TAR but inside Tibet's historical territory) lay in ruins. The people of Tibet suffered a devastating famine during the Great Leap Forward and numerous disastrous social and political experiments. In 1984 the Tibetan government-in-exile, operating out of Dharamsala, the town offered by India to accommodate the influx of refugees, announced that 1.2 million Tibetans had lost their lives as a direct result of the Chinese invasion and occupation. It was a Tibetan holocaust, and its effects are still being felt.

Given the extent of China's destruction and its genocide of the Tibetan population, most exile communities would embrace a call to arms. The Tibetan government instead developed one of the singularly most Buddhist pieces of legislation in modern history—the Middle Way Approach. The policy is designed to draw parameters in the struggle to regain freedom for Tibet, renouncing violence even in its subtlest, psychological form.

The policy's evolution can be traced all the way back to the time of the Buddha, when he rejected his privileged upbringing as Prince Siddhartha to become a wandering ascetic who practised self-mortification as a path to spiritual liberation. However, he came to realise that austerities of this sort were not a solution in themselves but that supreme enlightenment encompasses a path that we can all comprehend, a way by which we can understand the universe and live in harmony with all things in it. From this was born Buddhism's acceptance of the the Middle Way—a rejection of extremes, in this case between the asceticism of yogis and the hedonism of Prince Siddhartha's former life.

The Tibetan government-in-exile used Buddha's model to develop their own Middle Way Approach, designed to avoid the 'extreme' of independence on the one hand and the repression under which Tibet is currently governed. It seeks genuine autonomy for Tibet but works on the basis that both Tibetans and Chinese have legitimate needs and the solution to the question of Tibet's future should not create a winner and a loser. It also, bravely, acknowledges Tibet's political and economic limitations pre-1959—which can be summed up as a massive lack of infra-structure, including roads, electricity, sewage and piped water—while emphasising the truth that Tibetans have a distinct culture, language, religion and history. It holds to two non-negotiable stances: that under the Dalai Lama's leadership Tibetans will never embrace violence in their struggle for freedom, and that negotiations for Tibetan freedom encompass Tibet's pre-1959 territories, not the greatly reduced area deemed the Tibetan Autonomous Region by the Chinese.

The Dalai Lama first mooted the policy in an address to members of the United States Congress in Washington DC in September 1987. He suggested a five-point peace plan. It consisted of: the transformation of the whole of Tibet into a zone of peace, thus ensuring a buffer zone—in the form of a neutral Buddhist nation—between the subcontinent's two great powers, China and India; the abandonment of China's population-transfer policy which has seen Tibetans become a minority in the capital of Lhasa; respect for the Tibetan people's fundamental human rights and democratic freedoms; the restoration and protection of Tibet's natural environment and the abandonment of China's use of Tibet for the production of nuclear weapons and the dumping of nuclear waste; and the commencement of earnest negotiations on the future status of Tibet and on relations between the Tibetan and Chinese people.

Less than a year later the Dalai Lama addressed the European parliament at Strasbourg. In what was a surprise to many Tibetans, the Dalai Lama offered China responsibility for Tibet's defence and foreign policy while a democratically elected Tibetan government would preside over all social and economic affairs.

His address was both hopeful and pragmatic.

I am aware that many Tibetans will be disappointed by the moderate stand [this] represents. Undoubtedly, there will be much discussion in the coming months within our own community both in Tibet and in exile. This, however, is an essential and invaluable part of any process of change. I believe these thoughts represent the most realistic means by which to re-establish Tibet's separate identity and restore the fundamental rights of the Tibetan people while accommodating China's own interests.

The Dalai Lama concluded with this vision:

My country's unique history and profound spiritual heritage renders it ideally suited for fulfilling the role of a sanctuary of

peace at the heart of Asia. Its historic status as a neutral buffer
state, contributing to the stability of the entire continent, can be
restored. Peace and security for Asia as well as for the world at
large can be enhanced. In the future, Tibet need no longer be
an occupied land, oppressed by force, unproductive and scarred
by suffering. It can become a free haven where humanity and
nature live in harmonious balance; a creative model for the
resolution of tensions afflicting many areas in the world.

China has effectively ignored the offer but the Dalai Lama was right on one count. A fiery quarrel ignited within the Tibetan community, stoked up by Lhasang Tsering.

I explain to Lhasang Tsering that I want to understand why he objects to the Dalai Lama's proposal. At his invitation I spend the next several days sitting in a corner between the English–Tibetan dictionaries and an unwieldy stack of political magazines listening to his life history. Trying to get a fix on him, I ask where his family is from in Tibet, Amdo, U-Tsang or Kham? It is the equivalent of asking a westerner their profession—an indicator of who they are. But his answer is not so simple, his mother being from Amdo, his father a Khampa and he himself born far away from both his parents' districts, in remote western Tibet.

Lhasang's upbringing is marked by even more hybridity; he is the Christian-educated son of a tantric yogi who, upon the death of his own father, was told by the local astrologer that he must disrobe and marry in order to continue their family line.

With me balancing on a stool, Lhasang recites his history, making sure to enunciate each aspect of the circumstances that made him who he is. At first I am a little embarrassed by the way he replies to my questions, as though he is answering an inquisitor, but he ploughs through his past, ignoring browsing customers until they stand uncomfortably at the counter, disconcerted to hear such a personal tale as they wait to pay.

'In order to pay penance for breaking his monk's vows, my father did an entire pilgrimage of India, thirty full-body prostration *kora*s of Mt Kailash and a three-year three-month retreat in a cave there. On his way back he was in the central Tibetan town of Gyantse where one of the local aristocratic families had a sick, very old grandmother. They heard that he was a tantric master who could perform miracles so they asked him to help some of their servants and when that seemed convincing they requested him to attend to the old lady.'

Lhasang explains that when his father cured the woman the family asked the wandering mystic to stay, but he refused, explaining his fate. In an act of gratitude they offered him whatever he wished in their household. He told them he had seen one of their staff, an Amdo girl who was then in her late teens, and would like to marry her. So, in the manner of arranged marriages, they set off, not to the wild grasslands of Kham but back to the rugged mountains of western Tibet. It was here that Lhasang was born. Soon afterwards his father had two premonitions: that his own death was imminent and that a terrible danger was about to descend upon their homeland.

'As a boy I remember many people coming to my father with *khartas* requesting something and later on I realised they were beseeching him not to leave Tibet. In any case we soon left and went on a pilgrimage to Nepal and most of India, including the holy lake Rewasang, where Padmasambhava left for Tibet. Our family arrived in India at the end of 1958 or early '59 before the March uprisings in Lhasa [which precipitated the flight of the Dalai Lama]. While we were in a place called Mundi, celebrating the Tibetan New Year, my father passed away. As a lama he was cremated on the banks of the lake and it was while we were doing the long death rites that the first stream of refugees from Tibet began to arrive.'

Lhasang's widowed mother found work at a road labour camp in Manali and while the family was living there the Dalai Lama sent his officials around to gather school-age children. Lhasang got scooped up by the envoys and taken to Mussoorie to be educated.

'At that time Mussoorie had the best schools in India. After taking an IQ test I was among the students selected to attend the Wynberg Allen School. I was sponsored by American missionaries and was lucky to have had proper schooling. I did rather well in school and when I was in class in 1968 one of the turning points in my life happened. In an issue of *Reader's Digest* I saw an article about a raid into Tibet.

'It was about a man called George Patterson who had been working as a missionary in Kham when Tibet was free, so after the invasion he used his connections to help form the Tibetan resistance movement. The story talked about the way the fighters were trained by the CIA in the United States and then parachuted inside Tibet, making their way back to their base in Mustang.'

Lhasang couldn't stop thinking about what he had read; it seized both his imagination and his sense of injustice.

'These were the same men who were fighting in Tibet in the mid-fifties and who escorted His Holiness into sanctuary in India. I kept wondering, how will this struggle continue? These men are old, some of them will not live much longer.'

Lhasang decided then, in what turned out to be the dying days of the armed resistance against the Chinese, to dedicate his life to the cause of Tibetan freedom. He was fifteen and his sponsors were considering enrolling him at America's prestigious Johns Hopkins School of Medicine.

Two American tourists have approached the counter and linger long enough for Lhasang to serve them. They are each holding a bright blue copy of his book *Tomorrow and Other Poems*. They make some small talk, then Lhasang decides he wants to show them a poem that best expresses the sentiments of a refugee. As they stand slackly he opens the book, holds in it front of himself and in a beautifully resonant reading voice brings to life, unabashedly, '8x10', a meditation on how little it takes for a displaced person to feel they have a home. As he finishes, the Americans and I stare down in silence, words being too trite, our life experiences too comfortable, to comment on the passion and naked emotion with which he read. Lhasang hands them their change and turns back to me, ready to pick up his tale.

His sponsors, upon hearing of his ambition, went to Dharamsala to ask the Dalai Lama to intercede. Here Lhasang stops, as though still surprised by the promise of a vastly different life.

'But I went up to Mustang and I tell you it was a moving experience to live with those men who had given up everything for the sake of Tibet. These were the people who from the mid-fifties controlled over seven per cent of Tibet and who made it possible for His Holiness to escape. After they escorted the Dalai Lama into freedom they regrouped in Mustang to continue the fight. They set up sixteen bases and safe houses all down Pokhara, on the Indian border and inside India, but when I joined the numbers were really down. I would estimate there would have been less than 1000 able-bodied fighting men. That year turned out to be the end of military assistance from the CIA, hence the last year of the Mustang resistance. That was when Henry Kissinger, and later President Richard Nixon, visited Shanghai. Our suspicion was that one of the secret deals behind the Shanghai communiqué they signed was that the CIA would stop funding the 'Tibetan rebel bandits' as the Chinese called us. Some of the guerrillas were put in prison and matters blew up in the international media. Understandably there were many people asking His Holiness about what was going on. Were Tibetans in exile organising an insurgency? The Nepalese government made it a condition that for our leaders to be freed everyone must surrender their arms and close the bases. Finally His Holiness the Dalai Lama—and who knows what kind of pressures were on him—decided to act.'

The situation was so tense that simply sending a letter would not have worked. Instead the Dalai Lama sent his brother-in-law as an emissary, taking with him a taped message addressing the fighters. Lhasang was then in Dharamsala trying to convince the

Tibetan government to leave the situation as it was but by then it was too late. Back in Mustang the resistance leaders were tormented by what they heard.

'Here they were, hearing the Dalai Lama's voice, and they could not disobey him, but they had vowed to carry the struggle through to the bitter end. They could not surrender and they could not fight for freedom. Unable to find a way through their maze of feelings, some committed suicide.'

The rest surrendered and tried to merge back in with the burgeoning Tibetan society, trying to create homes in the muddy hillside village that was then McLeod Ganj. His tone still placid, I am unaware Lhasang has shifted gear. 'I suppose you know there was a Tibetan unit in the Indian army? They played a key role in the liberation of Bangladesh. My older brother was wounded in action. Today when we hear about the fighting in the highest battleground in the world—the Siachen Glacier— the soldiers are Tibetans.'

I am just being lulled into the sense of story when Lhasang roars at me. 'DAY AFTER DAY THIS IS THE ONE QUESTION THAT COMES TO MIND! WHY IS IT CORRECT FOR TIBETANS TO FIGHT FOR THE LIBERATION OF BANGLADESH AND NOT FOR THEIR OWN SURVIVAL!' The lingering customers and I are all taken aback at the ferocity that blasts across the quiet bookshop. Lhasang laughs bitterly and then continues.

'They have proven Tibetans were sent to fight in the Bangladesh war. Let's have some honesty. And the 1965 war with Pakistan. On my part I have no difficulty with this, that Tibetans die for India. I am happy and proud. BUT THE DOUBLE

STANDARD IS WHAT PAINS ME!' He again builds to a thunderous crescendo while the customers quickly flee the shop. 'I DON'T HAVE ANY DIFFICULTLY WITH TIBETANS DYING FOR INDIA BUT DIFFICULTIES WITH, ON THE ONE HAND, OUR LEADERS ACCEPT-ING ARMED PROTECTION [the Dalai Lama is accompanied by armed guards] AND ACCEPTING THAT TIBETANS CAN DIE FOR OTHERS BUT NOT FOR TIBET!'

Alert now to the danger of complacency I sit up nervously, but Lhasang tones down to reproach his fellow Tibetans. 'It may be they are trying to live up to the expectations of our new age friends. I'm sorry to have to put it like this. The truth is we were Buddhist for centuries but we had an army and capital and corporal punishment.

'People,' he says with resignation, 'should look at the real Tibet.'

'Time is running out for Tibet, the survival of Tibet is in danger. I try to alert concerned people about China's rampant destruction of the environment. They have been dumping nuclear waste in Tibet and, God forbid, Tibet is still seismically active. If there is one major earthquake, Tibet is the source of Asia's most important rivers and they would be polluted with waste and would bring it right down here.

'So whatever little my life is worth, and I know it's not worth a lot, I have decided this life is for Tibet. As I see it the survival of the dharma is not in question, the survival of Tibet and the Tibetan nation is in danger. The Chinese are playing for time and we are playing into their hands. It is to the credit of His Holiness and the government-in-exile that we have managed to maintain our identity. More than our ability, it speaks to the kindness and generosity of people in India to allow us to live as a separate people in their homeland. But today when I meet young Tibetans I don't see purpose in their eyes. They have nothing to dedicate themselves to. When I left school there was a sense of purpose. I wanted to fight and dying for my homeland was more than enough for me. Some of our leaders and elders blame these Tibetans for wanting to go overseas, but what have they got to dedicate themselves to?'

He turns to roar at McLeod Ganj. 'YOU CAN'T DEDICATE YOURSELF TO SURRENDER! Reading that article in *Reader's Digest* really did something to me,' he says.

He tells me that in their hearts many Tibetans want Tibet to be independent but feel they can't express this publicly, or even acknowledge it to themselves. I ask him, why not?

'It is the Dalai Lama's own personality and history. This is the fourteenth Dalai Lama—this is the second George Bush and he's not even a god. Tibetans wouldn't even consider not agreeing with the wishes of His Holiness. It is very significant when you know the power and position he has in the hearts and minds of the Tibetan people. But the government has failed to recognise that, deep inside, the Tibetan people wish for freedom. We don't have anything against China but we have the right to make our own mistakes. Not that if we get Tibet back it will be a paradise, but it shall be Tibet for Tibetans and I think we have that right.

'I faced more difficulties from my government than any other source I know. My own government undermined me in so many ways. The exile parliament made legislation about people not being able to participate in rallies. Individually there were people who offered to help me, and what really used to make me sad was that sometimes when I came up early to the shop an old man would look around to see if anyone was watching and then hold my hand. He had to look around to see if anybody else was looking before he could do that. And that is very sad.

'So in our most difficult of years we had a sense of purpose, which gave meaning to our lives. Now what about my children? When you give people nothing to look forward to, nothing to dedicate themselves to, you cannot blame them for wanting to go to the west.'

Lhasang talks of the time he and a group of intellectuals put out a newspaper that was very critical of the government and its policy. He tells me they received death threats because other Tibetans thought they were against the Dalai Lama. Again he fires up, 'At one point we were accused of serving the enemy's interests. They couldn't find fault with the writing and analysis so they said criticising the exile government and exposing its faults was serving enemy interest.'

I ask him who 'they' were, who made the allegations?

He pauses and looks down sadly, then mutters, 'His Holiness.'

Really? Publicly?

'Yes,' he says. 'We shut our newspaper down in the mid 1990s.'

I can see Lhasang has exhausted himself with history and the passion of his beliefs but he dutifully makes one last effort at staking out his stance.

'My political position is against surrender and compromise. It is against sitting here and hoping. The Middle Way Approach keeps us directionless and worthless. My shop is registered in my wife's name and when the call goes out to the Tibetan people for freedom I am ready to answer that call. But I will not waste a single day of my life to help make Tibet a part of China. That is in China's interests and they are doing it very well, they don't need our help.'

I ask him a question that I believe is at the core of much support for His Holiness. I start by apologising for the pain it must cause him. 'Do you believe His Holiness is the God of Compassion, Chenrezig, in a human form?'

He takes a deep breath before he answers. 'Um, I do not believe His Holiness is Chenrezig. I do not believe he is divine, I do not believe he is omniscient, I do not believe he knows the future. He didn't see the Chinese coming, how can he see the Chinese government coming?'

In fact, the Dalai Lama's previous incarnation, the thirteenth Dalai Lama, starkly warned Tibetans of the threat shortly before he died. He was very specific, announcing, 'In my lifetime conditions will be as they are now, peaceful and quiet. But the future holds darkness and misery. I have warned you of these things.' He further prophesied:

It will not be long before we find the red onslaught at our own front door. It is only a matter of time before we come into a direct confrontation with it, either from within our own ranks or else as a threat from an external nation. And when that happens we must be ready to defend ourselves. Otherwise our spiritual and cultural conditions will be completely eradicated. The monasteries will be looted and destroyed and the monks and nuns killed or chased away. The great works of the noble dharma kings of old will be undone, and all of our cultural and spiritual institutions persecuted, destroyed and forgotten. The birthrights and property of the people will be stolen. We will become like slaves to our conquerors, and be made to wander helplessly like beggars.

He finished: 'Think carefully about what I have said for the future is in your hands.'

But Lhasang continues, 'The way I see it the future is to be won through struggle and sacrifice. And I'm sorry to say this but I think His Holiness has been misguided and for the sake of the Tibetan people he must accept the mistake and restore freedom as a goal for our people.'

It is our final day and I rise from my stool and thank Lhasang. An unexpected curtain of shyness draws across his face and I feel the vulnerability of someone who is now cleaved open for the world to see. Lhasang, I know, is not a hardened revolutionary but a man who has lived his convictions and long ago accepted there will be hurtful consequences. He is an individual among a culture where virtue has become synonymous with conformity.

I leave Bookworm exhausted by the complexity facing the Tibetans and step out into the dusk, through the buzz of the market, past eagle-eyed Indian shopkeepers taking stock of the humanity weaving around McLeod Ganj, around tourists stopped dead in the middle of the street arguing over which restaurant to try, past the shadow of a large ornate stupa being erected in the middle of Jogibara Road. I turn into the narrow alleyways that will lead me home and make my way unobtrusively past the old people who sit in the fading light, their hands busily clicking *malas* as they silently turn their heads to watch a stranger go by.

6

DIVINE GOVERNANCE

He was concentrating on swinging the pots that billow wafts of incense over the chanting monks when the spirit first seized him. He started shaking then felt a jolt of electricity pass through him. It seemed as though he were floating away from the people surrounding him, becoming more and more distant from their presence and his own identity. The next thing he knew he was lying on the floor, staring up at the faces of concerned monks.

It was 31 March 1987 and the state oracle of Tibet, the deity known as Dorje Drakten, had chosen a new human through which to pass its prophecies, a modest monk called Thubten Ngodup. For three years, since the death of the thirteenth medium, Lobsang Jigme, there had been only silence. The government-in-exile had made extensive prayers and requests that the deity, who for thirteen centuries had guided them on matters of state importance, find a new medium through which to transmit its advice. By the time Thubten felt well enough to go outside and walk to the Tsuglag Khang he noticed people talking and pointing at him. The Dalai Lama and the Tibetan cabinet were informed and he was summoned to recount in detail his dreams and feelings in the lead-up to the event.

The monk who was known at his small monastery for surreptitiously nurturing stray animals in his room and mending broken statues told them he had been feeling increasingly mentally disturbed and short-tempered before his seizure, yet his dreams were incredibly peaceful and gentle. A short time later, after a special retreat and the blessings of the highest lamas in Tibetan Buddhism, he was asked to dress in the costume the medium traditionally wears when the oracle is being channelled.

He put on the twenty-two kilo brocade outfit and the moment the twenty-kilo jewel-encrusted headdress was placed on him he immediately fell into a trance. The weight of the headdress would kill an ordinary man, therefore monk attendants were placed nearby so that the second he appeared to be regaining his own consciousness it could be removed, lest it snap his neck. Soon afterwards thirty-year-old Thubten Ngodup was officially enthroned as the Nechung medium. For the rest of his life he would be required to channel a spirit that a select few—including the Dalai Lama, the government-in-exile and two monasteries—could call upon to help them see the future. The young monk agreed to forfeit his independence, anonymity and his health to be possessed by Dorje Drakten, the protector of Tibet since the eighth century. Tibetans everywhere breathed a sigh of relief.

I am slightly scared to be meeting the monk now known as Nechung Kuten. To be selected by a wrathful spirit and used to transmit prophecies leads me to suspect he will be like the spirit itself. I half expect to be taken to a dark turret in a decrepit mansion but have been given instructions to make my way to a house on the *kora* in line with the Dalai Lama's residence. It is surrounded by pots of carefully tended flowers. An attendant ushers me into the parlour where the medium is waiting.

A sturdy man in monk's robes stands up and offers his hand. He has a broad face and later I notice a beautiful smile. He tells me he has a cold but wanted to meet me because, he laughs, I have requested an interview so many times. A tree is growing through the middle of the room and I can see the house has been built around it; Nechung Kuten has carefully wrapped colourful plastic flowers and vines around the trunk.

I immediately see he has less the quiet, self-possessed demeanour of a lama than the enthusiasm of an energetic young man fascinated by the life around him. I am surprised to see he looks younger than his forty-three years—mediums reportedly have relatively short lives due to the toll on their physical health.

Nechung Kuten starts by explaining how Dorje Drakten came to be the protector of Tibet. He recites the history of when Padmasambhava introduced Buddhism to Tibet in the seventh century, when he called upon the oracle to leave its home in Outer Mongolia to come and live in Tibet. Later the abbott of Drepung monastery had a vision and told his attendants to go to the River Kyichu that runs through Lhasa to pick up a leather case that would be floating downstream. The attendants brought a box home and inside they found the heavy ornamental costume used today. Over the years thirteen people have been chosen by the oracle to be the medium; whenever they have donned the costume they have become the channel through which the oracle has served the government. One of the most important roles is that under trance they help find the reincarnation of successive Dalai Lamas. In 1959 the oracle was invoked during riots against the Chinese in Lhasa and it was then the Dalai Lama was told his life was in danger and that he must leave Tibet that night. Dorje Drakten left very clear prophesies about the escape route he was to follow into India.

The medium is sitting in front of me leaning forward expectantly. I ask him why he thinks the oracle chose him. He shrugs his shoulders and smiles. 'Because of our karmic connection,' he says simply. 'Days before the trance I am very nervous, not very happy,' he says with a frown on his face. 'I go there and monks are praying and sometimes doing *puja*. When I open my eyes I see each person and I hear the music and chanting but slowly it recedes, focus not very good, my feeling very tired.' He giggles. 'Sometimes people asked me what it felt like and I never knew. But once I went on a plane from Delhi to Ladakh and the weather became very bad, ooohhhhh, the plane went up and down. What is this word?' He pauses, and then says, 'Turbulence. That is the feeling in my stomach.'

He explains that to him it appears he simply falls asleep, that he wakes up later, often in another room with the monks taking off the costume. He opens his eyes thinking that only a minute has passed but when he checks his watch finds it is as much as an hour.

'After, my veins, they really feel numb and my heart is very tight. But maybe after twenty minutes I begin to feel very happy, I really enjoy that feeling,' he grins. He explains that later he can't remember what he was asked or the answers he channelled. It is said Nechung speaks only in Tibetan and senior monks say that in the past the prophecies were extremely poetic and difficult to understand but have gradually become clearer.

'It is spoken in the form of a poem in stanzas and prose style or a mixture of both. The language, however, is not like the common language; it is spoken with a tune unique to Nechung. I think different advice is given in relation to the weight of the issues involved and who is requesting the prophecy.'

He explains that some are made public, while others are highly guarded secrets and that he believes the oracle acts as a kind of divine colleague helping the Dalai Lama with his spiritual and temporal responsibilities.

I ask him about the sacrifices he has made to be the medium.

'I feel that if I am able to render good service, especially to the dharma and to Tibet, then my personal life is insignificant. Back in Tibet the medium was treated like a high person, no one could touch him and he used to sit on high chairs. It is like the Dalai Lama, once he would wear only brocade robes and people would not look at him. But since we came into exile the Dalai Lama has become more like ordinary people; it is the same with the medium. Many, many people come to see me each day; most are sick or unhappy or have money problems and want a blessing or a donation. I always try and give them a teaching on imper-manence and compassion. This makes me feel well and good. Sometimes it is a bit hard because I must be here all the time in case the government need me to go into a trance. Also I cannot go out alone, I always have monks with me. In the marketplace sometimes people bow at me so it makes it a bit harder.'

Nechung Kuten is well travelled and intelligent, our talk roams over his visits to Russia and the Antipodes. We fall into a discussion about his three dogs, one of which—a huge black and brown Alsatian—has been on the balcony staring at us expectantly during the entire conversation. He tells me about the time before he was a medium when he lived with three parrots and a dog. A family who lived nearby had a cat who was pregnant and when she had kittens he asked for one of them. However, they gave it to him too soon after birth and he tried to take it back as it could not drink the milk that he was trying to feed it through a syringe. Once the mother saw it and smelt the unfamiliar scent of a human, she refused to nurture it. He didn't know what to do. His dog, he said, had just had a litter so he placed the kitten on the dog's teat and hoped for the best. Soon the dog was nursing and cleaning the kitten as though it was one of her own. He was surprised to see as it grew stronger the kitten never tried to harm the parrots. Then one day he said a journalist turned up inquiring about a dog that had given birth to a cat—a joke he had been telling his monk friends about the menagerie in his room. He had to tell the newspaper it wasn't true but he explained the extraordinary relationship that had evolved through two traditional enemies nurturing each other. He relishes the story and laughs at the way the rumour spread.

I remember Tenzin's story. 'It's funny what people believe, isn't it?' I say. 'My friend was telling me about a bird in Tibet who gives birth to a small dog.'

The medium stops. 'Oh yes, but that is true. The bird is like an eagle, it is called a *Golega*,' he says. 'My teacher once saw the bird with her small dog. Many things like this happen in Tibet.'

The medium is now quietly coughing and the room is becoming dim. His dog has started to leap at the window, rearing to go for a walk. The medium simply lifts his hand an inch and the dog sits down patiently. I thank him for his time, offering him a *kharta*. It is dark and cold when I step outside and begin the long walk home. I am hit by such a wave of fatigue that on my way I consider having a quick lie-down underneath a tree. Dulled by tiredness, I rationalise to myself that beggars do it so perhaps no one will notice a westerner curled up in a dark corner under her jacket. I soon snap out of it and drag my feet up the endless stairs home, wondering what is wrong with me.

Much later I manage to catch a rare glimpse of the medium in a trance that had been recorded onto a video tape. Escorted by a phalanx of monks, he is led into the courtyard of a monastery to the discordant sound of Tibetan horns. Despite the shaky image, what I see is frightening. The medium, in a blindingly gold costume and heavy ornate headdress, seems to stalk around the forecourt with such volatile energy he looks like he might combust. Crude black hair swings out from the headdress as he shakes and quivers and spits out words. Gone is the placid monk Thubten Ngodup, in his place is something that is radiating a force not quite human. He almost seems electrified, but in seconds it is over and he is led away by attendants. As he departs you can feel the energy being sucked from the forecourt and a sense of normality returns. The camera pans over the crowd's shocked, silent faces before the video abruptly stops.

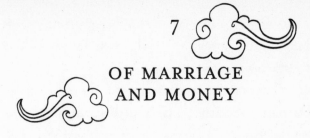

7

OF MARRIAGE
AND MONEY

A week later I am pouting in the mirror, stretching and puckering, trying to spread my lipstick evenly when Choying runs his hand lovingly over my chin and down my throat. He stops, cocking his head sideways. 'Oh,' he says. 'You have two of these,' gently wobbling the loose skin under my jaw. I am horrified. I know that Khampas prize directness, but I'm still trying to get used to his tendency to think honesty is always a virtue.

I complain, 'I do not have two chins! You can't say that to a woman, at least not a westerner.'

He pulls back, shocked, as though he has no comprehension of the logic of my argument. He disappears as I stare in the mirror, turning this way and that, trying to catch sight of the offending chins, but he soon returns bearing a picture of the Dalai Lama. He taps me on the shoulder then points at the Dalai Lama's jowls and says, 'No, these chins really beautiful, look the Dalai Lama also has. You very lucky. Very auspicious, I think, very beautiful,' staring at them in wonder.

I tell Choying that as much as I admire the Dalai Lama, it doesn't extend to wanting to look like him. I am a thirty-four year old woman, he is a sixty-nine year old monk; the aesthetics are a world apart. Choying, I can tell, doesn't know what to make of his strange western girlfriend.

Despite the poor start, I spend the day in a state of excitement. This afternoon is Kate and Tenzin's wedding ceremony. The restaurant has been hired, *chubas* sewn, crates of beer snuck into McLeod Ganj—to circumnavigate paying exorbitant local prices the boys went on a mission to nearby Norbulingka and smuggled it back to town—and plenty of meat dishes ordered for the guests. Despite the Dalai Lama urging restraint and a new push for vegetarianism, most Tibetans I know, having come from a place of scarce vegetation, are devoted meat-eaters and any occasion that calls for a celebration is judged successful or otherwise by the amount of mutton and chicken on offer.

For Kate and Tenzin this is as much a celebration of their relationship as a party to rejoice at successfully negotiating their way through the labyrinth of Indian paperwork required to get a marriage certificate. It started with a visit from the local policeman, whose blessing for their union was bought with a plucked chook and a bottle of whisky. For months afterwards I would go with them as they waited in line with all sorts of felons at the Dharamsala District Court for a judge to sign their marriage papers. The final hurdle was a small wooden box with a hand-written sign saying *Red Cross Lottery Donations* pushed across his desk by the paunchy chief superintendent, whose signature was needed to confirm the certificate. While I fumed at his barely concealed corruption, Kate, long reconciled to Indian ways, folded up a 500-rupee note and, smiling, told him the Red Cross was one of her favourite charities.

At four o'clock Choying and I, dressed in our finest *chubas*, stumble our way down the road, its stones loosened by the monsoon, towards the Himalayan Hotel. The open-air balcony has been decorated with tinsel and streamers and long tables laid out for the guests. We join Lobsang and Elizabeth, who in only two days will leave for Australia, in a queue to pay our respects to the couple. About to part, Lobsang and Elizabeth are inconsolable. They seem to have one of those relationships that is passionate at every turn, all emotions are amplified: their arguments, mutual frustrations, their humour, and their love. Elizabeth tells me that despite the way he tires her out, she loves the character in Lobsang. She also reckons that the challenge of living with him increases her opportunity to practise patience.

The first part of a Tibetan wedding ceremony involves the offering of *khartas* to an altar with a photo of the Dalai Lama and then around the necks of the couple who are sitting on low seats nearby. By the time we make it to the front of the queue both Tenzin and Kate are looking strained; their red, sweaty faces emerge from a huge pile of silk and synthetic *khartas* around their necks, lending them the look of immobile snowmen. I feel the pinprick of tears as I place a *kharta* around Kate. Like the other guests we drop envelopes full of offering money onto a small table placed in front of them, then back out of the room, careful not to turn our backs to the picture of the Dalai Lama.

Soon afterwards the couple emerge and take their seats at an especially reserved table, whereupon the Tibetan MC asks the assembled guests which of them would like to sing. He is holding a bottle of beer with a *kharta* wrapped around it to hand to the performer. The westerners stare at the floor while several Amdo street boys race towards the bottle. They stand in front of the crowd, strong and happy, and sing beautiful nomad songs, their voices undulating over high calls emanating from deep in their throats to low languid notes. One after the other Tibetans get up and take the bottle to sing; sometimes alone closing their eyes, sometimes spontaneously joined in by others swaying happily in their seats. Just when I think there is no one left, someone else will get up and launch into beautiful, unabashed nomadic wailing. Some boys get up and moonwalk, much to everyone's delight, some others have perfected break-dancing (a skill Choying has demonstrated to me in the privacy of our home).

The MC begins asking westerners to get up. I am mortified that I might be asked as my voice sounds like a cat being run over, but to refuse would be impolite. Thankfully a Canadian with a guitar gets up and sings an angsty folk song—the Tibetans politely nodding their heads—and a group of Australians sing 'Waltzing Matilda'.

As the beer is drained some Amdo boys get up the courage to sing English songs. A particular favourite is 'Hotel California'— which sounds more like 'Hoel Cal-forna'. Sung with all the passion of a Celine Dion ballad, they belt it out, flinging their heads back, mutilating the words until only the tune is recognisable. They finish, flush with effort and success. It is dark by the time the songs are exhausted and the tables are littered with empty plates and bones.

The Amdo boys then get control of the stereo and crank up the techno music. They dance for hours and hours, helped along by whisky whipped out from under their *chubas*. Choying and Lobsang, the only two Khampas, are slightly more restrained. They dance but, both being former monks, stay away from alcohol. It is twelve o'clock before the night winds down and everybody heads home. Another couple married. I feel great hope for their relationship. It seems that two years together has taken them beyond that initial fascination with each other's culture. Their shared cheekiness and willingness to compromise seems to be a recipe for happiness. I file that lesson away for Choying and I.

Later Kate tells me that she had been talking up a shy Amdo man, who was scratching a living selling *momos* on the street, to a Canadian friend of hers who had moved to McLeod Ganj to manage a charity. She said she finally introduced them on the dance floor, where they seemed to hit it off. She laughs, because at the end of the evening the happy suitor approached her, so thankful for her intervention that she had to hold him back from prostrating to her. She put her hand on his shoulders, turned him around to face the picture of the Dalai Lama, and told him that's who he might want to bow to.

While the Dalai Lama isn't free to wander the streets of McLeod Ganj in case he is swamped by adoring Tibetans, his image is everywhere. Out of admiration or craftiness, large portraits of the Dalai Lama hang in nearly every shop in McLeod Ganj, whether they are run by the Muslim Kashmiris, the reverent Tibetans or the Hindu Indians. At the postcard vendors that line Jogibara Road, pictures of His Holiness sell like hotcakes. Despite the ever-present robes and shaved head, it is possible to tell his age by the evolution of his glasses. Very early pictures of him show a young man just emerging from the influence of Chinese utilitarianism, with thick black-rimmed glasses; in the seventies, they become square veneer-brown plastic; and still later photochronic lenses cover his eyes. This decade they have been replaced by gold-rimmed frames.

If the Dalai Lama is an integral part of the Tibetan psyche, he is also vital to the political survival of those in exile. The Tibetan government-in-exile is in the unusual position of not being recognised by any government in the world but with a populace that looks to it for leadership, if not protection. To this end it is known officially not as a government but, due to the respect afforded to him, as a quasi-extension of the Dalai Lama called the Central Tibetan Administration. This means they are unable to pass laws and are reliant upon the goodwill of India for their existence. It is the Indian government that issues all official documentation to Tibetans, the registration certificates that allow them to stay in India and the identity certificates that serve as a passport for stateless people.

Ordinary Tibetans have come to accept democracy but largely want to be led by the Dalai Lama because they believe he alone can foretell the future. For his part the Dalai Lama has been quietly dismantling his political power while encouraging Tibetans in the art of democracy. What happens when a people accept democracy but believe they are already led by an omnipotent being? For the Tibetans the result is a highly idiosyncratic style of governance, characterised by the seamless overlap between

politics and religion that Tibet has practised for centuries—
although in exile it now has vehement critics.

A measure of the importance and the delicacy of the institution
of the Dalai Lamas became apparent the first time Tibetans in
exile voted on their future. On Uprising Day in 1995 the Dalai
Lama proposed holding a referendum to decide which method
Tibetans should adopt to get back their homeland. Tibetans
seemed to agree to the proposal but government representatives
were inundated by anxious people wanting to know if it was
compulsory. They were horrified to think that the act of voting
on the Middle Way Approach was, by insinuation, questioning
its main advocate, the Dalai Lama.

In the face of this collective panic, the government held an
opinion poll instead, allowing Tibetans to indicate their preference
for the Middle Way Approach, Independence, *Satya Graha* or
Self-Determination, or to leave the decision to parliament. To
placate them further, a fifth option was included: the unilateral
handing over of any decision about the course of the Tibetan
freedom struggle to the Dalai Lama.

In total 47 084 Tibetans voted. More than two-thirds either
directly wanted to keep the Middle Way Approach or devolved
decision-making to the Dalai Lama. The Dalai Lama accepted
the people's will and on 20 September 1997 signed a resolution
making it law. According to popular mandate the course of the
freedom struggle is in one man's hands. Many Tibetans breathed
a sigh of relief.

I visit the Chairman of the Assembly of Tibetan People's
Deputies, Pema Jungney, and ask if he considers this attitude to

be an impediment to the democratic process. 'Doesn't giving unilateral decision-making to the Dalai Lama mean people are relinquishing their own responsibility?'

He looks at me askance. 'All Tibetans have faith and believe in His Holiness. The majority of people have had belief in him since he was sixteen years old. Right now he is seeing the right way forward not just for Tibetans but for the world. So if we want a bright future it depends on His Holiness.'

I decide to try to interview Professor Samdhong Rinpoche, the first ever directly elected *Kalon Tripa*, or Prime Minister. He is a highly respected monk, a Sanskrit scholar, an admirer of Gandhi and a man who deeply divides Tibetans in exile. Some label him a Buddhist fundamentalist, others admire the way he has headed a stateless government, reliant upon the kindness of strangers. I send two emails to the Department of Information requesting an interview and, in order to facilitate my chances of success, say I am available any time in the next six months. They appear to fall into a void; for weeks I hear nothing. I wonder if the Tibetan government has adopted the Indian model—don't refuse requests, just ignore them. The silence is troubling because the email system is always malfunctioning in McLeod Ganj, so they might have got lost instead. I try to call but the phone lines are always congested.

A few weeks later, when I am starting to wonder what move to make next, I get a telephone call. The line is scratchy. 'Professor Rinpoche will see you tomorrow morning at 9.30 a.m.,' says a voice that sounds like it is coming from deep under the sea. I wonder who he is talking about. Professor Rinpoche could be anybody. A professor is common enough, and I'm in the town of Rinpoches.

'Are you there?' the voice bubbles up again. 'Yes, thank you, thank you,' I bubble back. 'Come to the Kashag,' it replies faintly. That's a vital clue. The Kashag is the Tibetan cabinet. I'm in. The phone goes dead.

The home of the Kashag is the Tibetans' best attempt at an imposing secular building. Three storeys high, it sits upon a hill in the *Gangchen Kyishong* or government area, a few kilometres down the hill from the market. Each department has its own premises surrounded by gardens replete with signs admonishing visitors not to 'pluck' the flowers. I arrive drenched from another monsoonal downpour. The reception area is deserted. I am drying myself off when the secretary sidles in with a steaming hot coffee. I explain that I have an appointment with Samdhong Rinpoche and she points me to a narrow stairway. It is hemmed in by two walls and, unbelievably, given McLeod Ganj's annual rains, is paved with shiny white ceramic tiles. I gingerly make my way up the stairs and through a door, squelching across the tiles as though in a pantomime, trying not to slide over. A Tibetan office peon intercepts me and asks me my business. Upon learning I am to meet the Prime Minister, he shows me into a large room with armchairs covered in Tibetan rugs arranged in a long rectangle.

Rinpoche has a reputation as a formidable intellectual with unrelenting honesty. He once asserted that if fifty-five per cent of Tibetans refrained from the ten nonvirtuous actions Tibet could be soon be free. Coming from a devout Buddhist this is a typical statement, but some Tibetans felt that from their Prime Minister it was a slap in the face. There are many sighs and whispers about how even in exile they haven't managed to get out from under the thumb of the monk class. Having read interviews where he has talked about the superiority of hereditary employment—the system of sons inheriting the jobs of their father that is the origin of India's caste system—and railed against the abject failings of western consumerism, I find myself looking forward to a robust interviewee.

When Rinpoche walks in I immediately realise that all my expectations are wrong. It is not a stern intellectual who strides into the room but a subdued renunciate. Like many Rinpoches he has a personal lightness of being, borne from a quiet confidence in the knowledge he lives according to ethics and governed by his desire to help others. I experience a kind of familiarity that it is possible to feel with many authentic spiritual practitioners, who possess an ease that allows the barriers erected between strangers to vanish.

He has brown eyes that sometimes appear green, bags under his eyes like miniature empty hessian sacks, and a small pointed gathering of hair on the bottom of his chin. As he lowers himself into a chair I notice he is somewhat elfin, with delicate movements. He instinctively wraps himself tight in his *zen* and sits up ready for me to begin. I offer a *kharta* and am surprised when he doesn't offer it back, the customary form of blessing. Instead he gently places it on the table in front of us.

I start by asking him how the government-in-exile is funded, and immediately notice he has a Hindi accent borne from years of living in India. 'That is a big question,' he replies, clearing his throat. 'We have three different kinds of resources. The first and foremost is not big, but is very holy. That is the Dalai Lama's Charitable Trust.' He explains that in 1956 the Dalai Lama visited India and, with the thought he might seek asylum, brought with him a large amount of his personal gold and silver which was then deposited with his friend, the Maharaja of Sikkim.

Another source is a three-rupee per month ($3 for those living abroad) voluntary tax paid by all Tibetans in exile. 'That is quite a huge amount these days,' he nods. The third source, grants from various NGOs and governments, including India, the United States and some from Europe, is the largest but most unreliable. 'I can't say it's regular because we have to apply every year. There is no policy, so they can deny it at any time. But for the last fifteen years it has been regularly granted and we hope it will continue in the future.'

I realise that as well as having legitimacy issues, the government-in-exile is in a perpetually precarious financial situation. I tell Rinpoche I am interested in the difficulties of operating as a government without a country. The Tibetan government is unable to pass laws or issue basic documents.

'That's right,' he says. 'Actually the government of India does not recognise the Tibetan government-in-exile but it works like this: the government of India says the Central Tibetan Administration is His Holiness the Dalai Lama so they recognise the Dalai Lama as an institution and his administration as an entity. It's a de facto kind of recognition and we have no problem with that. They ask very politely, "Please do not, ah, put on record the 'government-in-exile'," at least in correspondence with them. In that way everything functions very smoothly.

'But because there is no recognition of the government-in-exile we can't have any judiciary. The government of India keeps their eyes shut for our parliament and executive, but for justice it is very tricky because it is to do with the law. If something went wrong the government of India might go to an aggressive position. Therefore we put our Justice Commission within the Indian legal position of arbitration. The Indian law provides that anybody can appoint any other person as an arbitrator by mutual agreement. 'So we have,' he laughs a little, 'the Justice Commission, which we don't call a court to save the legal complications. At the Justice Commission, they can't hear criminal, property or civil disputes, they can only hear certain kinds of inter-Tibetan conflicts.' With these words I begin to understand how pervasive the disempowerment of exile must feel. Tibetans not only struggle to eke out a living in an already impoverished nation, and deal with the diabolical Indian bureacracy, but the administration they look to for guidance exists only meekly. They must often feel there is nowhere and no one to turn to.

What are the other difficulties of being a government that isn't recognised, I ask. 'There is not much if we don't make much noise,' he answers simply.

With that I turn to the difficulty of encouraging Tibetans to embrace democracy when they believe they are led by a buddha. Samdhong Rinpoche doesn't hide his surprise at the question and tells me the government is far from disappointed in the radical changes Tibetans have accepted in their forty-three years in exile;

after all, they have moved from a feudal theocracy to a democracy. But his next words give me an insight into how carefully they have had to extract the Dalai Lama from his traditional duties.

'In spite of the people's feeling, His Holiness very tactfully withdrew his powers almost to a negligible point and at this moment His Holiness uses his power almost not at all, almost everything is carried out by election. But as long as the present Dalai Lama is in the scene we can't expect any radical advancement from the people. His Holiness is a form of human being and he has to pass away. He has worked very hard so that when he passes away there should not be a vacuum. He thinks people should not be dependent on the Dalai Lama and I think that has been achieved.'

I ask Samdhong Rinpoche if he believes Tibet will be free. He seems taken back by the simplicity of the question. 'Oh yes. Of course,' he answers simply. I ask what he sees as the best-case scenario to get that freedom. Again, he looks at me and says forthrightly, 'The best would be as proposed by the present Dalai Lama.'

Then he decides to elaborate: 'That is, genuine autonomy within the People's Republic of China and the unification of all the Tibetan nationalities, which at this moment are scattered over more than five oceans. For that, democratic self-rule needs to be granted then the PRC can help with external affairs and defence. Tibetans themselves will decide all internal matters. That will be good for China, good for Tibetans, good for India and good for everybody.'

This brings me to a question that has been nagging at me for some time. If, prior to 1949, Tibet was independent, why should it not be independent again? Is this policy merely a political compromise with a country that already holds all the cards? Samdhong Rinpoche is quick as a whip. He explains that the current China-designated Tibetan Autonomous Region is less than one-third of the original Tibet geographically and population-wise. So, if the Tibetan government looks to regain the pre-1949 independent Tibet, then a large population of Tibetan nationalities and territory would be left under Chinese rule. 'Then it is a very small achievement, number one,' he says. 'Then number two, we would be a tiny nation between China, India and Russia, so it would be difficult to exercise our sovereignty in a real sense. So that is why His Holiness is looking for a bigger Tibet.'

I ask the Prime Minister about tensions that occasionally flare up amongst Tibetans in McLeod Ganj. Tenzin often arrives home with tales of fighting Tibetans. He says the trouble is mainly between newcomers and settlers—those families who came into exile first and who now own most of the restaurants and guest-houses. He believes the settlers have little tolerance for the newcomers and their needs that stretch the town's already scarce resources. For their part, newcomers like Tenzin can't understand why these families don't help their countryfolk more. I was often told that many Tibetans found it a matter of great shame that wealthy families preferred to keep their money and leave west-erners to sponsor the poor. I ask if it's because McLeod Ganj is overpopulated. He laughs and adds that 'People living here also have a lot of leisure. Too much time is a problem.' I want to probe further, so ask what he thinks are the particular difficulties and challenges for Tibetans in their third generation in exile. He answers with his legendary honesty as though he has long brewed on this question.

'It is a big challenge. The biggest concern for our administration is the personality development of the third generation. They don't want to work; they don't want to do any physical labour or hard job. There are many unemployed educated people who have been offered a number of jobs and they are not able to work or they are not willing to do this kind of job. So I don't know how to deal with them. This is our big problem. We are struggling.'

He sounds so disappointed with contemporary Tibetan society, so I ask him if he thinks it may be tied into the idea of a free Tibet becoming more and more distant for the third generation as they identify more and more with India. Again, Samdhong Rinpoche is blunt.

'I don't think so. They are not identifying themselves with India or Tibet. I think their minds are confused and during the last fifteen years they have been carried away by consumerism, particularly television and the internet. These make the younger generation's minds so clumsy they are not able to concentrate on one point for five minutes.'

As we are already on the subject of lost youth, I bring up the desire by what seems like the majority of Tibetans in exile to live in the west. Samdhong Rinpoche tells me they want to leave because they have been indoctrinated that money is the only way to have a good life, and that without it nothing can be achieved.

'But,' I say, 'with all the skills they learn overseas, won't their expertise benefit Tibet when it's free?'

Rinpoche laughs. 'We are thinking the other way around—now we must take advantage of them. They have gone out and now we can't bring them back. So we are trying to make them aware of the importance of culture preservation. We try to make them think of the future of Tibet and when Tibet is free to do something for Tibet.'

I thank him for his honesty, at which he smiles and laughs. Then I remember that before the Dalai Lama asked him to be a candidate for the first prime ministerial elections Samdhong Rinpoche was on the verge of retiring to a Krishnamurti community in Bangalore. Being Prime Minister was not a post he aspired to, but he felt that he should respect the Dalai Lama's wishes. I say to him that I hope one day he will be free to retire in peace again and he confides that his books are still in storage down there. He laughs, then leans forward, picks up the *kharta* and gently wraps it around my neck.

Later I begin to ponder Professor Samdhong Rinpoche's words. I wonder just how many Tibetans have married westerners and are beginning a second exodus to the west. I secure the phone number of Kate and Tenzin's lawyer, Mr Rakesh Narayanan. On a scratchy line from Dharamsala District Court he tells me he will have a look at the records and get back to me. He calls me the next day to tell me that between the first of January and November that year, forty western women married Tibetan men, a rate of almost one per week.

It would be easy to be cynical about this but when I look at both the disposition and predicament of many Tibetans I begin to understand a little more about the phenomenon. Like the rest of us, young Tibetans want to see more of the world and try new things. There is also little opportunity and much frustration in India. While the official unemployment figure in Tibetan settlements is six to eight per cent, up to thirty per cent of people are seasonally unemployed with only a subsistence lifestyle. Wages in the few jobs available in McLeod Ganj—mostly restaurant work—are driven down by cheap labour provided by Nepalese or Bihari migrants. The average wage for a cook or dishwasher is only around 2000 rupees or $60 per month. Yet the influx of westerners into the town has seen the price of food and accommodation rise. It is difficult to find a room with an outdoor, shared, cold-water bathroom and no kitchen for less than 1000 rupees. The conditions in exile are so dire that the ambition of many Tibetans is to move to the west and make something out of their lives.

A survey carried out in 2001 found that thirty-five per cent of people are willing to migrate to join family abroad. It also showed Professor Rinpoche was right: the emigration to foreign countries is considered lucrative, with over ninety-two per cent citing financial gain as the main reason for leaving. But there is another vital point Samdhong Rinpoche didn't mention. For young people who have left their family in Tibet, securing foreign citizenship is one of the few ways it is safe to return to an occupied country. Without the protection of a foreign government, if Tibetans return they will be imprisoned for the crime of leaving.

These factors are undoubtedly part of the complexity of attraction between Tibetan men and western women. Tibetans also come from a culture where marriages were often arranged, where the benefits of their spouse's financial circumstances were a natural part of the equation and did not preclude a genuine and loving relationship. Of course, as in all cultures, there are money-diggers and people marrying for all the wrong reasons.

Choying and I are walking through the main street of McLeod Ganj a few days later when Choying takes my hand. I am surprised. Tibetans generally show no affection for their partner in public. It is easy to mistake the body language between a husband and wife for that between two acquaintances. I tell Choying I have never seen another Tibetan man hold a woman's hand and tell him that he doesn't need to do it if it makes him feel uncomfortable, especially with the old people all around.

He looks at me. 'It's the twenty-first century, so what if I hold your hand?'

I'm embarrassed that I thought he would blindly follow convention. I think the subject is closed, but after a pause he continues.

'I know people look at me and think, there is another Tibetan guy using a western woman. That is their minds, I can't do anything to stop that.'

I am taken aback that he has voiced something I thought he was oblivious to. We continue holding hands, our small act of defiance in the fishbowl that is life in McLeod Ganj.

8

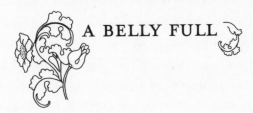

A BELLY FULL

I avoid buying a pregnancy test for the worst possible reason— because it means a trip down to Kotwali Bazaar and the chemist who adds another five rupees to anything a foreigner buys. But as the days wear on, the thought I might be pregnant looms larger and larger in my mind. We buy a test one afternoon but decide to wait until morning to try.

The next day I reassure Choying that I'm not pregnant. It is a brief flash of certainty. I come out of the toilet holding the kit and we both sit looking at it. Choying, being Tibetan and the ripe old age of twenty-seven (we think) and certain that the first woman he has met in his life will be the only woman, with the hopeful anticipation it might be positive. Me, like a rabbit caught in the headlights between reluctance for change and the secret wish for a child. We stare as the urine creeps across the white screen and a faint pink line begins to appear, growing darker and darker. I sigh dramatically . . . why must all Indian products be faulty? Then we stare a little longer. How could a little plastic stick be responsible for such dramatic news? I turn to Choying. He is wide-eyed. 'It's positive,' I say.

We spend the day in a surreal fog. We had already planned to go on a picnic with friends. Kate has borrowed Tushita's jeep and eleven of us pile into it to drive to a big grassy field about half an hour away. The men are all Tibetan and their girlfriends all westerners. The men immediately organise running races amongst themselves while the women gather to mock the underlying seriousness of the competition. It's barely concealed Khampas versus Amdoese. Choying and I catch each other's eyes, bewildered. He tries to escort me everywhere with his hand on the small of my back but I slap him away. Tired of running, the men organise arm wrestling, each with a ten-rupee wager. They then fall into reminiscing about Tibet.

At home it is *Yartsa Gunbu*—Summer Grass, Winter Insect—season, and all their families are harvesting this rare medicinal plant found only in the most remote mountains. They tell us about it with wonder. It is a moth-like insect that can be seen moving about in winter but they say it turns into a plant that leaves only a horn-like feature above the ground in summer. Part of me is suspicious about this transmogrification but by now I think anything is possible up there on the Tibetan plateau. Recently this strange creature has been used by Chinese athletes to enhance their training for the Olympics. Demand is so high and the plant so difficult to find it fetches between US$800–$2000 per kilo.

That night the full implications dawn on me. Choying doesn't have any documentation; no registration or identity certificates, and they take up to a year to be issued. Without these he cannot travel, and anyway, isn't it difficult for refugees to enter Australia, even with passports? I will have to have the baby in India if I want to be with him. But in the future where will we live? I am a New Zealander but my adult life and career has been in Australia. Anyway, what do former monks, whose qualifications extend to reciting prayers and beseeching gods, do for jobs in the west? Wash dishes in Chinese takeaways? Overnight my life has become a jumble of uncertainty.

Whatever road we take I see a morass of Indian paperwork in front of me. While the Indian government issues the all-important registration certificates that allow them to remain legally in India, in order to secure one Tibetans must have a birth certificate—something they are not given in Tibet. They must therefore say they have been born in India to get one. An industry of lies and deception has sprung up around the need to prove Indian birth. Applicants have to bribe a government office to find the name of dead parents, bribe the police to issue a birth certificate with a false place of birth, then fill out false papers, often with a made-up name, hoping the police won't check too closely. Most people with the means simply take the shortcut— hand over a plucked chicken and a bottle of whiskey to the local police superintendent who issues one in their name saying they were born in India. It gets around the need for proof. The identity certificate, or passport, is then based on this false information and another round of bribes ensues. But there are further complications because securing an IC involves interviews with the police. Tibetans must memorise an entire history of being raised in India should they be questioned. If they don't speak fluent Hindi, or fail in some minor detail of their created parents' background, they can be easily tripped up. The Indian government knows these untruths but to register Tibetans born in Tibet openly could provoke China's ire. Again Tibetans are caught in a political black hole.

I spend the night staring at the ceiling, mulling things over. For the first time in our courtship Choying snores. It is the sound of a contented man deep in sleep. For Tibetans, men are either monks or married, so for Choying, the news of impending fatherhood is an auspicious sign that he was right to disrobe. His life, after much turmoil, is on a new path.

The next morning I wake up to him gazing at me happily. 'Is it really true?' he asks. 'Are we going to have a baby?' His undiluted joy gives me a brief flash of happiness, respite from my shock. I answer, 'Well, yes it looks like it,' and give him a smile. We decide to walk to the hospital for a confirmation test. I tell him that Kate and Tenzin are trying to have a baby. He is thrilled. 'They are trying but we don't need to try and we get one,' he says, as though we are particularly clever. 'I think we are blessed.' We hold hands the rest of the way.

A realisation sprouts in my mind. Kamtrul Rinpoche and the Tara thangka. This is what I asked for, it has just come sooner— Tara has been true to her reputation for extra-fast delivery.

Delek Hospital opens at nine o'clock but we arrive at eight. There is already a small crowd of wan-looking monks and nuns and some laypeople. We hang around the wooden seats in the foyer. Whenever there is a rustle of paper people dive for the counter. Like most official things in Tibet, it is designed to make the supplicant feel small.

The counter has a glass barrier and in the bottom right-hand corner a small square hole where patients can crouch to speak to the office wallah. When nine o'clock finally arrives, a person appears at the other side. There is a scrum as the Tibetans push and shove to make it to the hole. Choying is in front, vying with a tall stringy monk. I think he must have got number one or two but later he emerges with an appointment for Weenessa Waller with the number eleven. We sit and wait. Counting the numbers is hopeless because people in government service get to push in ahead.

After an hour—Tibetans push their noses against the frosted-glass door, and try to creep in whenever one patient comes out and the next goes in—it's our turn. I tell the doctor I have had a positive pregnancy test. Her name is Marie. She is British, with cracked lips, but at that moment gives me a nice centre-of-civilisation feeling. She tells me to take a urine test and if it's positive, a blood test. I urinate in a small jar and take it to the laboratory. The man is nice and jolly, in five seconds he comes out and says to go and get a blood test. I explain that I only need one if I'm pregnant and he says yes go and get one. The penny drops.

We go to the reception, slightly dazed, hesitantly happy, then return for a blood test. The jolly man asks if I'll have the baby in McLeod Ganj, I say I think so; it's the home of the Dalai Lama. He is nice, calls me by my name, not a very Tibetan thing to do. After the blood test we get to push into line to see the doctor again. She tells me about the lack of facilities at Delek Hospital and the nearby options. She is relaxed, says to go easy on caffeine, get exercise, stay healthy and don't worry. I get a lump in my throat when she tells me that if I start bleeding there is nothing I could do or could have done to cause it. Miscarriages just happen.

Outside Choying checks again. 'We are are having a baby?' I say yes. He lets out a low whistle. He is elated and gently takes the bag from my shoulder. From that day Choying adds carrying my bag to the increasing list of chores he insists on doing for me.

Abortion, which may be a consideration for some people, is not even raised. For Buddhists all life is sacred and monks have been known to stop work on building projects for fear of killing earthworms. I've long endeavoured not to kill even that peskiest of creatures, the mosquito, so I do not think of terminating our baby. The pregnancy—and the fact Choying and I now have an unbreakable bond—are both part of our karma. It doesn't make it any less terrifying but it helps us accept that this is our future and it allows me to discard my habit of constantly agonising over where my life might go and simply join in Choying's delight.

A week later we visit the antenatal clinic in McLeod Ganj for our first official appointment. Outside the small concrete building is a queue of nomad women, tiny Tibetan babies and what look to me like pregnant grandmothers. The nurse immediately scolds me for not bringing my blood test information. Choying runs off to fetch it. After a half-hour wait we get to see the doctor. He speaks in rapid English with some Tibetan words so I have to concentrate hard to get his meaning. He tells me the first three months should be natural, no medicine. I agree. An attractive older Tibetan woman is listening in. Later Choying tells me she is a famous doctor who worked in China but escaped from Tibet. She is renowned for her knowledge of traditional Chinese medicine, Tibetan astrology and allopathic medicine but speaks no English so is hampered in her practice here.

The door remains ajar and now and then strangers poke their noses in to see what's going on. Choying leans into the conversation trying to glean what's happening. Later he recounts all my measurements and statistics verbatim.

I ask the doctor about antenatal classes. He doesn't understand. I say, 'Classes to prepare for labour.' He looks at me, shakes his head as though I am demanding a triple-decker chocolate cake and replies sardonically, 'Only in west.'

An old man wanders into the clinic shaking hands with everyone, uttering, '*Om Mani Padme ...*' but forgetting the '*Hum*'. He does the round then disappears.

I remember that Choying's mother still doesn't know he isn't a monk. When he calls her, she addresses him as Getsul, the name of the monk's vows he took. When I ask him why he doesn't tell her he says that he cannot be direct with his mother, he needs to tell his older brother who will convey the information via his wife. To tell his mother directly, to talk about these things, is not done. I get the impression Choying's mother thinks he's a lama. She is enormously proud of the monk in their family. Little does she know he's no longer a monk but will soon be a father.

Now we are sure, it is also time to tell my parents. They have long suffered the indignity of being in their sixties with no likelihood of becoming grandparents. My brother, who is two years older, is living it up in London with his wife and I always seemed to be the eternal spinster. However, I imagine their joy at my news will be somewhat mitigated by the fact they have barely heard I have a boyfriend, let alone will become a mother.

In McLeod Ganj, landline telephone conversations are a communal affair. Houses rarely have their own phones; instead people must line up at tiny shops to pay for a line to the outside world. In a nod to privacy most shops have constructed shaky plywood booths around their precious handsets. I search McLeod Ganj for a sturdy booth that won't broadcast my conversation but soon realise that the Indian phone wallahs observe the Hindu custom of being all-inclusive by blatantly listening in. I am mortified by the thought of spectators so head home prepared to pay the cost of a mobile call to New Zealand. My parents are thrilled, so taken with the promise of a grandchild they completely ignore the irregularity of the situation. Between tears and hiccups, I reassure them I am happy and that Choying is wonderful. They call back ten minutes later aghast, evidently having sat down and realised that I intend to stay in India to have the baby.

I slowly email friends the news and get immediate calls on my mobile in reply. From New Zealand to Asia to Europe it seems the news has been greeted with unseemly surprise. Several friends report that they screamed out loud then immediately dissolved into tears when they found out. Most are still getting over the shock that I have a man. One immediately buys me a subscription to an Australian pregnancy information site on the internet and reassures me it helped a woman in outback Africa give birth alone in a tent in the desert. Choying is happy that I have some foreign expertise to lean on but reassures himself that the pregnancy will go smoothly by constantly praying to Tara and sponsoring *pujas* at monasteries around McLeod Ganj.

We also have great hopes for the hospitals in the area. Most inspiring is Mapleleaf Maternity Hospital. The name conjures up kept grounds and wide porches with nurses in starched white uniforms and bat wings. Kate offers to borrow the Tushita jeep and drive us down there. It is in Kangra, around eighteen kilo-metres away. As we leave McLeod Ganj I imagine leaving in the throes of labour. The road to McLeod Ganj is potholed and single laned. Being India it has two-way traffic; big trucks, minivans, mopeds and tuk-tuks. Whenever one vehicle meets another on the road there is a brief standoff before someone reverses and their counterpart inches forward, half sliding off the mountain. For us there is the added attraction that Kate, a western woman, is driving. Mouths drop open; drivers sit dumbfounded instead of moving. It takes us three-quarters of an hour just to get to Kotwali Bazaar.

After Dharamsala the landscape changes. As the road curves down the mountainside we see yellow and green valleys lining a rocky river bed. We leave behind the maroon-clad denizens of McLeod Ganj and move into sari and creaseless trousers territory. Big vats of fat bubble in *dhabas* at the side of the road, men with huge ladles keep watch over them ready to dip in handmade candy. We rush by colourful fruit stalls. We have to wait as three cows mournfully move from the middle to the side of the road on a steep bend. We need to keep stopping and asking the way to Kangra, but Indians happily point it out. Tenzin says, 'India nice place in country, people very good' and it's true. The sun is shining and the airconditioning works and India is pleasant.

After an hour and a half we come to Kangra. I get out and ask a Sikh chemist wallah with an orange-hennaed beard where Mapleleaf Hospital is. He says, 'Mapleleaf,' and I silently rejoice. Indians always repeat the name you ask and you can tell whether they know it. The man before him said, 'Marplelee,' and pointed to a hill in the distance. We head out of town, past a roundabout and into the countryside. There looming on our right is a large blue building with terraced gardens and a huge hand-painted sign saying *Mapleleaf Hospital*. It is undercoat blue with scalloped balconies and many rooms with brown doors.

We walk up the stairs past the first gate but when we get to the second it is bolted shut. We look up. The rooms are all locked. There is no sign of life, despite the hand-painted sign listing their facilities and a claim they are a twenty-four-hour service. We traipse down again and ask a passing Indian if the hospital is still open. She says they are closed for lunch. Two hours later we are back but the place is still deserted. We stop and ask an Indian man and he says we must go to the back entrance up in the hills.

We drive up the road for five kilometres then loop back to where there is a small village and bulldozers ripping up the road. It is pure mud. We squelch through it and find the entrance, whereupon a toothless Indian woman in a sari stares at our muddy shoes and asks us what we are wanting. We say we have come to see the hospital and walk past her along a wide porch. To the left is a small concrete park with a stone circular bench. All around women in various stages of pregnancy are slowly wandering, clutching their bellies, looking pained. To the right are heritage-green doors that lead into dark rooms.

We ask if the doctor is in and a nurse says he is coming. We have joined the throng of Indian women sitting on the wooden bench when I realise they are all before us in a queue for the doctor. We decide to take a look ourselves. One entrance way has *ward* painted above it. I open the creaky door. It takes my eyes a while to adjust to the darkness. It is a large cement room: floors, walls and ceiling. Inside are ten old iron beds, the kind that you see in movie sets from the 1930s. There is a fluorescent bulb at one end and in the dim light I can see one or two patients being tended by relatives. There are large enamel bowls and instruments that look like they came from the nineteenth century. I back out.

I see a door marked *baby bathing room* and enter. It is the size of a cupboard and reminds me of the outdoor laundries in very old houses. Inside is an iron washer tub and mesh-covered windows that open out onto the walls of a steep incline. There is a gas ring on the concrete table, I presume to heat the water. A fluorescent light hangs over it. In another room, marked *matron*, is a big wooden desk. It too is dark, although I can make out a small brown card file siting on the desk. Outside in the courtyard is a washing line. It is full of newly washed yet undeniably blood-stained sheets. I find them frightening. A black plastic water tank sits in the corner, breeding mosquitos. The rest of the rooms are locked.

I double back, picking up speed past the caesarean recovery ward, which looks like a government hospice, and go to find

Choying outside. There is no way I am giving birth there, I say. I applaud the work they do. This is an Anglican missionary hospital and for local Indian woman it has facilities they would never otherwise dream of having access to—but I can't give birth somewhere that reminds me of a World War One vet's surgery. We return, dejected, to McLeod Ganj, wondering what to do next.

Soon afterwards Choying and I have just finished being frisked by a heavily pregnant Sunita, my beggar stalker, when we stop to rest on a roadside bench. We vaguely register the man next to us but politely ignore him. He is dressed in a big Rasta hat with woollen dreadlocks sewn into the brim, sunglasses, red flares and a floaty white top. He sits silently as we chat, then turns to us expectantly. A familiar voice comes out of the strange creature, asking if we recognise him. We stare into his face. I'm still trying to discern what this man wants when Choying asks hesitantly, 'Jamphel?' The face breaks into a triumphant smile. 'I knew it would work!', he says, hitting his thighs. He says he wants to get a western girl so he discarded his usual blue nylon business suit and thick gold chain, denoting wealth. He's sure western women go for a 'more casual look' and there's a particular girl he think he might be able to 'catch'. The disguise is also important, he confides, because he doesn't want other Tibetans in McLeod Ganj to know what he's up to. 'They always gossiping,' he says disapprovingly.

I'm sure Choying and I are radiating disbelief but Jamphel swaggers off to the bus station. Later that night Tenzin tells us the ploy was a success. He got a furtive late-night call from Jamphel, stuck in a hotel room with his paramour, wondering what to do next, asking for advice on what western women 'like'. He's horrified it might include something oral, a sexual taboo in traditional Tibetan society. He must have done something right: the next day he is a new man, and even in his nylon business suit looks as though a weight has been lifted from his shoulders. His lady friend gets on the next bus home.

Elizabeth and Lobsang invite us out to dinner. Elizabeth tells us about Dr Choedak, local astrologer, urine-analysis specialist and acupuncturist. But she knows Dr Choedak is in fact Kunga, a disrobed monk and former door-to-door toilet-paper salesman who is making a living out of naïve westerners' propensity for alternative medicine. He has set up a practice on Bagsu Road, and despite the fact that most Tibetans know he is nothing like a doctor, they keep quiet about his operation. Elizabeth recounts his latest tale of infamy. He recently met and proposed to an American woman who came to McLeod Ganj on holiday. She was about to return from the United States for the wedding. He had also been corresponding with a Japanese girl who decided to come to McLeod Ganj to visit him. Horribly, they would arrive at the same time. Elizabeth witnessed it all: Kunga running between two hotel rooms, trying to avoid the women meeting on the street, telling complicated lies about having to be at class when he was in fact arranging his marriage ceremony. Kunga's best friend has just married a Polish woman—also on a brief holiday in McLeod Ganj—who works as a shopping-centre manager. Leg, so named for his limp, spends his days trying to figure out whether the Polish currency is strong and what kind of income a shopping-centre manager earns. Lobsang and Choying are loving the tale until Elizabeth mentions Kunga is a Khampa. Both immediately go po-faced and stop laughing.

Each day it becomes more surreal that I am in India and I am going to have a baby. For some reason I have always equated a baby with wandering around pregnant in a western country where I could buy nice maternity wear and strangers could smile at me benignly. Outside of these constructs, I don't feel I am 'rightly' pregnant, so strong are the attachments in my mind. At night I still brew. My life has changed in a matter of seconds. I haven't had a boyfriend for years. Soon after I get one I am pregnant. What does our future hold? There are too many permutations to even imagine what is in store for us but my mind roams over them obsessively. It isn't until I think I might explode with worry that I start to get a grip.

One sleepless night I finally remember the Dalai Lama's teaching, 'The greatest degree of inner tranquillity comes from the development of love and compassion.' I start to relax a little. In the deep of night, my lover beside me, I think about the enormous range of Buddha's advice to help counter our wayward minds. He diagnosed 84 000 kinds of wrong attitudes and their antidotes. I sit back into some kind of perspective. My entire body relaxes. I suppose the shock of being pregnant is finally wearing off and I'm getting my sense of equilibrium back. I finally think about the baby I will have, not the difficulties surrounding it. Choying and I will be all right. Things will not go wrong because of circumstances, only by us losing sight of what is important to us.

It also dawns on me that I am only visiting McLeod Ganj and that one day, perhaps sooner than I think, I'll be back in the western world. I decide to spend a couple of days with Tenzin Palmo at Tashi Jong monastery, just to take advantage of her proximity whilst I can. I also hope being near someone I admire will reinvigorate a feeling of calmness.

Choying chaperones me on a rattly bus for the two-hour journey. Minutes into the ride, his head lolls to the side and he falls asleep, head back, mouth open. The Indians stare impassively. The conductor forgets to stop at the long road leading up to the monastery and I cause a ruckus when I see us go past, shouting out for the bus to stop, shaking Choying awake and trying to grab our bags. We jump out and head straight for the tea shop where we have a drink and feast on dried mango. We buy some bananas and then see a taxi that is driving up the long road to Tashi Jong. The driver kindly stops and we clamber in.

As soon as I see the monastery building I feel as though a weight has been lifted off me. I realise what a small town McLeod Ganj is, physically and psychologically. Recently rumours have been sweeping around that there are Tibetans living in McLeod Ganj who spy for the Chinese, feeding information back to Tibet about who is powerful in exile, and noting who has been granted an audience with the Dalai Lama so they can be arrested if they try to make their way back into Tibet. Like many things in McLeod Ganj the truth is illusive, but the rumour itself leaves a residue of fear and suspicion. It means ordinary Tibetans live under a yolk of insecurity, unsure whom to trust.

Here the sky is clear and you can see with sharp definition the top of the hills that surround the valley. The grass is tall and there are cows grazing everywhere, their shepherds lying in the grass or chatting to friends. We get a large white sunny room with windows and a door that looks onto a balcony. Below us is a grassy field where goats graze, and in between classes tiny monks from the young lamas' school flood onto the grass to play raucous soccer. They take off their tops to reveal scrawny chests and hitch up their robes to kick.

Choying hears there are people here from his village and that night we search the dark alleyways of the small Tibetan settlement to seek them out and offer them presents. We eventually make our way to a tiny house that someone has pointed out. An elderly woman wearing a worn woollen *chuba*, her long grey hair tied in plaits, ambles to the door. Choying explains he is from the same village and she invites us in, but not before tying up a vicious Lhasa Apso—a small, white and fluffy dog—that is snarling in my direction. It is a two-room concrete house. One room is a kitchen and the other a dining room with a fridge in the corner and a large altar taking up an entire wall. An ancient butter lamp provides a flicker of light. A rusty old wok is sitting on a pile of embers in the corner from where a mass of juniper branches sends out clouds of smoke. I can hardly breathe but everyone else is oblivious. We sit on a bed facing the woman and the man she introduces as her husband. He has bright white hair. She sits with her hand on his knee. From there on I am lost as the people don't speak Tibetan—which I can vaguely follow—

but the local dialect from their village in Tibet. Choying fills me in on their story afterwards.

The woman tells him that her husband, Palden, is eighty-two and that she has a second husband, Wangchuk, who is eighty. She lives with them both. The two men were monks together as young men in Tibet and escaped thirty years ago. They arrived in India to make a new life but they had difficulty finding a monastery to stay in so they both assumed lay clothes. Soon afterwards they met the woman, Karma Dolma. Polyandry is practised in Tibet, so both decided to marry her. Ever since, the three have lived together in harmony, trying to eke out an existence in India. Karma Dolma is now sixty and tells Choying that she is content and proud to have lived her life serving these two men. She says that soon they will die and she will also die happy. She is spunky and proud, they are shy and content.

The next morning Choying and I have breakfast then call on Tenzin Palmo. She is as energetic and perceptive as ever. She hugs me hello and is genuinely pleased to meet Choying. I am proud of the way he handles himself. His gentle disposition shines through his smile. At the very moment I tell her that I am pregnant, I begin to feel the seed of excitement that I am going to have a child to a man I love and feel destined to share my life with. As she congratulates us I feel the tears well up behind my eyes.

I tell her that I am caught between the western model of being overly concerned about the effect my diet is having on the baby and my natural instinct to know that I am healthy and that is enough. She says it will be all right; think of all the women who had babies during the war when things were scarce. She says the most important thing is to make the baby feel welcome and to let it know it is loved. To hear these words is a relief to my churning mind. I have a moment of realising the great advantage of having someone to look up to, whose advice you can trust—the essence of a student-teacher or -guru relationship. The best thing you can do, she says, is to work on your mind. It is the state of the mind, the way we perceive our circumstances, that brings us stability and happiness, and the best gift we can give to our children is not material advantage but raising them with some wisdom. The more progress a parent makes in training their mind in patience and compassion towards all beings, the better equipped they are to cope with the pressures of raising children. They can also impart some of their insights to help their children through life's endless trials.

Listening to Tenzin Palmo, I feel completely centred for the first time since I found out I was pregnant. She asks what I have given up. I say tea and coffee and the occasional cigarettes I used to sneak. She takes the Middle Way Approach...a bit of tea is probably all right.

As Choying and I rise to leave she tells me not to overexert myself. We take photos. I attempt to crouch in one. It is convention not to stand taller than your teacher, someone who is passing on knowledge that may eventually liberate you. I bend forward into a half-crouch. She looks at me and sighs, 'Stand up woman.' I stretch back into shape.

After some hassling on my part Choying calls his brother in Tibet. I feel increasingly bad that his family don't know he's no longer a monk, let alone that he will be a father. He needs to speak to his older brother so the information can wind its way to his mother. But his older brother is away in Beijing—like most people who are employed outside agriculture, he works in one of the Chinese government's many municipal offices. Because Tibet is under the communist system, the government is the largest employer in industries from factories to banking. We go to McLeod Ganj to use the telephone and after a rapid conversation Choying emerges looking victorious. I assume, proudly, he's told them the news. I am wrong. He is puffed up from making what he considers a radical move: calling another brother and asking whether he had heard of any rumours reaching their village about whether or not he was a monk. His brother said no, so Choying said, 'What do you think, that I am a monk or not?' His brother paused and said, 'I think you are still a monk.' Choying laughed and said, 'It's OK if you think that.' For now that is as far as we get in informing his family of the biggest event in his life.

I start to really take notice of McLeod Ganj, including the great mounds of rubbish that are collecting on the street. The way cows congregate around them, munching through paper bags with squashed tomatoes, rotten vegetables and used sanitary pads, and how a stench radiates from the piles, two or three on each major road. They start small then spread, taking up half the width of the road, and every day the mound grows. It transpires there is a garbage war taking place. A month ago the Dharamsala Municipal Council decided not to renew the garbage collection contract they had with the Tibetan Welfare Society. The TWS were paid 35 000 rupees per month for their work but a local

Indian man, Vinod Kumar, has undercut their price by 5000 rupees. But when the council 'went to survey the situation' they found the 'stipulated fifteen workers and one supervisor were not there'. For weeks they haggle and no rubbish is collected. The council desperately tries to seduce the TWS back into the garbage business.

I also notice the great quantity of young children strapped to their parents' backs or playing together in the street. Instead of lurid plastic toys they chase oranges down hills and spend hours examining everyday household items. Grandmothers and grandfathers pass the time playing with children in the back alleys. All the children speak Tibetan and, despite the difficulty of their circumstances, appear carefree and secure in Little Lhasa. It's hard to avoid noticing the butchers in McLeod Ganj too. Here they sit in tiny unlit metal cages on the side of the road. They crouch—as though they don't want to be there for any longer than necessary—in their cramped box with the innards, muscles, bones and heads of goats and sheep hanging from huge hooks around them. There is no refrigeration, so a fetid pong radiates from the little slice of hell. Like most shop wallahs they usually have a minion who stands outside cleaning entrails and facial parts and throwing them into a bucket, blood clots and all. Customers who line up on the road have to peer into the cage to choose the best cut of the carcass. Often they have to avoid the head, with its dead eyes staring out into the world.

Before I left Australia I made a pledge to give up meat for one year. I had been a vegetarian for eight years from when I was sixteen but then became vociferously carnivorous. Over the years I tried to give it up again but was too in love with Chicken Pad Thai and service-station sausage rolls. This time, though, I was determined to see it through. I promised myself that if I needed to I could eat tuna, but otherwise no meat or chicken. I don't know why tuna got picked on but it did. The reason I undertook to be vegetarian for one year was because of an email that originated from the Dalai Lama's office. It asked all his students to consider forgoing meat—for a day, a month, a year or a lifetime—and to dedicate the merit to all sentient beings and in particular the long life of His Holiness the Dalai Lama. I thought it was a doubly good reason for doing it and I decided that because I would be in India for the next year that was a perfect amount of time.

It is surprisingly easy here. Vegetarian activists in the west often say that if people saw how their meat was killed they would be so repelled they would give it up. But we are sanitised against such things; the means of production is so divorced from our lives. Actually seeing where our food comes from in the west is a difficult task—not so in McLeod Ganj. Every day that I must walk past the butcher I am happy I'm not eating meat.

9

MELA MADNESS

I know it is nearing the end of the monsoon because McLeod Ganj is gearing up for the *Mela*, the traditional Indian celebration that marks the official end of the rainy season. Stalls line the streets, slowing human traffic to a trickle; hand-wound ferris wheels laboured over by emaciated Indians block the smaller roads. A street dentist lays out a mat on the ground with a neatly arranged row of teeth. As I walk past he has his pliers deeply embedded in a woman's mouth, wrenching out a tooth. Behind him is a board with faded photos of happy customers. There is a cacophony of bands roaming the streets. They are all preceded by a prepubescent boy screaming out some song, followed by a man crashing the cymbals and another blank-faced sidekick banging a drum. Their modus operandi is to stand at the doors of establishments—and they can sniff out westerner money a mile away—and launch into the most god-awful clamour. The point is that someone, under the guise of generosity, will eventually pay them to go away. Everywhere you go the sound of hell's baying dogs won't be far behind.

On the last day of the *Mela* I go to the Tibetan Handicraft Centre to get a *chuba* measured. Choying has also decided it's time to for me to wear a *pungden*, the multicoloured striped apron that indicates you're a married—or in this case a taken—woman. Back when I subscribed to a rigid kind of feminism, I would keenly be on the lookout for signs of male oppression and would scoff at this kind of 'ownership', but age and experience has made me a bit less ready to judge. I want Choying and me to enjoy having the best of our cultures expressed within our relationship.

Choying buys some beautiful turquoise brocade with embroidered birds on it to make me a new *chuba*. As we squeeze past the stalls to get into the handicraft centre a small, buxom hippie woman behind me mutters, 'Wow, that sounds fantastic.' Then I hear it. The banging of the drum, the wailing, and the high-pitched wind instrument piercing the air. I make my way inside. By the time I manage to get past, a big hippie has taken control of the drum and is swaying his head like he's in an ecstatic trance. The woman behind me pushes in front and starts to sway and gyrate and swing. She has long black hair that falls over her face and she soon whips off her black jacket to reveal a striped boob tube. Indian eyes immediately bulge, shoulders being a forbidden erogenous zone in subcontinental culture. The duo pick up the rhythm, the flute man almost exploding with the air he is pumping as her boob tube slips lower and lower. The Tibetan tailors put their hands over their ears. One finally gets up and asks them to leave. But the big hippie is enamoured of the free-spirited picture he thinks they must be making and tells her to wait for a photo. Mercifully someone produces a camera and they all strike up again for a minute or two. The hippie woman hitches up her boob tube, reaches for her jacket and the posse moves on.

Once the *Mela* is over the days become gentle with sunlight and the mornings full of the sound of cicadas. The mongooses that live in the wood stack below our house emerge after weeks of seclusion, fat and playful. They find an old sock and play tug of war. Friends send me western magazines that I devour. I slowly get up the energy to reinvestigate the maternity scene thinking the madness is over. Instead I find it has only just begun.

Choying and I have decided that hope for having the baby in India is not lost. I have discovered a private Indian hospital down in Dharamsala that some western women have given birth in. It is known as Shukla after its doctor, although the sign hanging above it reads *Sai Mahima Hospital*. There is a big notice saying *Sex Determination Is Illegal And Will Not Be Performed*. In the months to come I will have to sign many papers stating that I will not ask the sex of the baby and that the doctor hasn't told me. Hospitals are fined 10 000 rupees if they reveal a baby's sex because in India, disappointed parents commonly abort girl foetuses.

Shukla is, by Indian standards, grand. A cross between a Spanish hacienda and an early Italian migrant's Sylvania Waters' dream mansion, rendered, of course, in cement. It looks like a large family home painted white with three storeys and a faux colonial facade. Outside, a minivan with a hand-painted sign saying *Emergency Ambulance* is parked in by two cars. Inside, the receptionist is perched behind what looks like the kind of veneer-panelled rumpus room bar found in *The Castle*. Next to her is a burbling fish tank and a noticeboard with faded letters from past patients praising the service. The pharmacist, on a break from prescription filling, loiters around the receptionist, cracking jokes in Hindi, scratching his crotch. Everywhere photos of a laidback Sai Baba, the famous Indian guru, look down. He sits on a rock, one leg resting on the knee of the other, his hand casually draping around his ankle. He is dressed in a white robe and headscarf. Behind him is a landscape of the rugged valleys of Himachal Pradesh.

I introduce myself to the receptionist. Like many New Zealanders I am cursed with terminal politeness. The receptionist looks at me witheringly and replies, 'Give me fifty rupees.' I hand it over. 'Wait fifteen minutes.' I shrink onto the waiting room bench. Pregnant Indian women waddle in and out, their husbands clutching water bottles and tiffins. A Sikh man comes to sit next to me and stares. Finally I get called into the doctors' room. It is through two narrow doors that meet in the middle, controlled by extra strong levers on each side. I can hardly prise it open before squashing my body through. On the other side four people are seated around a small desk. There is a grey-haired older man with a middle-class paunch; next to him is a woman with a short bob and crimson lipstick wearing a shalwar kemeez. A slouching woman, who in the nanoseconds my eyes flicked over her looks like an albino Indian but who I later realise is a westerner, and finally the top doctor, an older woman with strong straight black hair. I presume it's Shukla herself.

The nurse points to a stainless-steel stool. I sit. They stare. Minutes tick by. The nurse's eyes bore into me. I shift in my seat. I make a half-murmur. Finally the doctor next to me speaks up. 'What is it?' she says.

'Sorry?' I ask.

'What is it you are wanting?'

I realise the protocol is not for them to introduce themselves or make pleasantries but for me to state my case. I lay my file on the table and explain that I am pregnant and would like an ultrasound. They don't utter a word but signal a waiting nurse to take me behind a plastic shower curtain. Once there, she looks at me as though I am mentally challenged. The examination 'room' is between the shower curtain and the wall. There is a narrow high bed, an ultrasound machine and a rubbish bin.

The nurse takes my blood pressure and examines my uterus, pushing firmly on my belly. Then she tells me to get up. I rearrange my clothes and come back out into the doctors' conference. They stare solemnly; the woman with crimson lipstick beckons me to sit next to her. She begins to talk to me. For a moment everything in my world shuts down. I wonder where I am, whom I am speaking to. She stares at me. I stare back blankly. Then she laughs. 'Oh sorry, you are not knowing Hindi.'

'You will be taking these,' she says, pointing to a doctorly scribble on a piece of paper. I ask what they are. Her response is in such rapid English it sounds like a garbled pop song on fast forward. She sighs and tries again, starting slowly but building up into a crescendo of gibberish. I repeat what I think I hear her say. She looks at me for several seconds. Then sits back. 'You can go now,' she says.

'What about the ultrasound?' I ask.

'If you want, but you must drink a lot of water and wait for maybe one hour.'

'How much is it?' I ask.

She looks at me dismissively. 'I don't know...maybe 500,' she says.

I get up to leave, squeezing my body through the reluctant doors. The receptionist doesn't look up. 'Give me seventy rupees,' she says, her palm outstretched. I hand it over and say I think I will come back the next day for an ultrasound. 'You will have to give me 500 rupees,' she says.

Two days later I summon up the strength to go back. The receptionist is strangely happy to see me. Disconcertingly, the pharmacist welcomes me like an old friend. I almost jump out of my skin. I have to drink enough water until I almost burst. That inflates the bladder and moves the uterus closer to the surface of the skin, allowing the sound waves to hit the baby. I sit in reception, drinking litre upon litre of water. I must have the weakest bladder in the world so I am confident that within minutes it will be full. I gulp it down. Choying suggests I slow down. After an hour and two and a half litres I still don't feel like going to the toilet but desperately want to throw up. I run outside and like a fountain all the water comes back up, spouting out of my mouth and nose. I sit down in the sun, open my bottle and start again.

Three hours later I am still gulping it down. Patients are staring at me as though they are about to line up a brass band and herald me a water saint. I decide to tell the receptionist I am ready, although I don't feel any urgency. The nurse ushers me into the room again. The doctors point at the shower curtain. The elderly woman comes in and spreads a clear gel on my stomach. The minute the ultrasound scanner touches me, I desperately need to go the loo. I am scared I will pee all over the bed.

The doctor frowns and runs the scanner over my belly. I pray to Tara the child is all right. The doctor converses with the nurse in Hindi. I hear the word placenta. I raise my head but they ignore me. The doctor asks me if I've had other children. Sensing there is something wrong, I feel a wellspring of tears and struggle to keep them back. Then she tells me to get up. When I come into the doctors' corner they tell me to go and get a urine sample. I leave. Later I come back to the reception area. Choying asks me if I have seen the ultrasound. I say no. He says he has, the baby is normal.

I feel a wave of apprehension, mixed with fear and anxiety, pass over me, the residue of my worrying lagging behind the moment. I'm going to cry in the middle of Shukla hospital's reception centre but look at the receptionist and manage to get myself under control. Choying hugs me and whispers 'Thank you' into my ear. The wave rises up again.

I ask the receptionist if I should go straight back in or wait. She fixes me with a look, 'Do you want to see the doctor?'

'Yes,' I say. Through my incredulity I find my voice. 'I want to talk about the ultrasound.' She hands it to me. It looks like a picture of a giant worm. The notes underneath don't reassure me, the scrawled phrase 'Single living being'. I certainly didn't just want a blurry picture of a half-moon-shaped being without any information.

'Wait,' she says. 'Give me thirty rupees.'

'I'll give it to you after,' I say. She smiles.

I get called back into the doctors' room. 'You are all right. The baby is alive,' the crimson one says. I point to my file and ask what low-lying placenta means. 'Your placenta is below the baby if it stays there you will have to have a caesarean you have to see if you bleed maybe it will move up don't exert yourself,' she says in one sentence.

I am determined to get more information. 'How many women have this?' I ask. 'About twenty per cent at the beginning,' she says, 'but most of the placentas move.' She hits the file on the desk as though winding down. I grab it. 'What do all these measurements mean?' I ask. She sighs. 'This is crown-to-toe length of spine and the foetal heartbeat,' she says, double hitting the file on the desk and handing it back to me. I decide to look on the internet later. Right now I just want to escape Shukla hospital. I thank her and head for the doors out of Hades. The receptionist smiles at me. I pay her fine. Choying and I head out into the sunlight clutching the photos of our blurry progeny.

I check my email only to get a rejection letter from Venerable Taklha, the Dalai Lama's assistant. I had asked for an interview sometime in the next six months. He replies that they are cutting down the Dalai Lama's schedule because of his ill health. Anyway, he adds, his diary is full until the next spring. I remember the Dalai Lama's advice never to give up. I write a grovelling email back explaining I am only a phone call away should fifteen minutes become available. Within days I get a second rejection. The Dalai

Lama's health really needs to be looked after. They are sorry. There is no chance.

I console myself with a new commodity. Choying turns up one day with a dual-ring gas element from his old house. I feel like we have become a two-car family and am slightly embarrassed by our wealth. Choying also sets up an Indian home office for me on a rickety table out on the balcony. Everyday the monkeys leaf through my notes, eating some, screwing up others.

I also get my first censure. Choying and I have heard there are some people from his village who have just arrived in McLeod Ganj. They are staying at the Tibetan Reception Centre. All will want to meet His Holiness and once this has been achieved they will have to find their own accommodation. In the meantime they get much-needed health care and some orientation about the outside world.

The TRC is a large building with wide dormitories with row upon row of beds lined up next to each other. The new arrivals are sitting in groups talking, or walking around with bowls of hot water and distilled Tibetan medicine. The dormitory we walk into stinks of yaks, butter tea and unwashed bodies—reminding me that Tibetan nomads traditionally wash only once each year. Dark faces with rosy red cheeks raise their eyes to us. Choying stops to talk to his village people, chatting amicably and relaying the conversation back to me.

They talk not about the arduous journey they have made or the petty repression that governs their daily lives—that would be most un-Tibetan. Instead they tell Choying about the new road that connects their village to a nearby city. A journey that used to take several gruelling days over the hills on horseback is now easily made by government buses that ply the route. The new road has opened up Choying's modest village to trade and prosperity—now almost everyone owns a television. It can't be denied, as the Dalai Lama says, that along with the disasters the Chinese have bought a kind of progress to Tibet. A road network has connected previously isolated villages and glasshouses have guaranteed harvests, increasing some ordinary Tibetans' standard of living. But, I think to myself, it is an indication of their character that, despite material progress, the need to freely practise their spiritual beliefs continues to propel many into an uncertain life in exile. After all, in much of Tibet it is illegal to possess even a photograph of the Dalai Lama or the national flag.

After twenty minutes of smiling inanely at Choying's friends I notice that he has forgotten to introduce me, so I proffer my hand and say, 'Hi, I'm Vanessa. What are your names?' They stare at me in silence. Choying looks sideways at me and hurriedly winds up the conversation. He slinks off with me in tow. Outside I ask him what the problem is.

'You accuse them of being thieves!' he exclaims.

'WHAT?' I ask.

He says that in Tibet it is rude to ask people's names. Choying rarely refers to his friends directly but calls them 'that guy with the earrings' or just 'he', leaving me to deduce who he might be talking about by gleaning information later in the conversation. He tells me it has become even ruder lately because of the Chinese. When people are asked their details it is usually because they are in trouble with the authorities. His friends are former political prisoners and still bear the scars. Despite his assurances that I need not worry, I walk away ashamed of the position I ignorantly put them in.

My mother sends packages from New Zealand: maternity bras, underpants and chocolate bars. The underpants are g-strings. Choying's eyes fall on them. He picks them up holding them in front of me. 'What are these?' he asks querulously. I explain the function of the spindly strip of material. He stares at me disbelieving, then, in the high-pitched voice he reserves for moments of incredulity at western culture, says 'Oh my god!' then throws them back on the bed dissolving into hysterics. They go to the bottom of the drawer, never to be seen again.

We have told only our closest friends about the pregnancy but one day an acquaintance of Choying's congratulates him on the street. My jaw almost drops open. Afterwards Choying tells me the man is the nephew of the doctor who was present during our consultation. She rushed home and told him the good news. I'm astounded and annoyed at her lack of professionalism. Choying agrees it's bad but I sense he is a little bit more philosophical about the strange rules that govern life in McLeod Ganj.

10

BEAUTY AND THE BRUTALITY

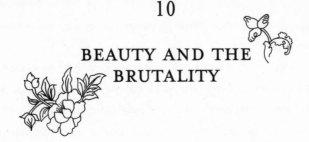

The morning of 10 October dawns with a fury. In the mottled darkness a clap of thunder breaks in the sky. The rain pelts down on the corrugated-iron roofs. The mountains, covered in snow, send waves of glacial air down the valley. It is a freakishly cold day at least one month ahead of the start of winter.

Soon vegetable wallahs will huddle around fires lit on the street and vendors will sit shivering under woollen blankets. The Kashmiri carpet sellers, cafe owners, and anyone with the means, will shut up shop and head to Goa, the only fertile tourist ground in winter. For the rest of us there will be no relief. No heated shops to duck into, no warm offices to take refuge in, only icy concrete rooms with landlords who forbid the use of heaters because of the cost of electricity, forcing the population of McLeod Ganj into acts of sneakery, tucking heaters under beds whenever footsteps are heard. Tuk-tuk drivers wrap their shawls around their heads and under their chins and zip through the bus station, in the dull light looking like a clan of mobile Mary Poppins. The entire population finds it hard to go five minutes without a cup of chai to warm up the body. Any Indian with a gas ring finds a spare metre and sets up shop. Huddles of humans wrapped in blankets bulge out from the side of the road sipping the sweet brew.

I wake up to a chill air and a town divided. Like clockwork, at this time of the year the town breaks into warring factions. In internet chat rooms, monasteries and cafes throughout the Tibetan diaspora, friendships are strained as accusations fly and arguments rage. It is the third annual Miss Tibet beauty pageant. And after the Middle Way approach, it has become the most bitterly divisive—and painful—subject for Tibetans in exile.

Tonight is the final, after two days of heats. As the big day has got closer, posters demanding Tibetans boycott the show have appeared on billboards. The posters, put up during the night by clandestine activists, claim contests where women show off their assets are offensive to Tibetan culture with its profoundly Buddhist persuasion. They also accuse the organiser of mimicking the worst of western ideals and humiliating Tibetan women. Next to posters advertising the week's events, someone has taken the trouble of printing out the contestants' photos with the words *Shame on You* and *Beggars* scratched across them.

The Prime Minister, Professor Samdhong Rinpoche, knows the contest is harmful to the global good press on which Tibetans rely. He is aware that Tibetans hold a special place in people's hearts, that they are seen as guardians of a unique spiritual heritage. In exile they are the vestiges of an isolated country where religion once flourished as the centre of life. The developed world, starved of spiritual depth, lends Tibetans a mythical air. This translates into support for the struggle for a free Tibet, and financial assistance for the government-in-exile. Without it, Tibetans would be just another displaced people. So to gamble with this reputation—especially in something so blatantly western as a beauty contest—is considered particularly dangerous to the Tibetan cause.

'Tibet is respected because of its spirituality and its cultural traditions in the world. The Tibetan cause stands on that basis. Just imitating western culture will never help the Tibetan cause— it will always damage the Tibetan cause,' Professor Samdhong Rinpoche told me when I interviewed him. Unsurprisingly he rejected beauty contests as anathema to the Buddhist view. 'We are firm believers in the fact that the body is the home of the conscience. Beauty is skin deep and there can be no such contest of individuals wherein inner virtues could be put to the test.'

This year the Minister for Religion and Education, Mr Thupten Lungrig, pins down the contentious issue for many ordinary Tibetans: the swimsuit round. He says the cultures and traditions of India and Tibet are somewhat alike and girls exposing their bodies is not considered acceptable. 'This is a concept of western culture and definitely alien to our society. Also, one wonders what is the benefit of organising all such beauty contests.' But as a government with no laws, they are impotent to stop it and can only look on with disapproval.

Their comments produce a flurry of debate on phayul.com, the most popular Tibetan news and current affairs website.

S.H.U.T the F.U.C.K up Samdhong Guri and Lungrig. Snap out of your illusory realm of hypocrisy. This is reality and in *reality, monks disrobe and have intercourse, Lamas take on wives, Tibetans flock to the West, the youth want a more active freedom struggle, and all the young men and women are into the latest fashion craze, including showing skins and tattoos. This is just reality. If you want to go back into past, just don't take us with you. We are good living in the future. And one more time, I'd rather support the four [sic] brave Girls than Give a damn to you two and your empty F******words.*

Gyatso. Location: NYC

For those of you who argue that this is not part of our culture, this is not in sync with our beliefs and traditions please remember we go with the times. Then a lot of what we are doing is not in sync with our culture. From food to dress. In old Tibet, people eat only the local products of tsampa, meat and diary products. Men and Women wear only chubas and keep their hair long. Traditions of polygamy, landlord, monastery ownership exist. So is that where we could go back. If holding pageant is unTibetan, then eating pasta, Chinese food, burgers, and wearing jeans, shorts, minis, and capris is unTibetan. Keeping hair in all shapes and colours is unTibetan. Still if you want to go back to preserving culture, do so. I and all my frds vote for the pageant, which I also agree.

Lobsang. Location: Toronto

I do not understand what the organisers of Miss Tibet contest would gain from this controversial issue. I think we have so many things to work out with respect to our main Tibetan issue. We have a democratic form of government and people could exercise democratic rights as enshrined in the Charter. But [the organiser] *should remember that we are not yet ready for such a contest and he should also realise that Tibetans are living in exile as refugees. He could have directed his efforts to a more meaningful work like helping Tibetan children get basic modern education. There are so many Tibetan families in various settlements/camps/pockets who cannot afford to education their children . . . I think* [the organiser] *should change his priorities and should stop creating a rift in our community. Beauty contest does not serve our purpose. Be a Tibetan because you are born to Tibetan parents. Ask your parents about it and listen to them if you are the son of your parents.*

Tenzin, Pema, Sonam, Jangchup. Location: Nepal and Delhi

The creator of the Miss Tibet pageant is a man who passes as the town's only spin-doctor: organiser of dance parties, head of his own production company and serial man about town, Lobsang Wangyal. Born of Tibetan parents he is a Sherpa—from the Nepalese area bordering Tibet—a fact many of his opponents revel in drawing attention to. All week he has been dashing around McLeod Ganj with five wannabe beauty queens in tow. The elderly people who sit in doorways spinning their prayer wheels day after day cluck in disapproval when they pass. The street boys' jaws drop. Western tourists surveying tantric implements in roadside stalls barely register the commotion.

When not escorting the contestants around, Lobsang can be seen roaring through the marketplace on his souped-up motorbike, sunglasses in place, his long lush black hair flying out behind him. I called him earlier in the week to ask to meet him and talk about the pageant. He didn't waste any time on pleasantries, demanding my qualifications. He perked up when I told him I was interested in writing about the pageant for a book, and acquiesced to a visit the day before the three-day round of competition began. His HQ is the roof of Ladies Venture Hotel.

I lug my now slightly protruding belly up the hotel's narrow iron stairs. On the roof under a blue awning is a long table surrounded by five polished Tibetan women. I recognise them from the defaced posters. Listening attentively to a distinguished-looking gentleman, they are all making tidy notes. Lobsang Wangyal is sitting at the end of the table. He looks up, stumped that a stranger has walked into their mist, but doesn't move from his seat. I walk the expanse of concrete, take off my sunglasses and introduce myself. He keeps his on. They are formidable. Huge pink wraparound sunglasses through which I see intense black eyes. They match his white *Pirates of Penzance* shirt and lollypop-pink stovepipes. In a conservative Buddhist town, where monks and nuns roam the streets, his dress sense is high camp. I once saw him in tight leather trousers.

One of the women holds up a note for me and points at the gentleman lecturing. It says *Professor Thondup Narkyid* and next to it is a shaky arrow. Professor Narkyid is the official biographer of the Dalai Lama. I try not to let my jaw drop. He is quietly explaining to the girls the current human rights situation in Tibet. Lobsang leans forward and whispers he has arranged a week of tuition for his 'brave and unique' girls. Their curriculum would be the envy of many ordinary Tibetans. The speakers include the director of the Tibetan Centre for Human Rights and Democracy, Geshe Kalsang Damdul; the principal of the Institute of Buddhist Dialectics; the former political prisoner, Palden Gyatso; a retired opera Master; and, lastly, 'personality development trainer' Sangetta Jain. Later, as part of a round in the contest, they will be asked questions about human rights in Tibet and their Buddhist faith. Lobsang has gone to a lot of trouble to ensure they are prepared for the rigours of the contest and they aren't made fools of.

I ask Lobsang how he responds to the criticism from a wave of new flyers that have been circulated around town in the past few days. In eccentric English they demand Tibetans boycott the event. A beauty contest, they say, 'demeans rich Tibetan culture and traditions and humiliates Tibetan girls'. But it saves the most vehement criticism for Lobsang. 'Living in a free nation and not trying to preserve one's own culture is unpardonable', it announces. It mocks his promise of keeping crowned Miss Tibets away from misdeeds, saying 'it seems to have become a ticket for getting foreign husband'. It brings up an issue painful for many Tibetans, that someone is using the name Tibet for individual and commercial benefit. Someone is making money off the country they cannot go home to and not spending a 'single penny' on social welfare. And it perhaps reminds people that one of the reasons why there is such a groundswell of disapproval around Lobsang Wangyal is that he once gave an interview to a journalist in which he boasted of sleeping with sixty-five western women a year.

He leans forward, his soft voice has a lyrical Hindi lift at the end of each sentence. 'Oh there have been few flyers,' he says. 'The people are very cautious, they don't like new things and they pretend that beauty is not important in our Buddhist culture.' It is a well-rehearsed argument. 'But you know, beauty is part of Buddhist culture. We believe that what you look like is the result of your past actions, it is your karma. If you did meritorious acts in the past you will appear as attractive in this life...we all get taught that, so I don't see how they can say it's not important.'

Technically he is right. All aspects of our personality, appearance, and everything from the smallest to the most momentous events in our daily life, are the result of cause and effect. That is the essential meaning of karma—that everything we experience has an origin in our past behaviour. But this is taught as an explanation of karma, an illumination of why things are as they are, not a reason to elevate its outcome.

He has another reason he thinks the pageant is significant. He claims the aim of the contest is to bring international attention to the plight of the Tibetan people. 'When one reads the words "Miss Tibet", Tibet is thought of as a separate entity and not part of China,' he says. 'Miss Tibet is a positive thing for Tibet. Any coverage of Tibet is beneficial.' He is every bit the restrained, thinking statesman. A model of reason.

In a particularly Tibetan twist, there is another underlying objection to the contest. Successful pageants need a large pool of beautiful entrants to choose from. That allows the women who possess all the exaggerated qualities considered beautiful to float to the top. It is a matter of eternal shame for Tibetans that around the world people see girls who are not the most beautiful women Tibet in exile has to offer. It magnifies the humiliation of holding the contest in the first place. Last year was the worst. To the mortification of supporters and opponents alike there was only one contestant. This year there were twenty applicants, but fifteen pulled out. The organisers blame family and community pressure.

It is time for the girls to finish their lesson. They clap their hands and push their chairs back in unison. Lobsang hands me a media pass and tells me to be at Sunday night's final.

Today is Sunday. By midafternoon the storm has cleared enough for Choying and I to wrap up and venture out. We decide to take a walk up from the bottom of Dalai Lama-Gi Road. As we are strolling we notice the way has been lined with prayer flags. More and more Tibetans, clutching smoking bundles of incense, are taking their place beside the road. Short-haired security guards and big Sikhs with dogs are scoping the area. We ask what the commotion is about and are told His Holiness is returning home any moment. We take our place on the side of the road, Choying helping some children light a small fire of juniper twigs that send out great billows of fragrant smoke across the road. We are fanning it when a murmur races through the crowd. A siren rings out and we see, roaring up the hill below us, a convoy of cars. We get in position. A white Ambassador sedan filled with well-built army men in khaki uniforms roars past, their eyes sweeping over us. An Indian flag flutters on its bonnet. Next is the gold Mercedes—donated by the Swiss Tibetans in exile—the car we have been waiting for. It drives past slowly and there, in the passenger seat, waving, is the Dalai Lama. He is about one metre away from us. Choying and I bend forward as His Holiness's car moves past. We look at each other and smile. I've always found there to be a strange feeling of peace when my eyes fall upon something that represents hope and goodness, as though it sparks a memory of the great potential in our lives. The moment is broken only as carloads of monks and officials roar past. When the convoy has passed, Choying and I join the throng of Tibetans who immediately head to off to do the *kora*, contented now that the Dalai Lama is home.

As we walk through the bus station we see a large yellow awning has been erected in one corner. Underneath are twenty silent protestors, wearing headbands, sitting cross-legged on the ground. A man with a microphone explains they are on a twenty-four-hour hunger strike called by the Regional Tibetan Youth Congress. It is part of an ongoing campaign to protest the imminent execution of a renowned Rinpoche, Tenzin Delek, who has been sentenced to death for a series of explosions in Chengdu, Tibet, during which one person died. Shortly after the explosion, in April 2002, Chinese police arrested a man called Lobsang Dhondup. They ransacked his room and found a photo of Tenzin Delek, and despite the fact that all Tibetans have photos of their lamas on their altars, they concluded that Tenzin Delek was involved. Both men were sentenced to death in December 2002 and, despite his protestations of innocence, Lobsang Dhondup was put to death soon after.

Human-rights organisations, including Amnesty International and Human Rights Watch, believe Tenzin Delek was framed because he is viewed by the Chinese as a threat to their control of Tibet. He has built many schools, monasteries and orphanages in East Tibet and is an advocate of the Dalai Lama's philosophy of nonviolence. He is also one of an increasing number of lamas drawing Chinese students into the study of Buddhism. Fearless in his attitude to the Chinese, Tenzin Delek was convicted in a closed trial. Both he and Lobsang Dhondup were denied access to independent lawyers. His death sentence is due to be carried out in two months. In Tenzin Delek's own words: 'I am completely innocent... I have always said we should not raise our hand at others. It is sinful... I have neither distributed letters nor pamphlets nor planted bombs secretly. I have never even thought of such things, and I have no intention to hurt others.' All around McLeod Ganj posters of his face remind people of this terrible situation.

By nightfall the storm has abated altogether, although the cold remains. I head off to the Tibetan Institute of Performing Arts, the largest venue in town. I wonder if all the calls to shame—and the 150-rupee entrance cost—will affect the turnout. By the time I turn onto TIPA Road the answer is obvious. Cars, taxis, tuk-tuks and motorbikes are banked up, hooting and cramming past each other. Streams of people are walking up to TIPA. At the entrance there is an unruly queue, flanked on both sides by *momo* vendors and curry sellers. Inside the courtyard is a large stage and a catwalk that reaches far into the audience. A red-carpeted stairway, leading down from the top of a two-storey building at the rear, opens into the middle of the stage. Huge signs proclaim Lobsang Wangyal Productions and Sangetta Jain's personality development clinic.

As the sound system pumps out pop songs, lighting pierces the dark night. The crowd—full of young Tibetan men and families—looks as though it is about to burst with anticipation. Suddenly fireworks explode. The MC, a woman with a flat nasal British accent, welcomes us to 'Misssssss Teeeeebet.' She drops her voice an octave and asks for a minute's silence to respect an outstanding Tibetan and one of the biggest supporters of the Miss Tibet pageant. As the audience lowers its collective heads she says they will soon reveal the name of the Tibetan they are referring to. I try to work out who it could be, mentally flicking past the names of all the political prisoners I've ever heard of. I don't think Tenzin Delek would have heard of the pageant, let alone support it. How intriguing.

Suddenly music roars out of the speakers. A puff of dry ice spurts across the stage. On the top of the stairs a spotlight falls upon a suited silhouette. In the haze a figure floats down the stairs, delicately stepping sideways to avoid tripping. As the lights roll up to shine on the face, I gasp. It's Lobsang Wangyal and he is wearing a bright orange two-piece suit, the shoulders heavy with padding. He strolls to the front of the stage, slowing raises his hands to his lips then flings them out, screaming out the greeting, '*Taaaaaaaaasssssssssshiiiiiii Deeeeeeeelllllleeeekkk.*' I immediately think of Spinal Tap and the folly of hubris. I look around at the crowd but they are gazing in rapture at the man in the orange suit. They break into deafening applause.

He walks down the catwalk with the microphone, his pinkie finger erect as though about to sip from a champagne flute. Gone is the concerned professional; in his place is a Tibetan Donny

Osmond. 'Weeeeeellllcommmme to Miiiisssss Tiiiiiiiiiibbbbetttt.' Every sentence he shouts out ends in an upward lilt as though he expects to be drowned out by applause before he can finish. Rapidly changing between Hindi, English and Tibetan, he doesn't take a breath, instead launching into a passionate defence of the pageant against 'that certain section of the Tibetan community so tunnel-visioned they are against the pageant and the swimsuit competition in particular'. Lobsang Wangyal owns the stage.

'I'd like to thank you for the minute's silence. It really was for a great Tibetan and the supporter of the Miss Tibet pageant... my father... who passed away in March this year.' He launches into an emotional eulogy for 'his greatest supporter', chides the drinkers and smokers in the audience and delivers a Buddhist homily about how all life is *samsara*.

'But,' he whispers theatrically before breaking out into a shout, 'theeeee sssshooooowwww mmmuussst gooooooo onnnnnnnnn.' He then introduces the all-Indian judging panel and the 'oooohhhhhh soooooo' he drops his voice to an intimate whisper, 'sssssssexy MC'. The crowd gains confidence, hooting and howling. Lobsang bows out as another puff of dry ice floods the stage and 'She's the One' belts out of the speakers.

From high on the staircase comes the first contestant, Sonam Dickey. In a stream each contestant comes onto the stage, resplendent in evening dresses. They each take the microphone and tell the audience how the Miss Tibet pageant promotes Tibetan culture around the world. One, a hospital worker called Kelsang Dickey, tells the audience how she was so determined to meet His Holiness—and enter the contest—she escaped from Lhasa to make it to Dharamsala. She aspires to be a model. Her eyebrows are almost plucked into oblivion. She is by far the most overtly sexual of the contestants.

In the midst of the crowd, the people around me cheering and clapping, I have a sinking feeling. I had been undecided about the virtues of a Tibetan beauty contest, but there is a well of disappointment rising in me as I see Tibetans embrace what so many westerners now find meaningless. All people have a right to entertainment, but to see such enthusiasm unfold for something ultimately so worthless is like deja vu. I have seen the girls and how they benefit from the attention. That cannot be denied. Just acting with poise and confidence in an alien situation is enough to widen their experience. It's a pity it has to be in a context in which ultimately they are judged for what they look like.

I stop the mental chatter and straighten up. Next comes Tsering Kyi, the sole entrant and winner of the 2003 Miss Tibet contest. Tall and slim, her features enhanced by stage makeup and a glittering crown and with a blue and gold brocade *chuba*, she looks every bit like a beauty queen She takes the microphone and launches into a defence of why she wasn't able to use the Miss Tibet platform to publicise the Tibetan cause. Finance kept her from entering many competitions. As she recounts what she was able to do with her year (dancing with the Save Tibet Foundation) the crowd begins to get restless. She chides them to be patient and continues. They begin to call out. She tells them off again. Being a beauty queen has given her some guts.

Finally, out comes Palden Gyatso, the monk who spent

thirty-three years as a political prisoner in Tibet. He is there to launch Tsering Kyi's book of poetry. Standing beside her under the bright lights with his shaven head and worn face he looks minuscule. In his modest robes he is overshadowed by her beauty and glitz. That is the topsy-turvy world of show business.

Next is the evening-dress round, followed by the traditional Tibetan costume round. Each woman looks stunning in brocade *chubas*, festooned with coral and turquoise jewels, huge chunks of amber on their heads and their hair woven in 108 plaits.

I use a break in the proceedings to dash back to the bus station and I arrive as the hunger strikers are rising from their seats and each picking up a candle. We are joined in a silent procession by more Tibetans, and slowly walk down Dalai Lama-Gi Road to the Tsuglag Khang, the candlelight throwing shadows on the corrugated-iron doors of closed shops. Dogs silently follow. Once we have circled the monastery, Tenzin Tsundue takes up the microphone and addresses the gathering. He tells us Tibet is undergoing a fresh wave of political repression. In Kham, three people have been arrested on the premise they were conducting political activities. A monk with the highest philosophical training, Khenpo She Tse, has been gunned down by the Chinese police. Tenzin Tsundue urges all Tibetans and their supporters to join the mission to free Tenzin Delek and to continue to pressure China over human-rights violations. With images of murdered Buddhist monks looping in my mind, I slip off back to the beauty pageant.

It is time for the judges to ask the contestants one unplanned question. Each girl comes back on stage to take turns: How would you describe Tibetan women in one sentence? Dhondup Wangmo: 'Cultured and well mannered.' If you had one million dollars, what would you do with it? Kelsang Dickey: 'Help the poor.' Who do you consider the most beautiful and why? Tashi Yangchen: 'A person with inner compassion, intellect, aura and charisma.' If you could change anything in your life what would it be and why? Sonam Dickey, in a moment that quietens the crowd: 'I can't be in Tibet.' How would you present the Tibetan cause to the world? Thinlay Dolma: 'It's not only the Dalai Lama's responsibility, it's our responsibility to raise the issue.'

The excitement goes to one judge's head. He rushes to the microphone and tells the girls he wants to ask them all one final question. It booms out across the sea of people. 'If you knew the price of winning Miss Tibet was spending one night with Lobsang Wangyal, would you enter the contest?' he chortles. It hits the audience like a lead brick. In a courtyard of 2500 people not a sound can be heard. Monks cover their heads. Mothers gather their children. Men stare at the ground. The contestants suddenly seem like young girls out of their depth. One starts praying. Unaware of Tibetan sensibilities, the Indian judge has just stumbled across the crux of Tibetans' fear about the contest: that it compromises the moral reputation of the contestants. Just as I think he might be lynched, an orange suit steps out from behind a column. 'Annnnndd nnnoooooooow the mmmmoooo-mmmennnntt yooooou'veee alll beeeen waiiiiiitiiinnnnnng foooooorr...' The girls straighten up. The crowd finds its feet again, cheering.

But at the last minute Palden Gyatso steps forward. He tells the audience that he is a supporter of Miss Tibet. That he has seen the old culture and the new and the contest is good for Tibetan women. He bravely brings up a sore point. 'These women are not prostitutes as some people have been saying,' he glowers. 'They all come from good families, they have all studied. One is from a family whose uncle is a high lama!' he exclaims.

Lobsang takes the microphone again. 'Aaaaandddd the wiiiiinnnnnerr iiiiiissss... Tasssssssshi Yanchgen!' he bellows. She steps forward to accept the crown. Lobsang dashes off to get an oversized cardboard cheque for one lakh—$3100 AUD— to present to her. Photographers rush forward, clamouring onto the ramp to get her photo. One burly man with a huge camera runs up to her as she attempts to parade down the catwalk in her new crown. In a flash the orange suit is there, pushing him off the ramp, holding back the media. But it is too late, he is overcome. It is only when two huge bombs explode, raining confetti over the unruly crowd, that people quickly retreat.

By the time Miss Tibet 2004 makes it back to the stage she is inundated with media. I run with my tape recorder to where she is standing. She pledges to bring international attention to the issue of Tibet, but admits it will be difficult. Miss Tibet cannot yet enter Miss World or Miss Universe; instead she is relegated to second-tier beauty pageants like Miss International Tourism. Still, she says any talk of Tibet helps. 'I will be able to tell the contestants about what has happened to Tibet so they may be able to go and talk to others.' After several minutes listening to her heroically answering the most mundane questions, I turn around to look at the audience.

WHAT

IS

HE

DOING?

Lobsang Wangyal has collapsed forward, his head bowed, alone on the stage. The music flares up. Inch by inch he raises his arms skyward until he is unfurled. He stands, his legs astride, his arms reaching up to the sky, his orange jacket flapping behind him. The crowd raise their faces to him. I guffaw. Has he gone mad? For a second he stands enraptured, his face raised to the heavens. The beat gets faster and louder. Suddenly he swings his hips to the left, then the right. He fixes his stare beyond the back of the crowd, does a small on-the-spot jog, throws his head back and proceeds to sashay down the catwalk, his hands on his hips. I look around to see if anyone is as open-mouthed as I am but they love the spectacle. At the end of the runway, Lobsang stops and dances like a man gone wild, throwing arms up in the air, whipping his head around and gyrating, intermittently pointing out at the crowd, fixing them with his disco gaze.

Like a flash of lightning it dawns on me. The figure that is so incongruous in a town like McLeod Ganj has created his own niche. In this low-tech town, where cow dung splatters the street and rubbish mounts up in festering piles, he provides the fantasy. And people are glad for it, no matter what the implications. Forty-five years in exile and they want some moments of distraction.

As Lobsang continues to disco, I pack up my bag and head back to the twinkling lights of this complicated little town.

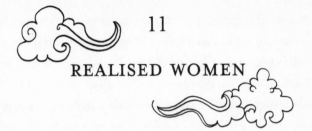

11

REALISED WOMEN

I decide to visit Dharamsala Zonal Hospital. Delek hospital in McLeod Ganj has birth facilities but no pain relief and no incubator. In short, if anything at all goes astray during or after delivery, you have to drive fifteen minutes down the hill to Zonal.

I have seen the outside of the hospital on my trips to and from McLeod Ganj and have always looked on with horror. A monolithic building, it looks like a post-apocalyptic nuclear shelter housing thousands of the burned and maimed. The brown concrete exterior seeps mould and decrepitude; washing hangs from the balconies where families congregate. As I approach I see a multitude of faces pressed up against grimy windows staring forlornly at the outside world. In the entrance way an abandoned wheelchair sits amongst crowds of people who seem to be just milling around. A man on a stretcher is wheeled through on an old iron bed, covered with brown blankets. The doctors look concerned.

I take a large concrete ramp, wide enough to look like it belongs in a car park, up to the next floor. The entrance to the maternity ward has an armed soldier sitting inside a metal concertina-style grille, open only enough for visitors to pass into a wide dim corridor. I step inside. Westerners are rarely stopped from doing what they like in India—the only time I have been held up is to satisfy Indians' endless curiosity—perhaps a vestige of colonial deference. The concrete corridor has only a faint light coming from the windows on the far side of the building, where I have seen the faces staring out. Streams of people are pacing.

I peek into a ward. Unlike the corridor it is flooded with blinding light from the bank of windows on the outside of the building. The fans sit idle and a fluorescent blue mosquito-repellent light flickers in the corner. Springless iron beds, with welded crosshatched iron bases covered by thin mattresses are lined up next to each other. There is no privacy, no bedside tables, wardrobes or telephones, only beds and buckets and what looks like three or more people jammed into a bed. As my eyes adjust to the light, I see they are the patients' families, many camped out on rugs beside the beds, tiffins at the ready, or sitting crossed-legged on the bed.

At Zonal people must provide their own linen, so each bed is a riot of multicoloured blankets jumbled with batik sheets and worn floral pillowcases. In amongst the people and fabric, patients are sunk into their beds. Empty plates sit on the ground next to bottles of water. In Indian public hospitals it is the duty of relatives to wash, cook and provide the daily care for patients. Doctors and nurses provide only the strictest definition of medical aid.

All the doors of the wards are left open with red handwritten signs designating their use in Hindi and English. I look into the antenatal ward. Each bed has a colourful blanket covering a prone shape with a jutting belly. It is ominously silent. I walk past the psychiatric ward, noting it is next door to the labour ward around whose door I poke my head. Obscuring the view is a line of flowery shower curtains but I can see four incredibly large-bellied women lying down on metal trays squeezed tight next to each other. One of the walls in the room is almost disintegrated from damp, and in the corner another mosquito repeller flickers.

I step back into the corridor as a woman in a blue uniform approaches me. I say in English that I am pregnant and am having a look at their hospital in case I give birth there. She squints and replies, 'Nam.' I say, 'Van-ess-a.' She says, 'Which ward?' I say, 'No, no, not patient, just looking' pointing at my eyes. She says, 'Next floor, eyes.' I say 'No, no' again pointing at my belly and holding up six fingers, one for each month to go. Then, shamefully, I mime giving birth.

A man with a bandage on his head steps forward, his eyes bright. Another woman in an apricot shalwar kemeez joins us. I appeal to them, saying I would like to look around. They smile sympathetically but have no better English than the nurse, who shakes her head in confusion and wanders into the labour ward. Crowds of Indians turn around to talk to each other about the strange pantomime they have just witnessed. I wander off down the corridor, unsure what to do, and duck into the first ward I see. The smell hits me at once, a combination of concentrated germ killer, fresh urine and stale faeces. The concrete floor is wet and a bank of yellow wooden doors stands open. A large bin overflows, a ring of sick around the bottom. It is the toilets. I gag and back out into the corridor. The man with the bandage is waiting. Except I realise it's a headband. He has a large white smile and stutters, 'My sister. Baby. Come.' He beckons me into a ward with *post natal* painted on the door and, beaming, points at a middle-aged woman in an olive green salwaar and yellow cardigan sitting up in a bed. She is holding a blanket near her stomach. She looks up, her gaze is beatific. She gently pulls down a corner of the rug as her brother murmurs, 'Half-hour' and I see inside all the swaddled clothes is a tiny yawning baby whose eyes are open and ringed by thick black lashes. As we both gaze down I feel a lump rising in my throat. The rest of her family step forward proudly, all eyes resting on the fragile little life wrapped in a blanket. For a second we all lean closer as though experiencing a miracle, a ring of warmth encircling us. My eyes begin to sting. I blink away tears. The family looks on kindly, nodding at me. Time stops in that instant. The baby gurgles. I thank them and quietly tread out of the ward, past husbands curled up sleeping on their wives' beds.

My friend sends me some pregnancy vitamins from Australia and I notice the amount of folic acid they recommend is 400 mcgs; right next to it is a warning not to exceed the recommended dose. My doctor here has me on 3000 mcg. Suddenly I feel radioactive. I immediately go to an internet cafe and write to the pregnancy website asking what dose I should be taking. They write back straightaway saying the daily dose should be 400 and anything over 1000 might be harmful. I close down the computer and wander home through the market. It is twilight and I feel as though I just got whacked over the head with a wooden block.

I wonder what I have done to the baby and myself. I feel as if I can't trust anybody with my pregnancy in this town.

By now it is freezing in the shade. Choying and I pull out the bar heater which was part of the modest collection of possessions that accompanied him when he moved in. It is of the smaller variety. I cling to it day and night. But unfortunately it has that peculiar Indian built-in obsolescence. It will go for a day then fizzle and die. I am obsessed with it. When it dies I almost feel like crying as I conjure up days and nights spent freezing. It's not like in the west where the workplace will be warm, or you can pop into shops or the car to get away from the chill. It is pervasive suffering, unrelenting, and very few people in this town get any real relief. My heater is like my lifeline and the fact it is temperamental makes it only more precious when it does work. Each time it breaks down Choying gets out the screwdriver and dismantles it. It always scares me when I see it in parts; it seems so vulnerable I can't believe it will get the will power to go again. But Choying always manages to resurrect it, at least for another day.

Each day we get our fruit and vegetables fresh from the market. Every day more and more shops begin to sell imported food aimed at foreigners: processed cheese triangles made in Poland, Pringles chips, SunSilk shampoo and big cardboard boxes of Cornflakes. But they are babes in the woods compared to the Osho shop, a tiny place that fits only one or two customers. One wall is taken up with tapes and books of Osho's teachings, while the glass cabinet that is the counter is filled with breads and crumbles and homemade cashew-nut biscuits. Behind it sits the man we call Mr Osho. Half of the western women in McLeod Ganj are in love with him.

The real Osho, or Bhagawan Sri Rajeneesh, was an Indian philosopher and guru who preached a fusion of Hinduism, Buddhism and New Ageism. He drew hundreds of thousands of followers to his communes and 65 000-acre ranch in Oregon, US, all attracted by his message of universal love and acceptance. Unfortunately for him, he was eventually evicted from the US on migration charges. Detractors dubbed him the Guru of Hedonism for his conspicuous consumption, which included a fleet of Mercedes and a massive cache of arms.

Like his guru, the McLeod Ganj Osho radiates love and acceptance. He has a small stutter and is always ready to push a fifteen-rupee homemade dark chocolate on you, for which he then expects payment. He guards a small fridge that houses real cheese. But it is the skill with which he has chosen the select imported goods that makes homesick westerner residents flock to him. He has balsamic vinegar, olives, mustard, tuna and French jam. Each day he gets savvier. I notice he now has capers proudly on display.

At first I try to limit my purchases; the imported goods are hugely expensive. But it takes so much effort each day just to get my hands on good food that finding the right nutritional elements becomes a full-time job. Like a bounty hunter I stalk the market and shops looking for nutrition. The only other place you can buy tofu apart from the Osho shop is at Jogibara village. There an Indian family churns up the soya beans each day and float the great slabs of tofu in a forty-four gallon drum. When you buy their tasty creation, they cleave off a chunk with a machete and wrap it up in newspaper for you. It is twelve rupees per half-kilo. But Jogibara village is a forty-minute walk down the hill and an hour's traipse back up. Every day I succumb more and more to Osho's charms. One day I go to him to buy some tuna. This time he tells me helpfully that it's more economical to buy the tuna in oil, as opposed to brine, because I can use the leftover oil for cooking and, he says, his finger pointing upwards with the weight of his bright idea, for massage.

Choying and I are chortling away about Mr Osho's advice when I think to ask Choying what we should do about the birth, given that we aren't having much luck around Dharamsala. He is succinct. 'I come from Tibet and you come from New Zealand, neither of us is born in India. The baby should be born in one of our places. I cannot go back to Tibet so the baby should be born in your country.' It has a beautiful symmetry to it and I immediately know it is true. He never tells me, and I don't realise until later when we go through the painful reality of separation, how much of a sacrifice this is for him. But, like me, he is disappointed with all the Indian hospitals we have visited. 'You can't go there,' he would say, shaking his head, after we emerged from each one.

I log onto a website about pregnancy in New Zealand. Up pops a web page from the Health Department. It lists the criteria for having a free birth, the options of birthing centres, an explanation of the follow-up treatment procedure and the rights of the woman. It is so comprehensive I am hit with a wave of reassurance. They have worked out the best way to comfort a pregnant woman. It has become so alien to me that my needs would be taken care of by the Indian bureaucracy, I have forgotten what to expect. I feel so happy. I remember that my mother said she had sent me a pregnancy kit. I can't wait to lay my hands on the graphically designed information pack.

We research our options about getting Choying a registration certificate. We make the decision that everyone I know who has the means has made before us. We pay baksheesh to a Tibetan woman with Indian police contacts in a small town far away from McLeod Ganj. This allows us to circumnavigate having to find two dead Tibetans in India who can be named as Choying's parents, and means his birth certificate can be truthful. For a couple of thousand rupees and a bottle of whiskey the police push through in a month paperwork that would take six months. Registration certificate secured, we now need to start the laborious process of obtaining an identity certificate. We hear rumours that we can buy one from a corrupt person in the Tibetan office— where it ends up after it has been processed by the Indian government—but the modus operandi is too awful. The card is someone else's that is almost completed but at the last minute a photo of Choying will be inserted in place of the real applicant. Choying will become this person and the office will tell the applicant that his IC has been lost. He will have to start the process all over again. It's too unethical; we decide we will take our chances and apply honestly. Both of us know this means Choying won't be with me when I give birth to our baby in New Zealand.

Choying's family still doesn't know he is to be a father. His preferred intermediary, his older brother, has still not returned from Beijing. He calls his second brother again. 'First I really embarrassed to tell. I asked him how he was, his wife and family,' Choying tells me. Then he came out with it. 'I have one secret thing to tell you but I'm really afraid to tell you because maybe you will be angry or surprised.' His brother replied, 'I think I know what you are going to say.' Whereupon my brave Khampa said, 'If you know about that please you tell me because I'm embarrassed to say.' His brother said, 'No way.' Choying finally got the words out. 'I'm not a monk.' His brother said, 'What?' Again Choying said, 'I'm not a monk.' His brother replied that he suspected it because when a businesswoman the family knew returned to Tibet from India she told Choying's brother he had hair rather than a shaved head. He had also pondered on their previous conversation when Choying asked if the village people had talked about him. His brother said, 'If it is difficult to be a monk that's all right, but I am worried about your situation.' Choying blurted out the next most important information. 'My girlfriend is not Tibetan. She is a westerner.' His brother said, 'As long as you love each other, that's all right.' Then he slotted in the big news. 'We are having a baby.' His brother is overjoyed. Despite the surprise of learning the family's only monk has disrobed, Choying's brother welcomes any new additions to their family, however far away.

Two weeks later, mainly to placate me, Choying calls his mother in Tibet. No baby or western girlfriend or lack of monkhood is mentioned but Choying assures me they both know what the call is about. Choying tells me he said, 'Mum, how are you?' She said, 'Everything is good, what are you doing?' Whereupon he answered, 'I am studying, everything is good.' Then his mother started crying. 'I am happy that's why I'm crying,' she sobbed. Choying understands that means she accepts everything. Then his mother told him she was worried about him as he is the one in exile. He said, 'Don't worry about me, everything is going good'—he would say that even if he was on his death bed.

Although the cold is testing me, it brings out the Himalayan aspect of living in McLeod Ganj. One day I see, like a mirage through the forest, some light shapes moving through the dark trees. As I look closer I see large, quiet, silver-backed monkeys that have moved down from the snow-covered mountains in search of food. They are stately and beautiful, unlike the smaller ratty variety that hang around my washing. Up to five feet tall, they move silently, avoiding humans. I catch only a glimpse. Later that week on a cold winter's night I see three precariously clinging to the outside windowsill of a house, straining their necks to see the human activity that is going on inside. It is only when they hear me pass that they jump down and run away.

Away from the woods it is a lama fest in town. Many teachers have returned from overseas and have made themselves available for people who want to consult with them. In addition the Dalai Lama is hosting a five-day Mind and Life conference with the imposing title, Neuroplasticity: the Neuronal Substrates of Learning and Transformation, to which many of Buddhism's most esteemed practitioners are going. Choying and I decide to go and see the renowned lama, Kirti Tsenshab Rinpoche, to ask if there are any obstacles to our life together or the life of our baby.

We walk to his monastery and ask at the office if he is available. The monk tells us to go up to his rooms. We arrive at a small outdoor terrace with terracotta pots and colourful flowers. A monk answers our knocks and enquires about what we want. Choying is bowed so low in respect he may as well be speaking to an ant. Meanwhile I peek up. We are ushered into a room where we prostrate. In front of us on a small raised throne is Kirti Tsenshab Rinpoche, leaning forward to hand us a blessed string to wear around our wrists. He looks like a small bird, with delicate bones and a radiant smile. In Tibetan he asks how he can help us. Although I don't understand the words, his presence is so peaceful I feel as though my heart is being zapped with light.

Choying recounts our situation, asking for advice on how to deal with the challenges we are facing. Kirti Rinpoche listens quietly, picks up and juggles the *mo* engraved with Tibetan script, then addresses Choying. In essence he advises us not to be scared of going slowly; we infer he means not to try bribery. He also advises us to offer a statue or *thangka* of Green Tara to a monastery in the name of our baby. Choying shakily translates, Kirti Rinpoche peering down kindly at him, sometimes murmuring, sometimes gently laughing. There is a glow emanating from him. In his presence I feel like I understand the essence of *Bodhisattvas*—the energy one gets from simply doing good.

Once again I decide to go down to Tashi Jong to see Tenzin Palmo but this time I am interested in talking to her about the position of nuns in Tibetan society. Over our discussion and five cups of chai, I learn that the serene faces of the nuns mask a raging battle for respect and status. What begins as a talk about nuns' place in the Tibetan hierarchy turns into an insightful discussion on the nature of womanhood.

One cannot help but notice Tibetan Buddhism is dominated by monks and lamas. The streets of McLeod Ganj are brimming with monks in Nike shoes and fashion sunglasses chatting with westerners or tapping on keyboards at internet cafes. Nuns, on the other hand, move through the marketplace as if they have something to do. Denied proper teachings for so long, nuns are rumoured to be excelling in their accomplishments, including the once male-dominated dialectic debating. This is a subject close to Tenzin Palmo's heart, as apart from establishing a nunnery to educate nuns from Tibet, Spiti, Kinnour and Lahoul, she has been pressing for nuns to receive full ordination, which has long been denied them in the Tibetan tradition. Unlike monks, all nuns remain technical novices even if they have been ordained for their entire lifetime. I had always presumed it was the same discrimination practised against women in most other parts of the world, but the answer is a little more complex and provides a window into the politics at the heart of Tibetan Buddhism.

Tenzin Palmo and I both take a seat in the waiting room outside her small office. She wraps herself warmly in her ʐen, asks about my health and then focuses her unwavering gaze on me. I begin by asking her why Tibetan nuns don't have full bikshuni ordination. She explains that historically it has never been part of their tradition.

'In order to bestow ordination you normally need at least five fully ordained monks and nuns and apparently five fully ordained nuns from India never made their way to Tibet when Buddhism was first established. It was a very difficult journey. So as far as we know full ordination never existed.'

So what was the typical lifestyle of a nun in Tibet in the recent past? Tenzin Palmo sighs. 'It's difficult to generalise because different people were in different situations. But basically there were two main divisions. The kind of nuns who lived at home and did prayers but mainly helped with general housework. They weren't educated but learned a few prayers by heart. Others lived in nunneries where they would concentrate on rituals or meditation. So a lot of nuns were quite realised women, it's just that others didn't get to hear about them because nobody thought they were important enough to write about.'

Given this lack, I ask, over the years did nuns in Tibet ever push for full ordination? 'If they did think about it they would be told either it wasn't possible or it wasn't something they would want anyway because there were so many rules to keep.' In Tibet monks with full or *gelong* ordination have 253 vows or rules they must observe and nuns with full or *bikshuni* ordination would have 364.

I ask what exactly full ordination is. I have been told that it is not possible to find out the specific vows they live by, as these are only for the eyes of those contemplating taking them.

Tenzin Palmo answers, 'Basically they were designed by the Buddha so that a person's conduct is in keeping with those of a renunciate—someone who has given up worldly ambition to concentrate on spiritual advancement. A lot are designed to ensure harmony within the ordained community. Others are made with the idea that conduct should be such that those looking from the outside—Buddhist laypeople—will continue their faith and those who don't have faith can develop it. One thing it is important to realise is that all the rules were made because someone broke them.'

She explains that the *vinaya*—the name of the assembled vows—is a fascinating document because it shows a picture of India 2500 years ago when Buddha, their creator, was alive. Each rule has a story behind it. Some vows, she says, derived from local customs, some were a response to a wayward student, and others were definitely created to keep people on the straight and narrow. I spy a back-door way to ask about the vows. So what are some of the rules that seem irrelevant now?

She smiles. 'Like for example you are only supposed to wash once every fortnight unless it is monsoon . . . and there is a vow about not eating garlic . . . but the story behind that is that one nun had a patron who had a garlic field and she wanted to take a few pieces of garlic to spice up her everyday alms. But then all the nuns came and descended on the garlic fields and ravished it and the patron was so angry that he went to the Buddha and complained about their behaviour. So the Buddha made a rule that no one was to eat garlic.'

And these rules, despite their origin, are still observed? 'Yes, more or less. Some aren't,' she replies enigmatically. 'A lot of the rules people quietly don't observe.'

I ask then, 'Where does the impetus come for full ordination among Tibetan nuns?' She explains that it was a British woman called Freda Bedi who started the first school for young lamas in Dalhousie and also started the first nunnery. 'She took ordination in Hong Kong in 1972 and then I took ordination a year later. So she was the first and then gradually people began to realise—especially westerners—wait a minute, how is it that we can we be ordained for seventeen years and still be just a novice when there are perfectly valid *bikshuni* lineages still extant in the world, in Korea, China, Taiwan, and Vietnam.'

Tenzin Palmo explains that after a while, some time in the 1980s, a few Tibetan nuns went overseas to take ordination. 'But unfortunately it didn't work. There were problems because they were usually younger nuns and of course more adventurous and when they came back into their own nunneries there was the question of whether they were senior because of their ordination or still junior because of their experience. Although the older nuns had a lesser ordination they were not about to put the younger nuns in front of them. In addition there usually were not five of them so they couldn't do the monastic rituals—called *sojong*—together. So basically they crawled back into the woodwork.'

She goes on to say that the other problem was the difference in lineages. When the nuns came back they had the Chinese or Dharmaguptika lineage, and this was not acceptable to the rest of the nunnery who had the Tibetan or Sarvastivada lineage. Looking at my blank face she stops.

'Let me explain the origin of lineages. Two thousand five hundred years ago the Buddha gave basic ordinations. Then because his teachings were taken to many different parts of India various lineages arose, these are called the eighteen schools. Of those only three are still extant: the Chinese, Taiwanese and Korean tradition called Dharmaguptika; the other is the Tibetan tradition called Sarvastivada; the last is the Theravada, or Sthaviravada, in Southeast Asia. The only one that still has the tradition of full ordination is the Dharmaguptika. So all the nuns that have full ordination have received it within the Dharmaguptika lineage.'

So given that many nuns now want the choice to have full ordination, what is stopping them? Is it just the forces of convention?

'The Tibetan argument is that they don't know the Chinese lineage is pure. They ask; "How can we trace it all the way back in documentation to the time of the Buddha showing that it has never been broken?" This is virtually impossible, because after the Chinese takeover of Tibet all the documents were destroyed. But nonetheless people have been diligently researching back into Chinese history the very best they can, and they have come up with the only time it was broken, as far as they can see, was during the reign of a certain emperor for forty years. During this forty-year gap there were no monasteries so outwardly there were no monks and nuns allowed, although of course some must have practised in private. Then after that the emperor died and another emperor came along who was pro-Buddhist and they all started springing up again like mushrooms. So there doesn't seem to be any reason...and I think it's extraordinarily insulting to say the lineage of the Chinese, Vietnamese and Koreans is not genuine. I mean if anyone said that to Tibetans...well...,' she rolls her eyes with a look of mock outrage.

Just then an urbane looking Indian man steps into the room and waits silently. As soon as Tenzin Palmo sees him she claps her hands in delight and introduces him as the nunnery site manger. He holds his hands together in namaste, while she hurries off to get her sidekick Monica, so the two can pore over building plans. She then turns back to me, intent on our discussion.

I ask her, is it just an excuse to keep nuns in their place? 'Of course it's an excuse. But people have been doing research; Chinese scholars have been doing research on this very subject because they want to help Tibetan nuns. They have not come up with anything to substantiate these accusations.'

'I'm curious,' I say, 'is there a block of lamas against this?' Tenzin Palmo nods. 'Opposition is huge. Conservative lamas say there wasn't full ordination for nuns in Tibet so there is no need to do it in exile. There is also an academic argument that bestowing ordination from one lineage to another is invalid. But this was solved when a progressive lama called Kenchen Pema Sherap suggested giving the ordination by Sarvastivada, or Tibetan, monks alone, despite the small innovation.

'Is that valid?' I ask. She nods her head emphatically. 'According to the *vinaya* it is.' So then that seems relatively straightforward you would think. 'What has happened since then?' I ask.

'I myself approached a high lama who I wished would help us do this. He is a scholar of impeccable conduct and great realisations and is a very good friend of the Dalai Lama. So I presented this to him and he said: "Very good, write down these points and I will take them to the Dalai Lama." He said previously he spoke to His Holiness about it and at that time His Holiness said the important thing would be to make sure the first ordaining masters were really excellent lamas, irreproachable. This is very, very important. Everything must be done with pure procedure so that there is no niggling. And so he assured me that whatever he could do to help the nuns he would do. It was very close to his heart but he needed to have something of the green light from His Holiness. You understand His Holiness is not able to say, "Yes, go for it" but he can nod his head which we take as affirmation. He is in a difficult position.'

I can't hide my look of confusion. I thought the Dalai Lama's word would be final. But as Tenzin Palmo explains, even though everybody looks to him for leadership, he is essentially the titular head of Tibetan Buddhism. Other lamas are responsible for running the monastic system.

'His Holiness is not the Pope. His word is not mandate for everyone. While everyone admires him tremendously for his own personal qualities, he doesn't want to be in a position and cannot be in a position where he appears to be unduly siding in a topic like this, which is very controversial. It will only stir up a lot of resistance. His Holiness has to be careful because there are many lamas, senior to him, who would resent what they would consider to be a gross and unnecessary innovation. It would create a lot of extra resistance, which is what we don't want. We just want to do it quietly and once it's done it's done.'

A canny smile spreads across her face. I begin to get a picture of the magnitude of the change and of the delicate procedure ahead, so I ask: 'If His Holiness thinks it's a good idea and finds ten impeccable lamas, will there still be resistance?'

'Yes, but so what? The important thing for us having done this is to make sure the nuns are really trained well and that they understand the monastic code and that they perform all the monastic offices faultlessly. Then no one can complain.'

I ask if it irks her that embedded in the *vinaya* are such rules as nuns always having to sit behind monks or bow down when they enter the room? 'No,' she says. 'I feel that one of the advantages of becoming a nun is that you can never become proud. And if it does irk one, one can just look at one's mind. Anything that is an obstacle can benefit you with the right mind. I mean as long as women get educated equally and have equal facilities for practice and equal facilities to be able to benefit others, who cares if you have to stand up and bow down? One of the problems of being a monk is that it's easy to become arrogant. Nuns rarely become conceited and that, from a spiritual point of view, is wonderful. I think the nuns have an advantage because whoever you are and however high you are you are going to get slapped down.'

Her answer reminds me of why I appreciate Buddhism so much. That it allows for a far more creative response to situations than I previously thought I had at my disposal. Instead of anger or frustration, a broader perspective is possible. Yet she is an example that this doesn't mean passivity.

I ask, given all the negotiations, how long it could take to achieve full ordination for nuns. She replies that it could be another two to three years. 'But you must remember it's only ten years since nuns became educated and it's only been in exile.'

We move on to fact that in exile nuns seem to be thriving while monks are disrobing at a high rate. Tenzin Palmo says that what kept nuns from gaining the same status as monks in Tibet was a lack of education and a lack of access to the kind of philosophical programs that monks had. Now that's opening up there is no stopping them.

'They are extremely well centred and, on the whole, they are better disciplined than the monks. Women on the whole are better at meditation, many senior meditation teachers have told me. Women have a natural affinity with meditation, they are much more intuitive. Men as a whole tend to be more analytical and pragmatic, going one step at a time. Women are more able to take a leap—they don't feel threatened by something which is beyond words.'

Part of the problem with monks, she says, is that there are simply too many. The Dalai Lama has said that out of every hundred monks, just ten should be in robes. 'Many are in there because they think it's an easy life, they get taken care of, and they don't know what else to do. They would be better out. I think a lot of women realise they don't want the life that many of their married mothers, aunts and elder sisters have. A woman knows that if she chooses the lay life she will be the one in the kitchen doing the cooking and looking after the kids. Also, to be honest, on the whole if women have a happy life and are studying and practising there is much less interest in the opposite sex. I don't think nuns even think about men. By contrast men, no matter how old they are, get the sexual urge much stronger. Some monks think, "Well, if I get married I'll have a wife to take care of me, there'll be easy sex, I can make some money and it'll all be nice and cosy."'

It has been a couple of hours when we decide to finish. The workers at the handicraft centre are now walking home in the twilight. I pack away my tape recorder and thank her for spending her precious time with me. She laughs, then has an afterthought.

'You know I think this struggle will be good for Buddhism, especially now when there are a lot of stories of the degeneration of monks and the bad behaviour of some lamas. People are so gullible. If someone has the gift of the gab they can literally get millions of dollars. It's sad also because there are exemplary lamas out there. They are not always the famous ones but the ones who genuinely do have a little monastery back in Tibet they are trying to save or build a little school. But you get others who get all this money and go and hang out at the Hyatt. It's sad but that's naturally going to happen. When you put lots of fertiliser down you are not only going to get beautiful plants coming up but also weeds.'

12

 BUDDHA AIR

We meet in the deserted dining room of Hotel Bagsu, hovered over by waiters whose boredom has mutated into a time-passing superciliousness with any customer unfortunate enough to want service. The man who weaves his way past the empty chairs towards me is gaunt, as though his energy has more urgent things to do than replenish his body. His thin face is decorated by a wispy moustache and goatee, and his long black hair is woven into a single plait hanging down his back, giving him the semblance of a South American Indian. Dark eyes are framed by black oval glasses and above these a red bandana is wrapped around his forehead. He was worn it every day since he decided to dedicate his life to the struggle to free Tibet.

Tenzin Tsundue is described as one of the best and brightest of the Tibetans born in exile. A writer, poet and activist, his parents were in the first wave to reach exile and worked as itinerant road labourers. Tenzin was born in a tent during the laying of the Manali–Leh highway and later educated at a university in Mumbai. Some years ago, determined to visit the country so often recounted in his parents' stories of life before exile, he went against the exodus, sneaking into Tibet on foot from Ladakh. When I meet him, Tenzin is in Dharamsala for only a few days before he must return to Mumbai where he is due in court to be tried on a case of criminal trespass. In 1999, during the visit of the Chinese Premier Zhu Rongji and much to the annoyance of the Indian government, he hung a banner demanding Tibet's freedom out of the fourteenth floor of the luxury Oberoi Hotel.

Before I can begin my questions, Tenzin clears his throat and, in a Hindi lilt fired up with a kind of no-nonsense conviction, asks me my reasons for writing about Tibetans. McLeod Ganj society has just been blindsided by an article that has appeared in London's *The Times*, by a journalist who stayed for three days and left disappointed when he found Tibetans in jeans hanging out in cafes, not in *chubas* doing *pujas* at the monastery. His story painted a picture of idle Amdo street boys passing time by seducing credulous western women, and ridiculed all those who had moved to McLeod Ganj to study Buddhism. Tenzin says that it may have been a passing story in the journalist's career but it easily damages the Tibetan cause, which rests so fragilely on people's perceptions of the Tibetan people.

I become aware of my own tendency to think a negative discovery is somehow superior journalism and stumble over my answer. Just when I think he has decided I am a bit confused, he asks me to try to publish some stories in the *South China Morning Post*, a newspaper that is based in Hong Kong but which reaches mainland China. This will help, he says, because it can show the Chinese the difference between old Tibetans and 'youngsters'. This is vital, he tells me, because older Tibetans are stuck with an image of Tibet in 1959; ask them what Tibet is like and they will draw their answers from this era. Their image of the Chinese is fixed as the way they were when they attacked and oppressed Tibetans. He describes younger Tibetans, raised in an age of mass media, as being more politically informed, but suffering a low morale. 'The sands shifted underneath them. They were raised to think they would fight for a free Tibet but in their lifetime the policy has become more oblique, it is hard to do anything.' My mind flicks back to a conversation I had the previous week with Choying when, in a rare outburst, he told me 'the freedom of Tibet is on my shoulders and I can't do nothing'. It left me speechless.

Remembering his frustration I ask Tenzin Tsundue what he thinks are the particular frustrations of the young people living in exile. He pulls a face. 'In a political sense I think we were reared to think that we would fight for an independent country and that we would have that sense of belonging from having our own country. There was also a feeling that we needed to go fast, that was the whole emotional and spiritual bonding of the Tibetan community of our generation. Now we feel that things have changed, we are asking for something called genuine autonomy, which is about living in China and having Tibet as an autonomous body within a larger country. Emotionally, we are unable to understand how to do that. Another thing is that because outsiders are all educated and informed about Tibet—especially people in the USA and Britain—it is really frustrating that these countries which have power just don't back Tibet.'

There is a silence. 'It's very, very frustrating,' he says.

I bring up an article he wrote in a magazine that said Tibet's freedom is tied to the success of the democracy movement in China. It isn't clear to me how they are related.

'Now it's like this. We would like to think Tibetans and Tibetan supporters would come up with this huge support movement and one day there will be this grand party and we would declare Tibet's independence and then in a magic sense China will say now we will release Tibet. I think this is not going to happen. Realistically we have to see how changes are happening in China. The issue is not so simple as the Chinese aggressively annexed Tibet in 1949 and we became part of China. No, it's not like that, it's 700 years of complexity and it's more racial than political. It's about the racial superiority the Han Chinese believe they have over the minorities. That's why they have a flag with one big super star and four small stars. They say the Han is the main star, the Mon is Manchuria, the Wee is the Islamic population, the Sun is Tibetan and the Min is Mongolia. They believe these are the minorities on whom the Chinese have the imperial inheritance overlordship. That is the basis of the Chinese claim of superiority.'

I ask Tenzin how an emerging democracy movement in China will affect Tibet. He suggests it needs to start with deconstructing this racial superiority, then, surprisingly, talks about how China's embrace of capitalism can make people more liberal-minded. But the best hope, he says, is the patriotic Chinese, who think that bringing freedom and democracy to China will help upgrade people's health and education and standard of living. This may filter down to the issue of Tibet.

In his book *Kora*, Tenzin Tsundue said the next twenty years would be crucial for the Tibetan people, when they might make one last desperate act to survive as a people. I ask him how he thinks that might manifest and whether it would only happen after the Dalai Lama dies. He gently chides me. 'In the Tibetan community it is considered an ill omen to think of a time without the Dalai Lama. But,' he continues, 'I think that we have to prepare for it.

'If His Holiness passes away in exile then we would be really in a desperate time and then I don't know how we are going to act. The issue of Tibet will definitely suffer. Now it is true that after His Holiness there will not be a unified leadership. Some people may take up violence, some may continue with nonviolent struggle. Presently I think Tibetan people have been looked at as the last resort of nonviolence and looked at as peaceful people. But if that time comes and the Tibetan people take up violence then I think the world will be shattered. The last hope of nonviolence will be gone forever so that will be a disaster for the world itself.'

There is a quiet moment as we both swallow the lumps in our throats. At times during our conversation Tenzin Tsundue floors me with his good heart, his humane intelligence and analysis. Sometimes I feel a wave of sorrow when he expresses himself . . . the loss of Tibet, the confusion of the future, the love the Tibetans have for the Dalai Lama.

Then I ask him his view on Tibetans moving to the west. Again he sees it from all angles. 'Many people do not see any opportunities in India so they take the opportunity from friends or relatives or a girlfriend or boyfriend from abroad to go over there. But then again there are some people who systematically scheme to settle abroad because they think it will be brighter and more prosperous. That's all about greed and leaving behind the struggle. There are some individuals who go abroad and find they were not really aware of the angst of living in exile when they were in India because they were living comfortably in the Tibetan community. In foreign countries they have to constantly speak a different language and live differently. There is nothing Tibetan in their life. I have heard from many people that they cry on the telephone saying, "I want to come back." These are sad stories of exile, when people want to find something and they end up with something else.'

This, I know, is true from my Tibetan friends in Sydney. The bulk of the community there are former political prisoners who have been granted refugee visas by the Australian government. For many, Sydney is the pot of gold at the end of the rainbow. On arrival they quickly take up multiple jobs, working slavishly in factories or restaurant kitchens to get some financial security and send money back to their family in Tibet. But as they years go by and their basic needs are met they find life in the west to be a constant round of work, sleep and the great Australian pastime, spending money. Thankful for their physical safety and their comfort, at some point they have to confront the question, is this it? Perhaps life in Tibet had more meaning. I worry that

Choying will eventually find living in the west dispiriting, but he tells me that as long as we are together as a family he will be happy—he isn't seeking riches or adventure.

I ask this man, born, raised and educated in India, how he defines being Tibetan. He laughs. 'It is the heartstring that, even though you may not be speaking Tibetan language or doing *puja* every morning, you have patriotism in your mind. That is Tibetan-ness.'

I thank Tenzin for his time and stand up to leave. As an afterthought I ask him his age and whether he is married. He answers no. 'I have never attracted any girls.' He is thirty; he says each day he works for Tibet, writing, organising rallies, meeting people. 'There isn't much to recommend it to a woman. No security, no income,' he says simply. I ask him how he gets funds and he answers that he lives off the sale of *Kora*. He points down to his worn black sweatshirt and faded jeans and says he has been wearing them for four years. 'Two meals a day is enough and I don't smoke or drink, only use the internet and that doesn't take much money,' he says.

At this we part and I walk home quickly in the fading light. I only just get in the front door when, to Choying's horror, I burst into tears. Tenzin Tsundue makes me indescribably sad. This young man who has sacrificed his life, all his pleasures, for the country he has visited only once. These, I come to realise, are the trickle-down effects of life in exile. Getting to safety is but one aspect of freedom; then there is the ripping apart of people's lives, the sadness that Choying won't be at the birth of his child, the guilt that many children in exile feel that they can't be near their parents in Tibet when they pass away…that a young man's joy in life is eaten away because of the burden of trying to get his homeland back.

As the cold encroaches, more and more businesses pull down their corrugated-iron shutters and lock up for the winter. The Buddhist exodus is following the annual pilgrimage route to the Dalai Lama's teachings at Sera Monastery in South India then to Bodhgaya in Bihar. Tibetans pack up their bags and radiate throughout India to buy and sell garments, jewellery and handicrafts. Already one of the most mobile populations in the world, in winter about two-thirds of the entire Tibetan population gets on the move. The streets, once packed, slowly leak people to the buses departing for Delhi. Choying and I have to go to Nepal to renew my visa and have decided to follow the Dalai Lama to South India, so we too join the line to leave McLeod Ganj and head down into the plains of India.

I am to fly and Choying will take the bus, a two-day two-night journey, which means we should arrive in Kathmandu one day apart. I thought Choying wasn't allowed to fly without an IC but at the last minute he secured a letter from the Indian Department of External Affairs requesting the authorities aid him on a one-month pilgrimage to Nepal, by land, sea (there isn't one) or air. By then it was too late to book him a flight and now I wave him off tearily at Majnukatilla on a rusty, stuffy old bus that will be his home for the next two days as he traverses India and Nepal. I then pack my bags for my flight to Kathmandu, one of the most stunning air descents in the world.

Despite the virtual civil war in Nepal, which makes any place outside the Kathmandu Valley under seige by Maoist insurgents, the flight is full. After one and a half hours of travelling above fluffy white clouds there is a collective intake of breath as we bank left and the ragged tip of the snow-topped Himalayan range comes into view. Too soon we are enveloped in vaporous clouds, only to emerge over a ring of green mountains, the exposed red of trekking routes clearly carved into the earth. As we slowly lower into the valley, red brick-roofed huts, small ponds and dusty roads come into view. The valley is so long and the buildings so sparse that for at least fifteen minutes we have an eye-of-god view, peering down on the human endeavours below. We see a shepherd leading his flock of tottering goats along a mountain track; a group of women, copper water-carriers on their heads immovable above their swaying hips; and further on a group of schoolgirls in matching red skirts and identical plaits running along the road, kicking up a dust cloud. As the pilot lines up the plane for landing I can almost touch the glistening gold coronets of the Tibetan *gompas* and feel the prayer flags snapping in the breeze.

As soon as I get off the plane and walk up the open-air corridor of Tribhuvan International Airport, past tiny Buddha Air and Cosmic Air planes that ferry adventurers to their assaults on Himalayan mountains, I realise a vague issue nagging at the back of my head is about to bloom into fruition. I haven't brought any foreign dollars, the currency the Nepalese government demands visitors use if they want to secure an entry visa. In a country that suckles on the milk of foreign aid, Nepal won't allow its own currency to be used.

I spot a group of lounging officials and ask if they have an ATM or accept Visa cards but they shake their heads with faux sadness and say, 'Only MasterCard allowed.' I have been in Asia long enough to know there are no dead ends that cannot be opened by the whiff of baksheesh. Sure enough, I linger at the vacant visa-application desk where within seconds an immigration official, his eyes bright with opportunity, sidles up to me.

'I help you,' he says quickly.

And yourself I'm sure, I think, knowing nothing will dampen his enthusiasm to help relieve me of some rupees.

'I get you money off Visa,' he whispers, his hot breath swirling around my ear lobe.

'OK, where?' I answer in a monotone especially reserved for this kind of creature.

Smiling like a snake that has just swallowed a rat, he says 'Baksheesh madam,' as his eyes latch onto a 500-rupee note in my wallet.

I attempt to regain a little control and quickly stuff the seducing note away. 'Three hundred, OK,' I say.

He acquiesces quickly, in a hurry to feel the warm comfort of cash in his hands. I can feel the attention of the other officials as they enviously witness their colleague execute a perfect catch. I dully follow the official through a barren forecourt to a dusty liquor shop. The manager takes my card and, in a perfectly choreographed routine, swipes it while saying he needs five US dollars extra. By now I just want to get out of the airport and stop bleeding cash, so I accept the affront in the hope of cutting my loses. Armed with thirty US dollars, I go to the now deserted customs officers where the snake, now 300 rupees richer, stamps my visa and tells me to enjoy my stay.

I emerge into the afternoon light and into what looks like a major protest, with hungry-eyed men waving placards behind a gate at the car park. It turns out they are touts. I get in a taxi and go to Boudhanath Stupa hoping my experience of human nature will be redeemed.

Boudhanath is one of the most gracious Buddhist stupas in the world. Stupas are three-tiered structures, with a square base, a hemispherical dome and a conical sphere topped with a crescent moon and a circular disc. They contain the relics of deceased spiritual masters but are also a spiritual landmark for Buddhists, representing the enlightened body, speech and mind of Buddha. Rich with metaphorical meaning, they provide a place to circum-ambulate or meditate. From miniature models to the size of buildings, stupas are dotted throughout the landscape in many Buddhist countries.

Boudhanath Stupa was built around the fifth century by a poultry farmer called Shamvara and her sons. Thirty-six metres high, it is said to contain relics of the Buddha himself. With the bright eyes of a buddha painted on its dome, Boudhanath is a magnet for believers from all over the world. It is situated within a large public square bordered by Tibetan shops and restaurants. Perhaps it is the way the gentle light falls upon the uneven grey stones smoothed by decades of circumambulation that draws so many people. Or it may be the sight of elderly Tibetans, barrel chests pushed stoically forward, ambling around the stupa with an uneven gait evocative of the miles they have walked along wide valleys and up mountains.

Each day there are two human traffic jams around the stupa. In the morning just before seven when the shops that encircle its courtyard are not yet open, hundreds of the shuffling faithful circle around it, swinging the ancient prayer wheels that line its base. Each day the music shop puts on the same CD, a soft chant of *Om Mani Padme Hum*, which slowly wends its way around the pilgrims. Tourists take up positions at the restaurants that look out over the stupa, while Nepalese and visiting Indians crawl all over its dome. At five o'clock the faithful again pour out of the narrow cobbled alleyways, meet up with their friends and slowly walk around the stupa, watching as the Buddha eyes that all day gaze out from the top cylinder slowly fade with the dusk. Women set up tables filled with salty butter candles and for two rupees you can light one as an offering. Ancient husband and wife teams, the crippled with their palms open for alms, yogis with long dreadlocks carrying staffs fashioned from trees, and an assortment of Tibetans in animal skins, fur-lined kidney warmers and thick woollen blankets worn as skirts do their rounds in companionable silence.

I sit at a Japanese restaurant, its carved wooden shutters opening out on the stupa. Boudhanath is the place where I first encountered Buddhism and it has a special place in my heart. It was here, nine years ago, after six months spent travelling in Southeast Asia, that I found a semblance of what I was looking for. I had seen so much futility, in Soeharto's oppressed Indonesia,

Mahatir's Malaysia and Lee Kuan Yew's tightly wound Singapore, I thought there was little wisdom to be found in the world. But at Boudhanath I came across a people who, despite losing their country, possessed an equanimity I had rarely encountered. A people dedicated to religion who had peace in their hearts. I wanted to find out where it came from. That was the start of a journey which has drawn me back today.

By the time I have settled into a routine of quiet contemplation, Choying arrives. I spy him from my hotel window walking up the driveway. He looks slightly crazed, shambling along carrying a dirty backpack, wearing orange tracksuit bottoms, a grey jumper and a large cowboy hat. He flops onto the bed exhausted. I want to be considerate but am so excited to be reunited, I mercilessly keep him awake with exaggerated tales of my travel. Our time apart was a taste of our upcoming separation and now I know how dire it will feel. Before he goes to sleep we vow not to waste any more time away from each other and decide to fly back to India together.

But first there is one major hurdle—the Indian Embassy. I have already had two tourist visas for India and I know they are reluctant to give three in one year. I hope my pregnant belly elicits some sympathy and line up outside the embassy gates at six on a freezing morning ready to make my supplications. Once let into the compound I queue again at a tiny window to get a visa application form. As I get closer I moisten my mouth ready for my entreaty but the office wallah isn't interested, stamping my application and telling me to come back in two days time to pick it up. I pass the time anxiously, wondering if I will be rejected at the last minute, but on the appointed day the man responsible for my final approval doesn't even flick through my passport, sticking my visa in and handing it back to me without looking up. Never have I been so thankful for the apathy of Indian office wallahs.

Choying has broken out in a skin rash and takes himself to the doctor. We arrange to meet on the walk around the stupa. I see him talking and gesticulating to a group of boys who stand around rapt in the tale he is telling. When I walk up to him he tells me, breathlessly, he has just had an 'objection'. 'Oh, so much pain the objection, I can't walk. Now I have really big bum,' he says jabbing at the place the doctor poked a syringe into him, his bevy of listeners nodding their heads in empathy.

Having had trouble finding maternity clothes in India—where women simply rearrange the wrap of their saris—I scour the Kathmandu markets for something that will accommodate my enlarged belly. I am about to admit defeat when I come upon a range of bright cotton skirts with drawstring waists and a line of delicate pleats at the bottom. Thinking they are perfect for pregnancy I buy three, olive, crimson and electric blue, and wear them in layers so different colours are glimpsed at the bottom. I spend my last few days walking the streets reading the minds of passers-by: 'She may be pregnant but she's still stylish'; 'Western women look so good being proud of their pregnant bodies.' Then one day a well-dressed woman sidles up to me on the street and raises her sari ever so slightly. Underneath she reveals the exact same skirt...worn as a petticoat! 'Madam,' she says, pointing at me, 'that is not dignified.'

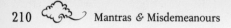

I have, it turns out, been wearing the equivalent of my underwear in public. The looks I took as admiration were in fact expressions of horror.

Choying and I skulk out of Nepal the next day, surrounded once again by Buddhist pilgrims ensconced on a Royal Nepal flight, all en route to the Dalai Lama's next teachings in tropical South India.

13

RESPITE IN A
MAROON-COLOURED
WORLD

A new city and a clean slate. Surely I can't go wrong in Bangalore, the town known as India's Silicon Valley. It is home to a breed of bespectacled, fleshy-bottomed computer programmers who have rendered their city as logically as a Linux code. Driving is not the haphazard affair that it is in the rest of India but runs along orderly lines—in opposite directions. Shops carry the names of global chain stores; airconditioned buses swish past carrying call-centre workers to colossal industrial parks on the outskirts of town.

Along with Choying—who delighted in the violent turbulence we struck just before landing and now believes flying is a great adventure—I catch a taxi along Mahatma Gandhi, or MG Road as it is known locally, past billboards advertising the zealous American evangelical Benny Hinn's upcoming Prayer for India, mirrored Intel and Amway buildings and roadside stalls where hordes of office apparatchiks are bargaining over nylon socks and polyester work shirts.

I feel as though I am halfway to the west, with brand names I recognise and small touches of sanity, like footpaths and streetlights and places where staff understand the word 'latte'. But of course it's still India, where looking at a child on the street can be risky. The pavement urchins stand before aluminium pans and sticks and, should they catch our eye, break into a routine of somersaults and other contortions, bending their bodies over each other like strings of elastic, then pop up and come and ask for money, or failing this, walk beside us trying to trip us up.

We have two days before catching a bus further south so decide to indulge in an all too rare pastime: browsing in an Indian multiplex. Although I don't do it at home, I've never been a traveller too proud to lunch at a foreign McDonald's or Pizza Hut so we take ourselves to Bangalore Central. Walking down MG Road my mouth drops at the sight of a woman chugging past on a motorbike. I have become so accustomed to gender roles that I can't help but stare at the sight of fashion emancipation: rushing in between the Muslim women in black burquas and elderly bow-legged men in dhotis are beautiful Indian women with long naked legs in tiny miniskirts, smooth slender shoulders barely covered by spaghetti strap singlets. The women have a swagger I have not seen anywhere else in India.

Everywhere are the signs of prosperity wrought from information technology. The streets are crowded with shoppers perusing Levi's, Benetton and Nokia shops, hair is blow-dried, moustaches flourish, fingers are podgy. Bookshops brim with titles like the *Seven Habits of Highly Effective People*, *India's Business Barons* and *Chicken Soup for the Soul*. At nearby Cubbon Park a pure-breed dog competition is in full swing. Yet interspersed with the modern throng are small Hindu temples.

Every now and then, along a crowded footpath, a human bulge will appear made up of old women in saris, young women in miniskirts, middle-aged men in suits and silk ties, and what look like aescetics, all clutching sticks of incense, mouthing silent prayers to the temple's deity. When I squint in, I can see a stone statue garlanded in orange flowers with small embers alight at its feet. Sandalwood smoke winds its way up from the offering plates and meanders out the door to mingle with the traffic fumes.

The minute we pass through the silent sliding doors of Bangalore Central I feel I have been beamed back to Sydney department store David Jones. My nose falls upon the delicate citrus and woody fragrance of Issey Miyake perfume as though it is one of the forgotten hallmarks of civilisation. I stroke the silk lingerie and glide past shelves staring at expensive trinkets, overpriced makeup and $100 leather wallets, humming along to the muzak I find a heart-warming reminder of home. While I feel I am being transported to my distant past, I'm vaguely aware it's not mutual. My Birkenstocks feel like wooden clogs on the white polished tiles, my faded cotton clothes stretched over my belly make me feel like a western pauper. The shop assistants eye me warily.

I get on the escalator to the first floor but when I turn I notice Choying, who has been following me around equally as hushed, is no longer with me. As I am conveyed up I see him far below waiting hesitantly on the ground floor, staring at the escalator's black steps as they fold into one another. Just as I am about to turn around and run down he steps forward with a do-or-die expression and clutches the moving handrails, whereupon he is shakily borne up to the next piece of solid ground. What a strange pair we are. Exhausted by the fluorescent lights and the bright objects of attachment, we stop for lunch at a cafe on the mezzanine floor. Choying wants to go to the bathroom so goes to ask directions from the staff. He returns, slumps down and adopts an exaggerated air of nonchalance. I ask why he didn't go the toilet and see a flicker of indecision cross his face. Within seconds, motivated by full-bladder-induced pain, he mutters something about another machine with a floor that moves. I realise he is talking about the lift, to him a completely unknown object full of pitfalls and trickery. We laugh at his predicament, but I have to remember that when I visit his family in Tibet I won't know how to ride a donkey from A to B or perform any of the essential duties like drying yak dung for the fire or sweeping the carpet with a broom.

My being five months pregnant doesn't stop men from opportunistically rubbing up against me on the street, as though the deserted footpath has hordes of people squashing them into me. It leads me to unsettling questions. I wonder if I am irresponsible travelling while I am pregnant. I am stuck between two cultural attitudes, the Tibetans like Tenzin's mother, who silently picked herself up, went out back and re-emerged some hours later to present her family with a new addition to their nomad troupe, or the email from my mother exhorting me to be careful of chilli, cracks in the pavement and nylon underwear. Mum and Dad, like everyone else in Australia and New Zealand whom I have told, are, in varying degrees, pleased, excited and slightly dazed at the rapidity of my conversion from single career woman to pregnant subcontinental wanderer. I've never seen another expecting western woman travelling. Does that mean it's unsafe or wrong? I feel in no-man's-land and can't decide.

I'm due for my monthly check-up so flick through the Bangalore phone book and ring some hospitals. Unfortunately I have to ring from the bus station where we have gone to book our ticket and there is so much noise most operators simply hang up. Finally I circle an advertisement for an obstetrician at a hospital I notice we had passed on the way. I call and an English-speaking operator answers. I explain that I am pregnant and in Bangalore for one more day and would like a general check-up with Dr Rao Malitha. She can't catch the name so I shout it two or three times in succession. Still she is perplexed and I can tell her dedication is waning; I'm scared I'm going to lose her. Then she says 'Oh, you want appointment with Dr Malitha Rao? Come tomorrow, ten o'clock.' I can't believe my success. The next day I bask in the company of a queue of silent pregnant women, for a moment indulging the fantasy that I am, in fact, quite normal.

Our bus for Kushal Nagar leaves at 11 p.m. but we end up at the bus station early. It is a teeming mass of village people, businessmen, beggars, cripples, con artists and other assorted elements of humanity. All the seats and available floor space are taken so we stand with our luggage next to where one belching bus after another reverses in, loads up, spurts some black smoke at us and rumbles off. I am a bus veteran but the trip south turns out to be one of my worst rides. It is like being tossed around inside a clothes dryer; every aspect of my being and all its reference points are rattling. The driver hurtles along roads so bumpy that despite an aching throat I cannot fathom leaning forward to pick up my bag and get a lozenge. I inhabit a dream in which I am paralysed and cannot even move my head forward. Friends surround me trying to help but I cannot flutter an eyelid let alone communicate my simple request. I wake up desolate and it is only when Choying lays his arm on mine that I feel some sort of connection with reality. With this the bus suddenly lurches to a stop. The lights blaze on. I look behind to see seats full of wide-eyed passengers sitting bolt upright as though we all just rocketed into space. As I stumble down the stairs I check my watch. It is 4.30 a.m., pitch black and we have just been dumped by the side of the road.

Before my eyes can adjust to the syrupy black night Choying has woken a snoring tuk-tuk driver and we are tearing along a two-lane road, bounded by flat empty fields. As the wind pouring in the canvas whips me awake, Choying points excitedly to the vista in the distance. Up ahead lies a shimmering city spread out over the landscape, its twinkling white lights matched by a canopy of bright orange stars in the night sky. Just then we fly by a line of majestic white stupas with golden coronets. Large gates with the eight auspicious Buddhist symbols wrought into the iron have been left open and we cross over the borderline into Sera Monastery.

Choying, who has developed the astonishing ability to see in the dark due to a lifetime of dodgy electricity and dim lights, points out how clean everything is, while I remain blind. Finally we come to a banner across the road that tells us we can go no further because of security for the forthcoming visit of His

Holiness the Dalai Lama. A security guard steps out of nowhere and tells us we must leave our tuk-tuk and walk from here. We heave ourselves out and start up the road, the plastic wheels of our suitcases rattling along behind us. Out of the darkness materialise robed figures, some pacing up and down, some still, facing walls, reciting in rapid Tibetan, making me feel as though we have entered a parallel reality, an elf-sized world that is serene and peaceful. I make out small, whitewashed houses, the tidy alcoves of their courtyards alight with candles that illuminate large ripe trees, dense with lush flowers. Dogs happily trot past or perch graciously next to their low gates as though waiting to welcome visitors.

At the end of the road we come to a huge white, gold and red building, with large copper prayer wheels on its roof and a wheel over the apex of its entrance. The entire edifice is so adorned with coloured fairy lights flickering on and off that it looks like a UFO about to take off. I catch a hint of pride as Choying whispers that it is Sera-Je *gompa*, his former prayer hall and the place where the Dalai Lama will be teaching.

The monastery is very much a part of Tibetans' identity. Founded in Tibet in the fifteenth century, it was partially destroyed during the Cultural Revolution but re-established in exile in 1970, and today it has as many monks living and studying there as at the height of its influence in Tibet. I try to pry out of Choying how he feels about returning here with a pregnant girlfriend but he is angst-free, telling me simply, 'It is good.'

We trundle up and down laneways cloistered by houses until we finally arrive at a small compound with two rooms that open out onto a tiny common forecourt. It is now only 5.30 a.m. and still dark but Choying knocks on an old wooden door and someone grunts from within. A light is switched on, the door opens and a monk steps out, rubbing his eyes. Behind him I see a room the size of a large cupboard with two narrow single beds separated by a hand's width. We tumble in and fall asleep on matching apricot sheets and pillowcases, which even in the fog of tiredness strike me as strange, given I've only ever seen Tibetans sleep on rugs covered with shawls or mats.

Perhaps it was the night that made Sera appear to be a haven of peace and meditation because by the hint of morning its real character takes shape. At first light I am awoken by the sound of hundreds of rubber thongs slapping on the asphalt laneway outside the room. I pull back the flowery netting to see a citizenry of monks—tall and short, fat and skinny, pale and black-faced—pass by. Soon after they have departed a group of adolescent monks stampede down the lane laughing, springing up to whack the branches of overhanging trees, their robes flying like capes behind them. Morning *puja* has evidently finished and they are going back to their *kamsens*—the large communal homes where monks live based on the region in Tibet they are from—for breakfast.

I rub my eyes and look around at our 'accommodations'. The room is tiny and filled with colourful collages of lamas and various pictures of the Dalai Lama. There is a mammoth picture of the Potala, the Dalai Lama's winter palace in Lhasa, onto which someone has pasted a picture of the Dalai Lama on the roof looking down on the city. Plastic flowers decorate an altar filled with water bowls and bordered by flashing lights. A poster showing a heap of fruit beseeches: *God Give Us This Day Our Daily Bread.*

I am still staring at the decor when the door swings open and a succession of grinning maroon-robed monks come in to slap a half-awake Choying on the back. They crowd onto his bed—studiously avoiding mine—fidgeting with excitement, exclaiming at his hair and taking shy glances at me. The gap between the two single beds is now like an obstacle course filled with gangly monks' legs blocking my exit. Worse, I have unbuttoned my fly to let my belly out and can't see my way clear to fiddling down there to do it up. Eventually it is impossible to fit any more monks on Choying's side of the room and one ventures to my side, perching at the very corner of the bed as though ready to spring off at the slightest provocation.

The last time they saw Choying he was one of them, a shaven-headed monk who spoke no English, knew few women, with the boundaries of his life circumscribed by monastic discipline and culture. Now he is back—speaking English, with 'fashion' clothes, hair and, with a pregnant western girlfriend, evidently a bit more experienced. The monks spend the next hour, before their first class of the day, questioning Choying, whistling and inhaling at his tales, occasionally stealing glances at me and, as if despite themselves, lowering their wide eyes to my bulging belly.

Finally en masse they all turn to me expectantly. They have a question. Choying translates: 'How many sheeps are there in New Zealand?' All eyes are upon me. I know this one. I have been asked it many times by Tibetans. I puff myself up in anticipation of the reaction. 'Forty-five million,' I say 'Compared to only four million people.' I bask in their sighs of admiration, their exclamations of *'Jo Wo Rin Po'*—swearing upon the name of Tibet's most sacred statue of Buddha, currently housed in Lhasa's Jokhang Temple. I am used to being mocked for New Zealand's sheeply situation and am glad to have found a people who instead look upon it as blessed with surplus livestock, their traditional measure of wealth. Then comes the crème de la crème of questions. 'What meat do you eat?' 'New Zealand is famous for its beef,' I say. 'A lot of New Zealanders like to eat really big beef steak from cows,' I say as they nod in apparent awe. Vanessa, I think, you are shameful.

Given the booster I need I manage to stand, zip myself up and stumble out of the room in one seamless move. Choying, who has been aware of my dilemma, points me to the small toilet block where, in the absence of a proper clean, I squeeze my belly under a cold tap seeking a bolt of refreshment. From the state of the muddy footprints surrounding the squat toilet I realise we share the facility with many others. While Tibetans are generally a tidy people they often have little concern for bathroom hygiene, coming as they do from a country like a refrigerator.

By the time I emerge again, large open-decked trucks loaded with maroon figures are pulling up and disgorging their human cargo—thousands of monks from nearby Drepung and Ganden monasteries—at the end of the laneway, each with their *ʒens* piled on top of their heads to provide some shade from the now scorching midday sun. Gaggles of teenage monks continue to scamper down the street, dodging the Indian men going door to door selling juicy portions of watermelon from dishes balanced on their heads.

I go for a walk past tiny kiosks with monk shopkeepers, internet cafes presided over by computer-geek monks, avoid monk rubbish men throwing their loads into the back of idling trucks, and past studious monk librarians rushing past with their books.

Back at the cupboard, another attentive shy monk serves us tea and freshly baked bread, cleans away our dishes and offers to boil water for my forthcoming showers. It signals the kind of hospitality we will be shown for the duration of our stay. One monk runs off to check where foreigners must register to stay here (most land gifted to the Tibetans by the Indians is near military areas therefore foreigners need permits to visit them); another offers to take us to the vegetable market in Kushal Nagar because, they earnestly tell Choying, I am pregnant and need good food.

Choying never introduces me directly but turns to tell me each one's name. He can't fathom how an hour later I can't distinguish one maroon-clad, shaved, shy, non-English-speaking monk called Tenzin—most take their first name after the person who ordained them, in this case the Dalai Lama, Tenzin Gyatso—from another.

We decide to take a walk to the *gompa* where the teachings will be held and set out with what will become our regular monk entourage. I soon feel like we are in a monastic version of *The Truman Show* as monks watering plants, jogging past, sitting drinking chai, all call out their welcome to Choying as we pass. As we turn from a laneway into the main road we come upon a semi-orderly 300-metre queue of ragged beggars sitting against the fence, their arms outstretched, beseeching people in their peculiarly refined whine. This, I realise, is the South Indian variation of what I always thought was a McLeod Ganj phenomenon. Their particular niche, or target market, is western Buddhists. Children dart from the dense mass of tangled cotton and dirty bandages and trail the westerners up the road trying to hold their hands. But giving to one causes a near calamity as the others complain and upgrade their pleading. I hear a particularly loud screech that seems to be aimed in my direction and turn to see a contingent of three McLeod Ganj beggars, a woman with betel-juice stained teeth and half a hand, her buck-toothed husband who has a prosthetic leg, and one of my favourites, a man who is always smiling despite walking on all fours because of some unidentified problem with his feet.

They smile and wave and we ooohh and ahhh at each other. The woman explains in broken English that she has a child at school in Bangalore and points at my belly grinning. From that day on I give them money each day, almost causing a riot of discontent among the other beggars who clearly think their counterparts have orchestrated an unfair advantage.

We turn into a wider road, the equivalent of the leafy streets of suburbia. Here landscaped grounds with large trees provide canopies of shade and stately multistoreyed homes have an air of wealthy stillness. Spacious balconies are lined with pot plants, while a breeze makes the curtains gently billow. These are the residences of the monastery's Rinpoches, many of whom are funded by inherited wealth or western sponsors. A Rinpoche, especially one with a *geshe* degree (the equivalent of a Masters of Buddhist philosophy which generally takes sixteen years of monastic study to attain), will be able to travel overseas to teach Buddhism and will often attract wealthy donors. This is particularly true of those with American or Taiwanese benefactors. The Rinpoches, who usually also have a class of Tibetan students at Sera, will then typically arrange sponsors for their students, thus ensuring a better standard of living within their close-knit group.

That night we go for a walk to the *gompa*'s courtyard where the monks have their nightly debating class. As we get closer we hear a cacophony of shouts. We enter the gates and come upon an incredible scene. Under the moonlit sky hundreds of maroon-robed monks, some sitting, some standing, are pointing, clapping and stamping at each other whilst vigorously arguing in sharp accusations and short rebuttals. There are four different schools of Tibetan Buddhism but dialectic debating is practised mainly in Gelug-pa monasteries, where the rules of engagement have been finetuned into a tactical game of verbal and intellectual jousts. The subject is always Buddhist philosophy. There is a responder who takes a sitting position, whose job it is to fend off attacks to the various philosophical and doctrinal positions that he has chosen or been forced to adopt. Above him stands the questioner, whose task is to act as an assailant subjecting his opponent to sustained attack. With a barrage of questions and challenges he continuously endeavours to catch the responder out and expose contradictions in his position. Each of the questioner's points is delivered in conjunction with a set action, either a clap, a shout, a stomp or a disdainful flick of the *mala*.

Monks must develop a colossal memory to recall all the philosophical positions and their refutations in this pressurised confrontation. The aim is to boil the ingredients down to perfect, unassailable logic. Debating is a way to hone these skills but the final goal—the reason monks spend years memorising vast texts—is the hope that one day, when repetition has burned the words into their consciousness, they will begin to grasp the meaning of Buddha's doctrine of emptiness.

Standing in the moonlight I have an epiphany. Devoid of religious texts to analyse and monks to debate with, Choying has taken to collecting my self-assertions and heart-felt declarations, memorising and categorising them in his mind, arranging them in order and then refuting the first proclamation—which undoes the second and the third, therefore exposing my complete lack of logic or consistency. Worse, it is carried out without malice, invention or exaggeration, just some simple mind exercise for him and a kind of trapped bewilderment for me. Having been raised in a family where politics is considered perfect dinner conversation I've always liked a good debate, but faced with his casual blitz I am silenced. I resolve to be mindful of what comes out of my mouth.

Early the next day, as per protocol, we rush in to secure some places on the floor, taping our shawls down onto the ground to mark out where we will be sitting for the duration of the teachings. Keeping one's space is a constant source of dispute among westerners—each day as new people arrive they try to squeeze into the territory other people have staked out. I am mortified on behalf of all westerners when whispered but potent disputes break out during the teachings as people argue over whose space is whose. Rivals fall into two categories: those who believe once you have staked out your space it is yours, and others—usually latecomers—who believe its a dog-eat-dog world and all space, even that marked with a person's name, is up for grabs each day. Hushed ferocious fights go on beneath the gaze of some of Tibetan Buddhism's highest lamas.

The next day the teachings begin. We get up at the crack of dawn to heat water, eat breakfast and pack our cushions and snacks. By the time we have reached the end of our lane we see a single-file line of monks winding around the streets. We hurry to the laypersons' line further up the road where we are all frisked and patted down by Tibetan security.

The first day opens seamlessly; many people have not yet arrived. As is typical of Buddhist events, at the last minute the teachings were brought forward by two days—although no one thought to change the information on the Dalai Lama's internet site; it is only those lucky enough to be in the loop that know. Like a school of fish folding backwards and towards in the pull of the tide, Buddhist students must constantly adjust their plans to changes in the schedule. There is a certain level of acceptance that if one doesn't find out, it is due only to karma; blame is rarely meted out to the organisers themselves.

On a raised dais sits the chubby, bespectacled twenty-one-year old reincarnation of the senior tutor of the fourteenth Dalai Lama, Ling Rinpoche; the stocky, smiling former Abbott of Namgyal Monastery, Jhado Rinpoche; and one of the oldest and most venerated lamas, having had a traditional upbringing in pre-Chinese Tibet, Denma Locho Rinpoche, who is said to be an emanation of the wrathful deity Yamantaka.

We pick our way across the field of people to our spot, thankful that no one has encroached upon it. Just as we sit down, the horns blow and everyone rises as one. In the distance we can see a procession of monks with yellow brocade *zens* and golden bow-shaped hats. The low tone of conch shells and cymbals clatter with the discordant notes used to herald the arrival of a great teacher. The monk at the front, while trying not to turn his back towards the Dalai Lama behind him, grasps a large bunch of burning incense sticks used to make the air through which His Holiness moves fragrant with scent. Craning our necks we make out the Dalai Lama's figure, the gait he adopts when he moves through crowds, peering into the throng to see faces he might recognise, a broad interested smile never leaving his face. Again, just the sight of him lifts my heart. Even better, good advice is to come. Words that I can chew over, analyse and use in my life. He climbs up a small ladder on to the throne, lowers his head and makes a thorough inspection of the crowd in front of him as in unison we all prostrate and then plonk ourselves down.

We open with a prayer then, as he will for the next week, the Dalai Lama begins by giving off-the-cuff advice to the people who have gathered to hear him. He has to accommodate the population of *geshes* and monks, many of whom are advanced practitioners of Buddhist philosophy, ordinary Tibetan laypeople and the full gamut of western students and first-timers. He is always aware that many Tibetans have undertaken the arduous journey from Tibet especially to attend teachings and fulfil a lifelong desire to see him and will soon have to go back to their repression. They will hold this experience among the most profound of their lives by virtue of having laid eyes upon him.

Speaking in Tibetan and translated by a monk called Ven Lhakdor, the Dalai Lama begins by telling us that he is happy to be here and feels a strong connection between teacher and student. He tells us that he has very few accomplishments and that the reason he has decided to give the teaching is to restore lineages that are in danger of degeneration. He has a microphone clipped to his robes and two on stands in front. He keeps his cotton dharma bag to his side and occasionally fossicks through it to fish out his handkerchief. In two columns in front of him on lower benches sit the *Umze*, or chant master, who leads the prayers, and a large number of attendants.

Next, as per convention, the Dalai Lama tells us how the lineage of transmitting these teachings has been passed down to him. He welcomes the monks and the 'ordinary publics' and tells us of the need to scientifically examine the teachings, to be very careful to investigate our teachers to see whether they are worthwhile. He also warns against practising the dharma by only propitiating the deities.

Just then a phalanx of monks appear carrying large battered metal teapots. They tread through the crowd, standing on shoes and limbs, dispensing plastic cups and spilling either sweet or butter tea into them. After we bless the tea I put on my headphones and find the English translation frequency. For a moment there is a crackle that penetrates through the prayers, but then I realise it is the Dalai Lama laughing because, out of sync with the *Umʒe*, he began chanting the wrong prayer.

He tells us it is very easy to be a Buddhist physically; to hold a *mala*, to go around the temple and to do prostrations, but that the real practice is to train the mind in compassion and to treat all beings with equal concern. He speaks of the constant fear of Tibetans in Tibet that they are watched wherever they go. The Dalai Lama says that sometimes when they visit him and there is no one else in the room they look around as though there is a ghost in the vicinity, they are so used to being spied upon.

He mentions the nice environment at Sera, and remarks that McLeod Ganj is small and dirty, 'still many foreigners live there and say they find it very peaceful and say they have a nice time'. Then he turns his attention to the monkhood saying he knows there are many monks here but only a small number with conviction based on teachings. A good monk, he says, needs reasoning and to understand the art of syllogism and to be happy to lead a modest life. 'A monk should spend his life in studying, reflection and meditation. If you merely wear the saffron robes and get contented with it, it's a big mistake.' Further, he says that if 'something has gone wrong with their ordination' they should not pretend.

'Right from the time of the dharma kings they allowed two types of practitioners, lay and ordained. If you can't carry on with the ordination then it is better to disrobe. There is nothing wrong with it because you can continue with dharma practice, you are not banished from the community.' This is a revolutionary statement to many of the older Tibetans and I know it makes Choying happy that he made the right decision years ago.

The Dalai Lama says he understands the challenges of monkhood, then much to everyone's delight confesses that when he was much younger there was one line in the text he had to memorise which, despite himself, he never could. Heaving with laughter he says he got so frustrated at this particular line that one day he scratched it out with his fingernail. The crowd roars.

The teaching lasts six hours during which I spend the last sixty minutes fidgeting nonstop because of the discomfort of being pregnant and crossed-legged on the floor. At the end of the first day, at four o'clock, we leave the *gompa* and take the laneway home. Already organisation is full tilt with monks scrubbing and chopping vegetables, boiling water and sweeping the courtyard. The monks ask us if we would like some tea and ask what I require for dinner. They confess they don't know what westerners like. Do I need eggs every day? Would I like a glass of hot milk in the morning?

The first night I ask if they have any needle and thread. They quickly find some so I decide to sew some cord to my *pungden*, or wifely apron, so I can tie it around my ever expanding waistline. But with the thread comes a pair of willing hands. Unlike many of the others, Tenzin Tashi is well built and muscular and it is he who seems to be in charge of attending to our needs. He sits down in the dim light and for a while doesn't look up as he concentrates on hand-sewing my apron. After one hour he holds up the finished product, a perfectly executed accomplishment. We later learn it was he who, upon hearing about 'foreigners' ways', arranged for the apricot bedsheets to be sewn by the local tailor and placed upon our beds.

I learn that these monks, who were together with Choying in the same monastery in Tibet, and who over the years have escaped in groups of two or three, have known Choying since he was a child. Tenzin Tashi was the first to escape, leaving one night thirteen years ago during a period of relative freedom in the Chinese political reign. He is now a parent-like figure to the entire contingent. Backed up by the second arrived, Tenzin Karma, he looks after the others with a strict fatherly concern.

Choying's *kamsen* is without a teacher because he died young. He was also never in a position to get sponsors for those under his care. I know they have to scrape money together for daily living, yet when Choying and I raise with Tenzin Tashi the idea of sending them money he says simply that they are looked after, the monastery provides them with food and of course their lodgings. They have little need and no aspiration for anything else, aside from when they are sick. Then there are no funds to fall back on. This is where Choying and I think we can help. I want to give them money straightaway but Choying has a more thoughtful approach. 'No, let's save money in New Zealand to be able to give it to them exactly when they need it,' he says. I have to put aside my desire to be seen as generous and admit this is the more discreet and practical solution.

While I am watching Tenzin Tashi sew, Choying is catching up on all the monastery news. He excitedly passes on to me that one of his monk friends has been elevated to the position of *geko*, explaining breathlessly that this means he has the authority to beat any of the 400 monks from their *kamsen* for any perceived infraction of the rules. If a monk fails to show up for *puja* for example, he can expect three strokes from the stick. This form of discipline 'keeps the monastery beautiful' Choying tells me. When I ask if the beater is disliked—after all he is first amongst equals—he is incredulous. 'No, he do this for monastery, not for himself.' Around Kushal Nagar are squads of lama police, empowered to check whether monks have a pass that allows them to be away from the monastery. If caught without one, they are fined 100 rupees. If caught at the nearby popular picnic and swimming spot they will definitely incur a beating. Choying tells me that his monk friend can keep thousands of monks in line.

I know one of the things on Choying's mind when he thinks about moving to the west and having a child is the dreadful rumour he has heard that you are not allowed to hit your children, that the police might come and take you away. He is horrified and wonders how you keep the child from becoming wild or disrespecting its parents. 'Khampas' ears are in their bottoms,' he says, pointing at his posterior with a great pride in their hardy character.

The next day's teachings are supposed to start at 9 a.m. but the Dalai Lama is ready by 8.45 a.m. This time he opens by talking about a recent meeting he went to with western monks and nuns and how they spent much time complaining about the behaviour of the lamas who took sexual and financial advantage of foreign students. He advocates putting announcements in all the media telling everyone about their wrongdoing because 'they are not following the way of the Buddha'.

The text we are studying is called *Bodhisattva Bhumis* and describes in meticulous detail the discipline needed and realisations achieved at each of the ten levels that a person travels through in order to reach enlightenment. After eight hours of sitting cross-legged on the floor soaking up the Dalai Lama's insightful teachings, yet squashed against other sweaty westerners, I finally unfurl and head back to the cupboard. I come upon what looks like a commotion. A friend of Choying's has returned to the *kamsen* triumphant. The word has spread: his job was to replace the fabric that sits on top of the Dalai Lama's cushion and he has managed to keep the one to be discarded. The monks are all excited: together they will send it back to Tibet to have pride of place at their monastery. The next day a monk called Tenzin Dorje goes into town and buys fifteen metres of white cotton he will lay down for the Dalai Lama to walk over on his way between the rooms and the *gompa*. He will take the one that is already present and send that back to Tibet too.

Each day the monks get up and cook our breakfast, attempt to wrest any domestic chores from Choying, rush home to cook us lunch in the hour break and dream up dinner dishes they think will appeal to me. Every night there is a power black-out and inevitably a maroon figure will emerge from the darkness bearing a candle. My every perceived whim is anticipated in advance. Keen to spend time with Choying they are in our room at every available second. If I stifle a yarn they immediately move outside and hang around the small concrete fence. I drift off to sleep content with the sound of them chewing the fat, laughing and exclaiming '*Jo Wo Rin Po*' in the Tibetan cadence that I have come to love.

At Sera I begin to understand the Buddhist concept of treating all beings as though they are your mothers. The idea is drawn from the belief that as we are all reincarnated countless times we have shared numerous different relationships with every other sentient being on the planet. At one time they may have been our mother, someone who gave us the gift of life, who forsook her comfort to carry us in the womb and who nurtured us into existence anticipating all our needs. The aim of every Buddhist is to treat all other beings, whether they are friends, family, enemies or strangers, with the great kindness our mother showed to us. The idea had always been slightly academic to me but it comes alive when I see the way the monks look after me and Choying.

One night the monks take Choying and I out for dinner in Kushal Nagar. Despite their poverty they are offered small amounts of money each time they perform a *puja*. Benefactors also offer them money twice a day for the duration of the Dalai Lama's teachings. The cash seems to burn a hole in their pockets, so taking us out to dinner becomes the fashion. Because they talk in Tibetan, I can contribute nothing to the conversation and am busy indulging in fantasies about what I will eat back in Bangalore when Choying interrupts me to translate for the monks. They say that since Choying escaped from Tibet, they are his only family in India and that they miss him and don't want him to go. They say he is a good person and they have asked him to always be honourable to me and to take good care of me, never to drink alcohol or hurt me. He translates this as if they are talking about someone else completely. Meanwhile I am floored by their openness and splutter back that I understand.

Slowly the individual personalities of the monks come into sharper focus. Most of Choying's friends are *gelong* or fully ordained monks, and in the next couple of years will become *geshes*. I ask them one by one what they would like to do after this time. Most are embarrassed at my question and answer that it is up to their karma what will happen to them in the future. But eventually they all tell me they want to go back to their monastery in Tibet to teach what they have learned to the monks who are not allowed to study properly. It reassures me that while many laypeople and some monks in McLeod Ganj desperately want a new life in the west, the strongest and most important tradition will still continue in the Land of Snows.

Tenzin Dorje, the scowler, is a particularly hard character. Unable to speak English, short and wide, he is like the housewife. One of a contingent of monks who serve the monastery rather than study, or 'not intelligent enough for Buddhist philosophy' as Choying puts it, he is in charge of all the household business. For days he has been rejecting all my offers of sharing food—although not meals I have already started on, as it is against the rules for monks to eat food already picked at by a woman. Finally I try the bright orange processed cheese balls available all over India and to my surprise he takes one. I offer again and he eats, so each time I pop one in my mouth I offer him, thinking we have finally made some connection. I smugly tell Choying that I have found what Tenzin Dorje likes ... cheese balls—but am immediately deflated when Choying answers nonchalantly, 'No, he just doesn't know if it is all right to keep saying no to westerners. He doesn't like the taste.' It becomes just another of my gaucheries.

Tenzin Dorje refuses to address me directly, but I have noticed that Choying pops out with new suggestions of what he thinks will make me more comfortable immediately after being with him. One day Choying tells me from now on the paper will be delivered every morning as the monks have discovered I am a newspaper addict. A man on a motorbike stops at our gate each day and Tenzin Dorje appears to receive it. Usually I am sitting on the bed eating breakfast but one day I have just finished in the bathroom when I see the newspaper exchange. I put my hand out for it and start to make thankyou noises when Tenzin Dorje marches straight past and hands it to Choying in our room.

Tenzin Dorje understands we like papaya and each day he brings one to our room. But before we can finish the last one he turns up the next day bearing a larger one, until eventually he presents us with a five-kilo beast that must be carried with a rope tied around a plastic bag. Little does he know the supply has banked up faster than we can eat them and there are several half-eaten papayas under our bed, which Choying forces himself to gobble in order to make room for new ones.

One night Tenzin Dorje comes into our room to chat to Choying and we show him our photos from McLeod Ganj. I mock some pictures where Choying and his friends, convinced it is cool, have taken themselves to a photo studio, chosen a 'nature' backdrop and struck weird karate-like poses in the hope of looking like Jackie Chan. Tenzin Dorje finds it hilarious and we laugh as Choying attempts to defend himself. The next day I say goodbye to him as I leave for the walk to the *gompa* and turn around just in time to see a flush rise up over his face. I had given up hope of being friends but our shared mockery of Choying makes me realise he is just plain shy and has taken a bit more time than the others to adjust to the presence of what must seem like a very forward western woman living in his monastery. That night he relents and allows me to help him prepare dinner. Together we fetch water and line up the vegetables for washing and chopping, then he notices the cauliflower is full of tiny writhing mites. Neither of us will kill them so together we spend a painstaking half-hour picking them out. Unable to communicate with a common language, it is a silent duty, but somehow I know we have become closer.

The next day Sera is alive with talk. The umbilical cord that connects every Tibetan to McLeod Ganj has delivered some shocking news. A fire the night before has destroyed a row of shops, a restaurant and guesthouse near the bus station on Dalai Lama-Gi Road. All made of wood, they were the businesses the settlers set up in the early days of exile. Thankfully there was no loss of life but sadly there is one significant casualty. The Magic Shop is no more.

A long-life *puja* is traditionally held on the last day of the teachings and I have to say my body is glad to be off the floor as I have begun to feel I have a football lodged in my stomach. Minutes after the Dalai Lama leaves us with some final advice— that the essence of Buddhism boils down to always practising *Bodhichitta* or altruism—huge open-decked trucks crammed with monks, depart the monastery tooting their horns and whipping up the dust in their wake.

It's time for Choying and I to return to the mountains of Himachal Pradesh, both a little sad at leaving our friends in tropical South India and heading into a vigorous northern winter. As we get on the bus Choying leans over. 'Thank you darling,' he says. However, the truth is that I didn't realise how much I needed to restore my battered faith in the monkhood until I visited Sera Monastery and saw monastic life flourishing. It is, as a western monk Sherab Gyatso said in *Exile as Challenge*: 'The Tibetan monastic world defies both idealistic and cynical expectation; neither do we have here a world of pure spirituality nor of Machiavellian intrigue. It exists not on the community's periphery but very much in the thick of it. It is alive and vibrant.'

Monks, I decide, belong in monasteries, not freelancing on the streets of McLeod Ganj.

14

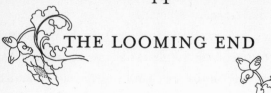

THE LOOMING END

We step down from the bus, once again at the McLeod Ganj bus station. Dappled sun hits the sodden earth while up high, fresh snow glows on the mountain peaks. *Momo* sellers stand bleakly with their hands stuffed into their pockets behind towering infernos of tin steamers. Peanut sellers have replaced boys selling quarts of coconut, their mobile carts smouldering with small ash fires on which they stir woks full of cracking popcorn. Dark-skinned Kashmiris in long woollen *kurtas* and embroidered wool skullcaps have set up makeshift tables selling almonds and walnuts, dried apricots and raisins. Next to them are more tables stocked with fur hats and baby booties, watched over by hawk-eyed Tibetan women knitting furiously with scratchy wool. Over the valley, eagles fly low to catch the upward currents of any warm air needed to glide over their hunting ground.

I immediately notice the gaping hole on Dalai Lama-Gi Road where fire has eaten the row of shops. Scavenging children the colour of ash play amongst the charred remains of overhead beams and glassless window frames, hunting through the mounds of black cinders for treasure. Cows, relieved of their diet of rotting vegetables and cardboard boxes, graze lazily on the potassium-rich soot. In all, ten uninsured businesses were destroyed but, I notice wistfully, even fire didn't have an appetite for the Sulabh International Public Toilet, one of the most ungodly latrines in McLeod Ganj. Next to the rubble its yellowing tiles still rise proudly aloft. The toll wallah sits timelessly amidst the steam that emanates from its rank urinals, still collecting the two-rupee usage fee, unmoved by the tragedy next door.

I hear that Jamphel has opened a restaurant called Yak Cafe on Jogibara Road hoping to lure in hungry and, perhaps, available foreign women. He has rapidly moved on from wanting a western wife and has instead discovered the joys of casual flings with the numerous women who pass through town for two or three days. When I see him he looks both too bright-eyed and worn out from all the effort of keeping up.

We house sit a friend's room for two weeks and discover that our neighbour is a lama much sought after for the accuracy of his divinations. Like Kamtrul Rinpoche he throws *mo* to advise people on what actions they need to take to clear out obstacles to their goals. However, unlike many lamas who teach or head monasteries, this is the extent of his council to the hordes of Tibetans who line up at his door each morning. Before we became neighbours I had visited this lama on behalf of an Australian friend of mine who has been trying to have a child for many years. When I asked for a *mo* to help her he addressed me, saying it was a bit difficult because—although I hadn't told him—he could see she wasn't a Buddhist, but he would try to help her. Like a well-oiled machine he threw the die three times, peered at its message and then reached for a stack of pre-printed advice forms on which he wrote down instructions, folded it into four and handed it to us with a smile. Reaching into a box and selecting a pendant he also said she needed to wear the image of a deity over her heart and sponsor a *puja* to clear out any obstacles. As Choying translated, I spied a large modern gas heater in the corner of the room and was momentarily distracted by envy until Choying gently nudged me back to reality. We offered a small donation and left the lama smiling cross-legged on his bed. I emailed her his advice and packed the pendant off in the mail. She thanked me and said she and her husband would also try IVF.

Living next to the lama, I realise how many people come to his door and why he has finetuned his process. From 8 a.m. a steady assortment of uncertain ruddy-cheeked newly arrived Tibetans line up beside Amdo street boys and burly businessmen in slacks and ties, next to shy young women holding newborns seeking a blessing and a divination, and burly men in *chubas* holding *khartas* or plates of piled oranges as an offering.

The lama has a civilised routine, throwing *mos* in the morning and in the afternoon sitting quietly on the balcony contemplating the valley that spreads out below us. He must be in his late fifties, with a wide malleable face that easily breaks into a smile that extends, like a cartoon, almost from one ear to the other. Under his robes he has wide hips and he walks with slow movements as though he is still adjusting to having an oversized body. He speaks only Tibetan and in the two weeks I live next to him I never see him go beyond the balcony; instead the world comes to him. Confronted with the masses that want his help, I wonder if this is really Buddhism, this constant attempt to use tools like divinations to make our lives better. From the lama's side he no doubt feels he is helping people, but for me Buddhism is melting down to the truth that a person alone must transform their mind through the hard work of controlling the extremes of attachment and aversion. Consulting a *mo*, however promising, will never be a substitute for the hard work of disciplining the mind.

I rarely venture outside it is so cold. When I do I experience an entirely different McLeod Ganj. Monks cover their heads in tall fur hats giving them a curiously Cossack-like appearance; the street boys have ditched their low-slung jeans and, like the older men, have adopted voluminous sheepskin-lined *chubas*. Even the cows have changed appearance, dumping their thin pelts and wandering the windswept, artic streets in new plush winter coats. The dogs pile on top of abandoned fruit stalls, sleeping all day on the hessian sacks that cover the ledges once piled with grapes, bananas and oranges. Everywhere Indians crouch over small fires lit in cut-off oil tins, feeding any wood they can find into its flickering flames.

Only Balu, the town's drunk, seems to stay on the street. Deprived of his unwitting bus-station paramours, he has taken to standing outside the bottle shop with a small block of wood pointing it at any direction a human emerges, as though he is directing them with a remote control.

The sweater brigade comes out in force. Selling sweaters is the fall-back position of many a Tibetan refugee, around sixteen per cent of the population. Like the well-trodden religious pilgrimage, the sweater trail is as old as the Tibetans' settlement in India. Sturdy businesswomen flock en masse to Ludhiana where they purchase great bales of machine-knitted woollen sweaters, in the sensible cut long adopted by civil servants, then disperse to any place where they might find shivering citizens. McLeod Ganj is a prime target, with its comfort-deprived westerners. They jostle for street space with the sock and ski-jacket merchants who peddle used clothes with the same shady look as drug dealers—wanting to get rid of stock before the authorities make an appearance.

One day I decide to visit the Dharamkot pizza restaurant with Kate. We take a tuk-tuk up to Tushita and then walk down a wide track into Dharamkot village, a sprawling hamlet of hotels and Indian mudbrick houses built into the mountainside. In summer Dharamkot is flooded with crusty Israeli backpackers who have just finished compulsory military service but have not yet shed the intensity of war. They party, smoke and haggle with a furious passion, rendering the village virtually unapproachable during their tenure. Encouraging them to remain Jewish despite their interest in Buddhism, the Israeli government is building a large new synagogue that will house the village's permanent Rabbi. But for the moment the cold has driven them and their roaring Enfield motorbikes down south and Dharamkot has retreated back to being a sleepy Indian village.

The icy air carries the muted sounds of village life: children playing, dogs barking and occasionally the hammering of an industrious labourer. We walk through tracks cut into the hillside, past patches of delicate yellow canola flowers. Now and then a herd of indecisive goats, unsure of how to pass us on the narrow track until the shepherd walking behind them emits a chirping noise or snaps a switch of deodar in the air, lunge past us fearfully. Three donkeys chump on grass, and a small square white Shiva temple with a pointed circlet stands bright in the cold air.

The pizza restaurant is owned by an indigenous Gaddi family and is open throughout winter. We sit outside in the last remains of the sun and devour three-cheese pizza and chocolate fudge cake. The resident black cat shoots past and runs up a tree pursued by a large aged black dog. I know from previous visits the cat is an experienced tormentor, the dog its victim. Alternately meowing mournfully and wrapping itself around the feet of customers, it cannot help itself but draw closer and closer to the fumbling hound until the poor beast, compelled by genetics, lumbers up to chase after it. Like groundhog day each episode ends up with the dog wandering dejected away from the tree as its nemesis settles in a hollow in the trunk grooming itself, vastly satisfied.

I am beginning to look like the ratty kid from next door, all flicked-back lank hair and freckles. I have seen what Indian barbers do, basically cutting a shape in the hair, be it an oval bowl or a simple square. The local Dogra Beauty Salon doesn't sound promising. I know there is a bona fide hairdresser in Dharamkot because I have seen posters around McLeod Ganj. Kate and I walk along the track and down an embankment, passing three huge boulders where a family has erected a blue tarpaulin cover and laid mats on the floor. Large steel pots sit jumbled next to the ashes of an open fire and a person wrapped in worn layers of cotton is curled up nearby gently snoring. At last we come to the gate of Om Tara House, said to be the hairdresser's residence. Four dogs start to bay in our direction but we are desperate— neither of us has had a haircut for six months. Choying has been begging me not to cut my hair; to his Asian eyes a woman is only a woman when she has a lustrous mane to prove the distinction. Unfortunately I have straight fine hair always in danger of being 'thin' and am constantly trying to fluff it up somehow, while he in turn always tries to smooth it down against my head, making it look like a limp curtain.

We see the hairdresser shelling peas in the sunlight; her three dogs, reassured they've done their duty, have dropped back off to sleep behind her. Dragging a chair out into the sunlight she pours warm water from a small bucket over my head as I lean over, then places a plastic curtain around me. No shampoo, no asking what I did on Saturday night, no product placement; I love the low-key style. Instead she tells me about the Moonpower course she runs and how for two days in May, when the full moon is in Scorpio and herbs are especially potent, it is good to pick walnut and stinging nettle and make a tea to rinse your hair in. She swears it makes hair stronger. She also advises against washing hair on particular days. She has large steel clips that look like oversized diaper pins, which she uses to hold the hair back. My hair slowly falls on the ground as she stretches, snips and gathers, all the while telling me about her cat's diarrhoea. As the inches fall away I feel as though I am taking off the layers of India and getting a hint again of the person I have been for the past ten years. The dogs snooze and harrumph in their dreams, wake up and take three steps only to drop themselves back down on the veranda again.

After twenty minutes my hair is cut and dried by the sun. She takes me back into her house to her bathroom where she proudly produces a small hand-held mirror in which, if I stare into her mounted mirror, I can just make out the back of my head. She has done a good job—and I am relieved that she is a woman. An Indian man with scissors might have strayed too near a buzz cut.

On 14 January Students for a Free Tibet carry a story saying that Xinhua, the Chinese government news agency, has claimed that Tenzin Delek 'has abided by the rules in jail and committed no further crimes' and that his case would be reviewed by the Sichuan Higher People's Court on 26 January. This is often a prelude to a sentence being lightened. Tibetans everywhere are hopeful, even those that remain on day-long hunger strikes for Tenzin Delek in a tent in the corner of McLeod Ganj's bus station. Later we hear that his sentence has been commuted to life imprisonment. It is a significant victory but I wonder how much of a reprieve Tenzin Delek feels it is to face the rest of his life in a Chinese prison for a crime he did not commit.

With my ticket booked and issued Choying and I begin to count down the days until we are separated. We have long known that I have to leave before I am over seven months pregnant; that is the latest most airlines will carry expectant mothers. I will go to New Zealand, where the baby will be born and where I can wait for Choying, who will remain in McLeod Ganj until his papers are sorted out. There has been no word about his IC since we lodged the application. We have been waiting for a visit from the Shimla police, ostensibly to check that he really lives at the address on his application. Once that is ascertained his file is sent around to each police station in the state to check whether he has a criminal record. This is the point at which the collective Indian bureaucracy falls asleep, awoken from their slumber only by the smell of baksheesh. The trick, we have been told, is to find out the file number and physically follow the application around to each port of call, offering fistfuls of rupees for a smooth, painless passage.

Back in McLeod Ganj, however, I discover it much easier to get things done in winter. Phones are answered, appointments easily given, there is no queue of customers at the post office and people, starved of company, want to talk—even to a journalist. Despite this I am becoming brittle in my feelings about the town and its increasing preoccupation with money, from the *barfi-* or sweet-wallah who short-changes all tourists to the post-office man who quotes me three different, escalating prices for cargo postage, to the tuk-tuk drivers who automatically switch their meters on to night rates in broad daylight if they see a foreigner approach.

I go in search of Jimmy Nowrojee, the last in a breed of Indians who were here before the Tibetan incursion. His haunt is Nowrojee's General Store, a once-grand establishment, now partly boarded up, that looks out onto the bus station. Heavy-lidded with wobbly jowls, the complimentary halves of his top and bottom row of teeth missing, Jimmy Nowrojee sits on a rickety old stool overseeing a large wooden desk filled with scraps of paper, receipts, folders and yellowing newspaper clippings. His black knitted cap matching the dark circles under his eyes and his cushion almost shooting out from under him, he rests heavily, his belly almost as round as mine. A faithful attendant, his face creased into a worried frown, stokes the charcoal burner at Jimmy's cumbersome feet with a pair of large iron tongs.

Jimmy leans into me, smelling for the entire world like an old walnut and says, 'He's a good one, he does everything for me,' before jutting his chin in the direction of the shopfront boy: 'This one is stupid, he always tells me, "I am not your servant."' He lurches upright, rolling his eyes in disbelief.

Through the open doors, customers can be seen coming into the dim cavernous Nowrojee shop where time has stood still since the 1950s. Ignoring the enamel signs advertising Nestlé's Famous Cocoa, Royal Palace Biscuits, the large scratched jars of forlorn boiled lollies that could easy swallow a human hand, and antique glass-topped counters displaying a range of ancient foodstuffs, they silently exchange two rupees for one of the Hindi or English newspapers spread out on the round table in the centre of the shop. Now and then a supplicant comes to the door of the office, his hands folded in prayer, and murmurs '*Namaskar,*' or hello, to Jimmy, whose face lights up with a roguish smile. Just like the old days.

In his hands is a large old photo album decorated with faded roses. He is fumbling with its thick cellophane-covered pages, ignoring ones that are stuck together, passing the square sepia photos of his father astride a pony outside their shop in pre-

Tibetan McLeod Ganj before he comes to the page he is searching for.

'You see this is the one,' he says, stabbing his finger at the picture. 'This is the day Dalai Lama-Gi came to this town.' The black and white photo shows a crowd of orderly-looking but bewildered Tibetans whose colourful clothes have all faded to white, standing neatly behind a rope outside the shop we are in now. What is now the outer edge of the cacophonous McLeod Ganj bus station was then the shop's wide wooden balcony, alive with Queen of the Night and hydrangea blossoms and painted signs swinging from its rafters. In front of the obedient crowd, a vista of dirt provides a swept smooth Himalayan front lawn, groomed for the arrival of the Tibetan god. A road to one side marks what was then Nowrojee Road, now upstaged by Dalai Lama-Gi Road.

'That day was a pleasing day. We had seen some bad days. I would look at my brother's face when there was no one here, only my sister-in-law. We lost everything in the Partition, back then we were the only store but the Britishers left and there were no customers.' Then veering back to the album, 'Of course photos were not allowed, his [the Dalai Lama's] life was in danger then and there was a lot of agitation by the Chinese but I took this one.

'The Tebeteeans were polite then not like now,' he says, knocking my arm conspiratorially. He sounds disrespectful but there is an undercurrent of affection for the people he has spent most of his life around. 'Now they have so much rude behaviour they learned from foreigners. They get a free flow of money from sponsorship. There are some good ones, but money is everywhere. Money is a curse.' From his nearly bankrupt business Jimmy can see how detrimental the free-flow of money to Tibetans has been. He has seen people use it well and watched horrified while others have squandered it.

He turns past some more pages until I see a photo of a young man cuddling a tiny leopard resting on his shoulder. It is a young Jimmy, with lush black hair, deep black eyes and collared shirt tucked into pressed slacks. He looks like an Indian Clark Gable. I ask him if he ever married. 'Twice I lost,' he wheezes, 'I was engaged but when you lose money you lose everything. I am the last of my father's five children. Now I just want to be left to die peacefully. I am alone here.'

Jimmy tells me he is unhappy in McLeod Ganj, where he has no business and few friends. He is also discontent at the passing of time that has seen the world outside the shop's doors turn from a sleepy yet refined hill station where baby leopards could be cuddled and the Nowrojee dynasty possessed the sole automobile, to a licentious town full of western spiritual bravado and Tibetan entrepreneurs. But as Jimmy says, 'The problem is you can only see the bad ones, but the good ones are still there.'

With winter here and many of the deep-pocketed westerners gone, a lot of the Tibetan street boys have run out of funds. Choying and I are constantly asked for loans that it never crosses their minds to repay. I am starting to feel uncomfortable with the way I am perceived by some of them: that as a foreigner I am a bottomless source of money.

We also get some awful news, which reinforces my decision to decamp to New Zealand to give birth. A Tibetan woman who was pregnant and had a complication-free birth at Delek Hospital got into trouble when her placenta took too long to come out. The doctors, unable or incompetent, couldn't act fast enough and she started haemorrhaging. She was transferred to Zonal Hospital in Dharamsala, which somehow managed not to treat her adequately and she died, leaving a distraught husband and a motherless newborn. It is a chilling reminder of how incompetent some of the medical professionals here are. Zonal Hospital is, ironically, a teaching hospital.

Each day McLeod Ganj feels more and more like a staging post on a modern-day Silk Road. Gone are the Amdo boys' 'high fives' and 'yo-bros', now the population reverts to old customs. The elderly poke out their tongues in greeting in an age-old Tibetan custom meant to prove their innocence of any mischief or of reciting non-Buddhist mantras. Afghanis in turbans and Tibetans in *chubas* and bowler hats wander the streets in a medley of fur, sheepskin and wool. Emboldened by their dominance the old people stare freely at the now rare passing westerners, sometimes venturing, 'America?'

People flood into McLeod Ganj from Tibet and I begin to recognise each region's facial features. I can spot Khampas by their long dark eyes and moon faces with cheekbones so high and wide it looks as though all their features have migrated upwards. They almost always have a swagger; I often catch a glimpse of a dagger swinging from their hips, mostly used for household tasks—occasionally for settling disputes.

In anticipation of *Losar*, the raucous Tibetan new year, Lobsang—free from Elizabeth's restraining eye—heads down to the Norbulingka to buy 20 000-rupees worth of beer and whisky which he and his sidekicks store with a local family. One bottle is fifty rupees but their hauling it back to McLeod Ganj—in defiance of all local laws—will net them seventy rupees and *Losar* anticipates a lot of thirsty Tibetans. Tenzin does the same with dried meat from Delhi although his journey is far more treacherous. As part of the opaque meat licensing system, the authorities have deemed it illegal to bring meat over the border from Uttar Pradesh to Himachal Pradesh and the buses that ply the route are regularly stopped at midnight and each person's bag searched by the police. Jail is a distinct possibility in the absence of baksheesh. All over India, people break out in a cold sweat at the thought of the mammoth bribe the police will demand for their complicity should they find any illegal business. It would take at least double the contraband's worth in rupees to get rid of the police should the whiff of hi-jinks float across their noses.

Tenzin Dorje, who is coming up to McLeod Ganj from Sera, telephones us. He has a small problem, he says. He has been arrested and is sitting at a police station three hours south of Delhi. '*Jo Wo Rin Po*,' Choying exclaims incredulously, so I ask him for a simultaneous translation. He says that Tenzin Dorje had a 350-rupee ticket in cattle class for the train from Bangalore to Delhi but met some monks who asked him to come to their section. He knew it was dangerous but wanted some company. The police came through the carriage and found he was in the wrong seat. Tenzin Dorje was hauled out and taken to the station where they demanded a 300-rupee fine or one month in jail. He told them he would go to jail—after all there were no classes at the monastery, everyone was on a break. It wasn't what they were seeking and after some haggling he bought his freedom for 100 rupees. He was calling to say he would be in Delhi that night.

It is freezing and bleak outside, a blanket of fog creeping its way into all the cracks and crevices of McLeod Ganj. Inside our home the heater has finally blown out and Choying is on the floor dismantling it, aiming for its fourth resurrection. As the minutes roll by my extremities begin to feel the chill, then a blank hard coldness creeps up my legs and arms.

Tenzin Dorje arrives at 5.50 a.m. He seems shocked into silence by the climate difference between the tropical south and the freezing north. We usher him in and offer him tea and a rug. His flimsy monk's robes are useless against the cold so he pulls his maroon polar fleece out and puts the hood up, joining the gangs of people in McLeod Ganj who once looked like monks and nuns and now look like Little Red Riding Hoods. Eventually it is so cold he puts on an assortment of lay clothes left by some street boys, stretching them into all sorts of shapes to cover his body. What was once a funky baseball jacket is pulled down and tucked under his bottom; hip-hop jeans that once slung off the hips are hitched up to his portly waist. The look is completed with red knee-high gumboots.

With two suave porters, Tenzin Dorje helps us move into our new room next door to Lobsang, and at the bottom of the largest flight of stairs in McLeod Ganj. It also has the first full-length mirror I have seen in months. I am shocked and fascinated by how big my stomach is, and the way it protrudes like the front of a bullet train, but am placated by the thought of the geyser in the bathroom that will offer us a hot shower. For the past few weeks we have had to rely on solar power that doesn't heat up the water until the afternoon.

Discouraged from moving by my now unwieldy body and the winding stairs that separate me from the shops, I decide to dedicate myself to a mini writers retreat; just me, the computer and bar heater.

But before I can take advantage the power goes out during the night. Even through my sleep I can feel that any limb I put outside the bed covers is chilled within seconds. When morning comes, neither the heater that I turned on during the night nor the geyser is going. A thick layer of condensation frosts the windows. Choying opens the door and shouts. Outside is a vista of white. The trees' limbs are heavy with snow like a department store window display, the hills outside our room covered. Snowflakes whirl around his head as he stands staring out exclaiming at its beauty. It is eerily quiet, the snow heaping silently onto the soft fluff that covers every surface like goose feathers in an eiderdown, belying the brutality of the cold. He goes to wake Lobsang and Tenzin Dorje next door whereupon I hear a lot of '*Jo Wo Rin Po*'s.

When he comes back he stands on the threshold with the snow falling behind him. 'Today I remember my home,' he says. 'There it snows all over but when sun coming, all finish.' He is not usually sentimental but I can tell he is truly homesick and loves anything that reminds him of life in Tibet. He puts on some gumboots and tramps outside, recruiting Tenzin Dorje to get some batteries for the camera. Choying makes a snowman for me on the fence outside our room except it looks more like a Tibetan statesman with an erect bust and broad shoulders. One of the Indians is playing with the local black dog, throwing snowballs at it. It is scampering around, thrilled at getting human attention at last, not sure if it is part of or the subject of the fun. When the man tries to bury it in snow, the yelping dog runs into our room under the bed, lying low to the floor, looking victimised.

Nothing will stop Choying's enthusiasm for the magic outside that is so reminiscent of his home. Even the discomfort is somehow familiar to him, resting easily on his shoulders. My own joy, however, is tempered by frustration at the fact it is freezing and there is no electricity. The bathroom which I previously saw as minimalist with its white tiles now appears as an unwelcoming igloo, the bank of windows that I imagined would let in the sun, a double-crosser acting for the cold. A ferocity I didn't think I had emerges if Choying forgets to close the door when he comes inside, oblivious to the glacial rush of air that further lowers the room temperature. He looks at me in alarm, not sure how to deal with the creature huddling on the bed surrounded by lumps of blankets, spitting out invective. Later when I apologise he tells me, 'That is all right, my friends told me some woman get angry when they are pregnant.' I wonder if it is really that primitive.

I am a child of comfort, taking a journey in a world of inconvenience. I have discovered I can bear it good-humouredly only for as long as it remains a novelty. I sit in bed trying to enjoy the beauty of the snowy landscape but am angry at India.

It is a useless, draining rage. I eat an entire packet of chocolate chip cookies while Choying feasts on long ribbons of dried meat brought illegally from Delhi.

Tenzin Dorje returns with bad news. Up in McLeod Ganj the shops, without power, are all shut. There is no way to buy things, aside from one stunned Kashmiri vegetable wallah, raking in the rupees from a throng of customers vying over his wrinkled frozen vegetables. The streets turn into a playground with people doing nothing aside from throwing snowballs at each other. I had invited some friends around for dinner but none of the shops that sell ingredients have opened.

Stuck with our impotent bar heater I now understand why the local Indians have not embraced this technology but prefer to rely on charcoal fires lit in sawn-off cooking-oil tins.

Tenzin Dorje, Choying and I climb fully clothed into the only warm place, bed, and spend the afternoon huddled together. It allows Tenzin Dorje to ask, via Choying, a question he seems to have been brooding on for some time. 'Are there trees on the moon?' Despite very agile brains, many Tibetans haven't received the same kind of knowledge that has floated around the western world for decades. I explain that the moon has a different atmosphere, so things that grow on earth cannot survive there. 'Are there people there?' I say no, not as far as we can tell; humans cannot breathe the air on the moon. He and Choying have a long impassioned debate in Tibetan, during which I hear the words '*Lo Zambuling*', the Tibetan word, used in mandala offerings, for the world system offered symbolically to a buddha. This names four planetary systems of which earth is only one. Other beings are thought to inhabit the other universes, although they share few of the characteristics of human beings. I explain that western scientists have discovered planets in our solar system with their own sun or moons, just as the earth has its own sun and moon. Tenzin Dorje hoovers up the information, fascinated. Intrigued by this revelation of unworldliness, I explain that western scientists only believe what they can see whereas Tibetan Buddhism believes in the existence of things not visible to the human eye. Satisfied, we all fall asleep.

Later that afternoon Choying and I decide to go for a walk to the bus station. I leave the room wearing almost every article of warm clothing I can find. Four and a half feet of snow has fallen, the biggest snowfall since 1991, and we labour up the stairs clinging to each other. McLeod Ganj is like a fantasy park: snow drips off every surface like a tiered wedding cake, occasionally plopping onto passers-by from tree branches that have grown too heavy.

The start of the hill from Jogibara Road has become one huge slide that newly arrived refugee children from Tibet are hurling themselves down. I slip and slide everywhere while Choying holds my arm in a vice-like grip, alarmed I'll fall and in the process making me feel like a petty criminal on day release. I am both touched and slightly embarrassed by his display of concern. Everyone can see.

The landscape looks extraordinary, the entire mountains covered in white with only peeks of green foliage to break up the colour. Dogs stand in the middle of the street, their coats covered with a sprinkling of icing sugar like snow, staring at the people shuffling past. Tiny newborn puppies huddle and push each other to get underneath their mothers' stomachs.

Shops have now opened and at first raise the price of candles 100 per cent then start to run out as new supplies from Dharamsala cannot be brought up. As a blanket of darkness falls on McLeod Ganj I am escorted home. I look out over the town and the mountains. The ground is luminescent but all signs of human habitation have been wiped out, except for the occasional flickering of an orange fire.

My mobile begins to run out and my computer flickers with warnings that the battery is low. We can do nothing but sit in bed under our highly flammable Chinese velour blanket, recklessly playing cards by candlelight. I ask Choying if Tenzin Dorje is disappointed he came at this time but again I underestimate the Tibetan capacity for discomfort. 'Oh no, he says he is so happy he came, it reminds him of Tibet. Once he went up to Manali especially to see the snow but it was too high up in the mountains. He thinks this is very special.'

The next day there is still no power. That means no way to dry our wet socks and towels even if there was hot water for a shower. Friends who went for a walk call by to say they saw too many power lines broken by falling trees to expect the power on any time soon. I have an appointment to see the rabbi overseeing Dharamkot's Jewish population, but apparently the snow has made the village impossible to reach. The mobile service here is also no longer working, although that is a regular occurrence, so I must traipse up the stairs to a phone shop to call him and explain my predicament.

The following morning—still no power—I lie in bed grumpily, conjuring up accusations of India's inadequacies. In a mammoth effort I get out of bed and sit on a nearby chair, huddled under a blanket. The rot has set in. I stare out the window, my teeth chattering, resentful at the cold and my truncated existence at the bottom of the hill. By the time Choying comes home from the market I am on the verge; two minutes later I start to cry, wailing that I want to go home, that I can't stand it any longer.

I can see by his flustered look that Choying feels impotent, this crying woman in front of him, her hollow boasts about being a sturdy New Zealander revealed for the flimsy fantasy they are. He takes me out for a walk to McLeod Ganj. It takes at least half an hour for me to get up the stairs but thankfully the missile throwers have worn themselves out and technically it is safe. We go to the telephone shop and wait in line to call my father for his birthday. After half an hour listening to someone else's conversation it is my turn. I dial New Zealand and on hearing my mother's voice promptly burst into tears again, bawling about the cold. The Indian men turn away. My mother starts to cry too, worried that her only daughter and prospective first grandchild will be mummified in Himachal Pradesh. Dad comes on the line oblivious, telling me about the Australian Open in progress. I sniffle and wish him happy birthday. The Indians evidently feel it's safe to turn around and continue their business, graciously ignoring me.

Exhausted, I shuffle back out into the bus station where Choying grabs my arm again. I notice the *rudarudarud* of a generator and follow the sound to an internet cafe where I email my friends plaintively. Australia is burning under thirty-eight-degree heat while I slowly go blue. I smile encouragingly at several small Indian electricians clinging to the side of the wooden powerline poles, ferreting in small knapsacks for tools to fix the mangled wires. At home I bury my head in a book, knowing that I have exhausted my 'character building' days. I have finally found my limit and, at six months pregnant without a hot shower or my beloved bar heater, it's not that far beneath the surface.

But just as I am losing myself in the book's plot there is a slight fizz and a bright blinding yellow light comes on. I jump up and run crazed around the room, flicking on the heater, plugging in the computer, jamming the mobile recharger into the socket, switching the geyser on. I have to stop myself from calling New Zealand with the good news. Suddenly India isn't so bad after all.

But I know I can evacuate to the west—for many Tibetans this is all there is.

15

THE RELUCTANT RINPOCHE
AND LONG GOODBYES

Right from my first encounter with Ngari Rinpoche, the Dalai Lama's younger brother, I know he is different. First I call and unbeknown to me it is he who picks up the telephone. I explain that I am writing a book about McLeod Ganj and am seeking an interview with Tenzin Choegyal, alias Ngari Rinpoche, the reincarnation of an influential lama. The well-rounded voice asks me who else I have interviewed, laughs when he hears the names, saying, 'Ah, the usual suspects,' before adding that it is Ngari Rinpoche speaking and yes, I am welcome to come and meet him.

Ngari Rinpoche lives at Kashmir Cottage, a hotel in the woods above the Gangchen Kyishong, or government district. I walk there on a dappled morning grateful that, today at least, there is respite from the cold, and at the entrance to the compound pass a large tethered bull-mastiff which, in the traditional Tibetan nomad style, is wearing red fabric tied around its neck. It barks furiously at my intrusion. I meekly call out and a man in a small office answers. He is middle-aged and weathered, with thick white hair and a swarthy face. A walking stick sits nearby and he is in a chair with folded blankets covering most of his body. He says I am early, it is 9.55 a.m.—my appointment is at ten o'clock—and I may have to wait. 'Please sit.'

A younger man emerges within a matter of minutes and leads me up some stone stairs to a large residence. It is designed to look stately with a wrap-around balcony and many doors and quarters but somehow appears unimposing and down-to-earth. Wrapped up in all my expectations of Tibetan culture I expect to be met by a monk in folded robes who, although he is reputedly very modern, still has the stately demeanour of a lama. Instead, the man who walks along the veranda to meet me is compact, with a long face and tinted square glasses. Although at fifty-seven he is twelve years younger than the Dalai Lama, Ngari Rinpoche looks strikingly like his sibling except he is dressed in grey slacks and a grey polar-fleece zipped up the front. He looks like the Dalai Lama in the guise of a rural real estate agent, precipitating in me a second of panic—have I come across the wrong brother? I am momentarily unsure of my bearings until he smiles at me and I notice he has a missing tooth in the front of his mouth and therefore can't possibly be His Holiness.

Ngari Rinpoche immediately strikes me as beautifully ordinary. He quickly warms his hands together before shaking my own and leads me to a room off the veranda with large couches overlain with Tibetan rugs. He asks me to sit wherever I like and seems solicitous of my welfare, asking about where and when I am giving birth even before I can ask any preliminary questions.

He has the same voice and intonation as the Dalai Lama and the identical habit of breaking into deep chuckles when struck by some absurdity. He is unguarded, keen to talk about Buddhism, Tibetan society and a culture he has come to regard as both highly admirable and bogged down in superstition.

Before I can even begin he talks about how being refugees has affected the psyche of the Tibetan people. 'If you look at the plight of refugees and you hear any person's story there is discontent, and from a Buddhist point of view discontent is the very nature of our cyclic existence so that way, to use an American term, it's "no big deal". But then being displaced has some particular features. You don't have a sense of belonging and there is no sense of security in terms of legal status, and then of course everything is foreign to you and you are labelled as some kind of a specimen...isn't it?

'But in another sense having no country and no security calls upon an individual to reach deeper in ourselves and find some other kind of strength and that, I feel, really promotes spiritual growth. It all depends on how you look at it...isn't it?'

I take a breath and wonder if the batteries on my recorder will go the distance. I am also a little parched. Thankfully he asks if I would like some tea, 'It is very easy I can always just ask for a cup. I have a small guesthouse so I am one of the permanent residents here.' His laughter bubbles up.

I say to him that he has probably talked about it many times but I would like to find out about his life. 'My life,' he repeats quietly. 'I was born and marinated in Buddhist culture, OK, but I never took it seriously until I was in my late thirties. I will explain why.'

He says that he was recognised as the Ngari Rinpoche as a young child and at seven was put into a monastery where he learned to memorise texts and debate. After the family escaped from Tibet in 1959 he was sent to a boarding school in Darjeeling, where he stayed for nine years. 'It was difficult for me because it was the first time I had ever really been parted from my mother,' he says.

He goes on to explain that after school he went to America to study as a career counsellor but there he had the first of many personal setbacks. The young Rinpoche found it difficult to adjust to life in Seattle. 'I was there for three months then I came back and I think I underwent a spell of depression. I felt like a college drop-out. For me, having a big ego and not completing college was a big problem.' It was, he says candidly, 'one of my monumental failures'.

After returning to India he tried several different careers: exporting clothes, working as an errand boy then teacher at the burgeoning Tibetan Children's Village—the school and orphanage—and at one stage in the private office of his brother, the Dalai Lama, before, he says casually, 'I went into the army as an airborne commando'.

I can't help but exclaim at this. The Dalai Lama's brother, a precious Rinpoche raised in the traditional manner in Tibet enlisting in the Indian army as a paratrooper? He stops. 'You didn't know?' I shake my head. He explains that he served for two and a half years until he discovered the corruption of an Indian general. After exposing his superior, he took early retirement.

For the second time in his life, Ngari Rinpoche started to feel the onset of a deep depression. He sought the help of Tibetan and western doctors and, while stable, once again joined his brother's private office, this time as the Dalai Lama's personal secretary.

'I did that on and off for ten years. Then I did nothing for a while because I wasn't feeling too good. You see before my illness was this depression, and then later on I acquired bipolar symptoms. I left the job and again took treatment then I came across some doctors who really understood my case and they prescribed lithium and ever since I have been on lithium.'

I ask what exactly lithium does and he says it dampens a person's synapses so they can remain emotionally steady, without the highs and lows of bipolar disorder. After a brief spell as a member of the Tibetan Peoples' Assembly he chose to recede from daily life. 'Then, since 1995 I didn't do anything, maybe living the life of a hermit. I stay at home and I study and I sometimes give talks,' he says.

I am taken aback by his honesty. I say that many people in the west have depression, either a chemical imbalance or a kind of extreme dissatisfaction with their life. He swiftly points out his illness is the former. 'It is chemical. The so-called blues don't last more than a week, not all the time unlike this kind of thing which keeps on going and the main manifestation is to lose interest in everything.

'My goodness me, it's horrible,' he says. 'When it hits you first and you don't know what is happening...but it has brought something positive in a way. When I meet someone who is depressed I can relate to them, talk to them and make them laugh and appreciate. Sometimes I go to Delek hospital to meet people who are depressed or they come to talk to me. Some are raving mad.'

We stop speaking for a couple of seconds, until I say that is so awful, to lose interest in everything. He agrees. 'Among Tibetans there are quite a number of people who are depressed but we don't talk about it. A lot of the older people think they are possessed by bad spirits and just consult lamas. Tibetan medicine now accepts the chemical involvement within the dynamics of cause and effect.'

I ask him if he thinks the origins of his depression could have something to do with the burden of being both a Rinpoche and the Dalai Lama's brother. He thinks quietly for a while. 'Probably it comes to not finding a personal worth. Then again it stems from some kind of craving. Having failed the prescribed image, that of a Rinpoche, I jumped ship, I'm a deserter. Although I didn't do it young enough,' he says before bursting into laughter. I ask him if, as someone who has been identified as a prized reincarnation, he remembers anything of his past life.

'I became a hostage as Ngari Rinpoche from the age of four. I don't remember anything about my being special and so on. I don't remember anything about past lives, my earliest memory is from five or six,' he says dismissively.

He then tells me that many Rinpoches have too stately a life and too much wealth, which they share only with their own retinue. In fact, he says, Tibetan Buddhism suffers Rinpoche-overload. 'I mean, anybody in any culture can be born a Rinpoche, they don't need to be recognised by the Tibetan system. They can do just as good, be just as altruistic, anonymously,' he says.

It takes me aback to hear this simple and unassailable fact. Just as it is possible to forget that the Christian Church doesn't own God, or can prove their priests are a conduit from above, Tibetan Buddhism can't claim that all Rinpoches are a part or a product of their system.

I ask Ngari Rinpoche if he could conceive of a life where he stayed in robes and lived more like other Rinpoches. He answers that he would never have been able to make it. 'I don't think I had a vocation to be a monk, a Rinpoche who stayed in a monastery. I don't know. I have tried. I tried until the age of twenty-five. I always thought the transition to India, when we lost Tibet, was easy for me but it probably took a toll. Things happened so fast.'

Ngari Rinpoche is so obviously different from other Tibetans I ask him what his relationship with other people in the upper echelons of Tibetan society is like. 'I stay out of it,' he answers bluntly. But the question opens up his dissatisfaction with some of the Tibetan community. His appraisal is tempered by his innate sense of humour and understanding of the great many positive aspects of his culture.

'Our greatest challenge today is pretension both political and religious. I don't want to sound like a Buddhist fanatic but all our ills lie in not understanding Buddhism while claiming to be Buddhist. For instance, I am sure you have come across Tibetans who say, "This life is not important," they think it's highly spiritual. But what the teaching is saying is don't get distracted with the *things* of this life, not life itself.

There is, he says, a lot of pretending going on in Tibetan society. 'Call it politeness, call it Tibetan protocol. Our culture is nothing but protocol and *khartas* and *momos*, although I must say it also has something quite extraordinary.'

Before I can agree with both his analysis and his conclusion he stops.

'Some of my views might have shocked you. I am sincere but maybe it is my mistake. That's OK. So you must have heard that I am a big mouth.' I try to reassure him, saying that I had heard he was honest and had an interesting perspective having been both an insider and a self-imposed outsider.

Given his attitude to many of the manifestations of faith I ask him if he has a teacher. 'His Holiness. He calls me a modern Buddhist.' I ask if that is a compliment. He laughs heartily. 'I don't know.' Then I ask the scorcher. 'As one of the people who is personally close to the Dalai Lama, do you believe he is a manifestation of the enlightened buddha, Chenrezig?'

He is taken aback. 'Oh, now that is hitting below the belt,' he says, then laughs. 'Maybe, but one with human faults and qualities. He is a form of human being therefore not perfect.' I ask if these faults could be manifested as a lesson to us instead of coming from his own side. 'Oh, you have become a Tibetan', he giggles.

'He is very skilful in teaching; there is something if you are perceptive enough. Just to be with him you learn something. He's a great teacher, a great teacher. But he is just a simple person trying to do a job as the Dalai Lama. And then of course his very position entitles him, or he is obliged to uphold the faith, and this part of the duty is something very natural for him. He is very inclined towards spirituality. He's really into it, that's his main thing. I have seen that in him since I was a child.'

Tenzin Gyatso came from a family of modest farmers, not an aristocratic lineage. By his recognition as the fourteenth Dalai Lama, his entire family were thrust into a position they would never have dreamed of, so I ask Ngari Rinpoche if his life in Tibet was insulated. 'No, in the monastery all the Rinpoches had to wear regular dresses and obey regular rules,' he says.

'So as the Dalai Lama's brother you were not naturally accorded anything else apart from expectations, not seen as part of the royal retinue or anything?'

'People treat you well; you get the best of treatment, very privileged,' he says. But I ask if that was the same way that any Tibetan aristocrat would have been treated? 'That's true, that's true more or less, nothing more I suppose. Yes.' So you weren't taken around on a palanquin? He laughs. 'No, no, no.'

I look at my watch and realise we have been talking for two hours. As I make noises about leaving Ngari Rinpoche asks me to mention in the book the Tibetans who have remained in Tibet. It is them, he says, who have made the greatest sacrifice.

He then picks up the topic of my baby again. I explain I am going home very soon. 'You know,' he says rising from the sofa, 'the biggest teacher in your life is your child. You learn so much about yourself.'

As he escorts me along the veranda he advises me not to ride scooters and to take vitamins. Then he asks me if I think it's a boy or a girl. I say, 'I don't know but it feels like a boy.' Shaking my hand, he replies, 'Whatever it is, I hope it is in good health.'

As I walk down the driveway I turn to wave goodbye. He is standing on the balcony watching me go, looking for all the world like the Dalai Lama in civilian clothes, albeit a more troubled man.

Ngari Rinpoche's inquiry about the baby reminds me that I must go to Delek hospital for my twenty-eight-week blood test. By then, the second snowfall of the week and its companion, a lack of electricity, hits us, but we have no choice. We arrive before the doctor on duty and sit shivering on the waiting benches, listening to the delighted sounds of the taxi drivers snowballing passers-by. When the doctor, a young Tibetan woman, arrives I request a full blood count as advised by my midwife in New Zealand. She is unimpressed, saying that's not what they do in India. Frankly I don't care, the standards here are so low, and simply ask her to sign the lab form. But there is another hold-up. Despite this being the main hospital in McLeod Ganj, the paper-pushers won't turn on the generator; the hospital is, in effect, dead. Although I am usually reluctant to foist my western idea of how things should work, I think a hospital can reasonably be considered an essential resource. I politely tell the office staff that electricity is necessary for a hospital to function, wondering if they can decode the meaning—that I am asking them to turn the forsaken generator on. My perspective falls on deaf ears. We wait for two hours until they decide there are enough patients to warrant putting petrol in the generator and only then will the lab take my blood. But such a queue has built up that it takes a further two hours for them to process it. I sit there shivering, increasingly furious. I resolve that having had disappointing experiences with McLeod Ganj's medical doctors, I will try traditional Tibetan medicine to see if its practitioners have any wisdom to impart to me in the countdown to the birth.

The Men Tse Khang, on TIPA Road, is one of the exiled Tibetans' most successful undertakings. On early mornings I have often wandered past and peered through the closed grating to see their doctors performing an early morning *puja*. The consultations start at nine o'clock but appointments cannot be made. Instead, customers come and take a wooden slate with a number painted on it and wait anxiously, lest anyone push in, for their turn. Because traditional Tibetan medicine is based on both an analysis of pulse and urine, the first 'stream' of the day being the most fruitful, the numbers are put out the night before so customers can take one and effectively assure themselves of an early place in the queue the next day.

Choying and I, however, arrive at 9 a.m. to a few monks and nuns waiting on white painted benches clutching their numbers with the usual disempowered aura of any Tibetans waiting for official business. The long waiting area has benches facing one another and today the sun is streaming in. One of the walls has a large *thangka* of the blue Medicine Buddha and a framed portrait of the Dalai Lama under which are seven offering bowls filled with medicinal herbs. The wooden blocks, which hang on a twisted wire, are already showing number twenty so we take it and sit down. There is only one doctor working today, her placard reading *Dr (Mrs) Choedak*. Outside her consulting room a crowd of newly arrived Tibetans are gathered, pressing their heads against her closed door, looking for the entire world as though they would like to ram it down. An old *momo-la* is at the front and the minute the door opens to emit a patient she dashes in— without a wooden block, I notice. The door immediately opens and she is ejected back out to wait with the rest of us. I am, sadly, chuffed and turn to smile smugly at Choying. He smiles back, the first time I have seen him acknowledge, however obliquely, how naughty some Tibetan grandmothers are. Usually discretion and national loyalty come first.

A woman comes and explains to the new arrivals that medicine is dispensed in the afternoon; the morning is the time for consultations. The crowd wanders away confused. Number 22 decides to leave and goes to put his block on the hanger when number 25 spies the potential and does a quick swap.

After two hours we are seen. Dr Choedak sits at her desk, flexing her stockinged feet at a bar heater underneath her desk. There is a small examination table and a blood pressure monitor on the desk and a bookshelf that holds Tibetan texts below a picture of the Dalai Lama. She is wearing a *chuba* and a *pungden* covered by a black and white chequered flannelette shirt. I explain that I am nearly seven months pregnant and would like a check-up before I go back to New Zealand where any kind of Tibetan medicine is difficult to obtain.

Throughout the western world it is illegal to buy Tibetan medicine without the prescription of a physician. This is because the medicine needs to be registered and approved for sale, which is highly unlikely in New Zealand or Australia. Despite centuries of investigation, analysis and use—medical texts which remain an important part of a physician's six-year training are hundreds of years old—proper clinical trials have not been carried out.

Dr Choedak at first explains that they don't have ultrasound and asks whether I have been getting check-ups at the hospital. I reassure her that I have. She takes my right wrist and, holding three fingers on the outside of my veins, juggles them in turn, feeling my pulse. She asks me about my appetite, then presses down and lifts up. She then takes my left wrist and repeats the same. She is feeling the pulse rate in each of my main organs in turn, trying to narrow down where there might be a block in my system.

Pressing down on my left wrist where she can detect the pulse of the kidney, she turns to Choying and says amusedly, '*Pu darpo duk.*' A happy flush passes across Choying's face. I ask him what he is smiling at. 'She says the pulse is like that of a boy.' He is pleased as this confirms a dream he had soon after I became pregnant that I would give birth to a baby son.

As Dr Choedak continues to press on my veins she tells me that I should not eat cold food or drinks, raw vegetables and to avoid potato and papaya. I remember the vast quantities Choying and I consumed in South India with a second of regret. Dr Choedak stops and tells me that according to Tibetan medicine there are certain things I can do to help me during labour. She said that because of all the pushing involved, the body's *lung*—wind or spirit energy; Tibetan medicine is about finding the equilibrium of the five elements (earth, water, fire, wind and space) and the three energies (wind, bile and phlegm) that make up our bodies—is thrown off its usual pathways and can flee through the crown of the head. She says, careful to explain that this is very much a Tibetan belief, that it is beneficial to put melted butter on the crown during birth to contain the wind inside. This prevents the onset of fatigue felt by many new mothers. She says that in the lead-up to labour it is good to massage the small of the back with oil as this is where the muscles start to separate to allow the birth canal to open. She also advises me that afterwards it is detrimental to take a cold drink, but weak black tea can be restorative. She says, softly, that Tibetan medicine is preventative and classical medications involve jewel pills that contain vegetable and animal products, metals, minerals and precious stones. There are prophylaxis such as Rinchen Dangjor and Rinchen Tsotru that promote a long healthy life, and specific remedies for the strengthening of the immune system, for cancer, altitude sickness and psychosomatic and psychiatric diseases, which Tibetans refer to as 'diseases of civilisation'.

All this advice seems more humane than our other experiences with the mainstream medical system. Choying and I head home more confident we know what to do.

We are talking about how we will celebrate *Losar* and whether we will hold a farewell for me when the idea of an engagement party creeps into our plans. 'We could make judgement party,' is actually how Choying puts it. 'Judgement?' I say. 'Yes, you know like getting married,' he says confidently. 'Are you talking about getting engaged?' I say with a smile. He says no, having only heard one syllable of this unfamiliar new word. 'We not gay.' Eventually I explain the concept of a marriage ceremony. The more we talk about it the more excited we get. Sitting on the edge of the bed we grin at each other. For a moment both of us are newly shy, like when we first met.

We consult the astrological calendar and see that the day Choying and I think might be suitable, the second day of *Losar* celebrations, is noted as being especially inauspicious to start something new. Choying calls Tenzin and they rush off to check with a lama about what day is auspicious. They return an hour later. The lama checked the astrological dates and found Monday to be beneficial, apparently many things will come to us if we create merit on this day in particular. Today is Friday.

Before I know it, a Tibetan wedding and judgement day is underway. Choying, who I thought was as relaxed about our unmarried state as I was, is bursting with happiness and goes to call his family in Tibet. From the day I met him, the inkling I had that Choying and I would be together has developed into a certainty. We were so sure of each other it seemed a low priority for us to make anything official, especially since we had such a large event looming in our lives. A part of me was also proud that, unlike so many of the couples around us, we hadn't rushed into marriage. But having made the decision I realise how good it is for the two of us to make the commitment. It feels somehow as though we are completing the circle that has bound us, and it will sustain us in our time apart.

One by one we pass our friends on the street and put the word out. I am surprised by how happy people are for us; they seem to think it has been a long time coming considering we have been living together and are about to start a family.

Kate and I decide to book out a newly opened Thai restaurant so we don't have to do too much work ourselves, especially since she has discovered she is two months pregnant. Like I was, she is both shaky and blissful.

Two hours after booking the restaurant and buying rings we are standing at a tiny bakery near the bus station, ordering 'Ultimate Love', a garish red and green Hindu-style wedding cake. Meanwhile Choying has gone to see two Tibetan friends of his who married in a lavish ceremony a month ago with a request to borrow their *chubas*, as the tailors are already working day and night on *Losar* clothes. I meet him at home and spread out on the bed are the most ornate electric blue and red brocade *chubas*. They are so rich they look like the kind of clothes Tibetan royalty would have worn a century ago. The previous bride is a lithe thing and I worry her *chuba* won't wrap about my belly, but it does, with room to move. I have a turquoise necklace and some earrings Choying gave me for Christmas; we are only missing the tall fur hats loved by Khampas for such occasions. Four hours after we made the decision, almost everything is under way. Although the wedding will be in name only—there is no time to apply to the Indian courts for a certificate—in Tibetans' eyes a public ceremony means it is all sewn up.

Before I know it I am a Tibetan bride with a beaming Khampa fiancé and a baby on the way, getting dressed for Judgement Day. When I reflect on my life in the past year I no longer feel overwhelmed by events as I did at the beginning of my pregnancy.

Instead I feel fortunate that, in a sense, the baby, not me, chose when it was to be born. Had it been left to me I would have kept debating the relationship and delaying having a child because it was my habit to think that I could control things. Somehow becoming pregnant feels like serendipity now—the catalyst for an important and entirely natural turning point in my life.

Monday morning dawns. It is raining with a ferocity I have not seen since the monsoon, leaving Choying delighted. Sighing to himself as he stares out onto the bleak waterlogged valley he tells me, 'Oh really good, very auspicious.' Lobsang arrives early and heads straight for the mirror, practising his singing while shamelessly checking himself out. By the time I get to the restaurant to help set up I am drenched and it is hailing outside. The taxis won't be able to make it down Jogibara Road to deliver guests. Still Kate, Tenzin and my Tibetan teacher, Pema, arrive and we arrange the tables then all decamp to a storage room to get dressed in our *chubas*. Pema, being a Khampa, has been assigned to dress me; she knows the subtle nuance of a sash being tied too low around the hips—according to Choying that's Amdo style and all about looking nonchalant. 'Khampas,' he says, 'wear them on their waist because they are serious and hardworking.' She soon discovers, however, that I no longer have a waist. Instead she must tie it the only place there is an indentation, just below my breasts. The voluminous electric blue brocade gown is puckered in the rear, creating a huge back bump to match my forward one. Unfortunately, instead of a looking like a beautiful bride, I have the appearance of an imperial hobbit.

By the time the wedding is to start a few bedraggled guests have made it through the door. We pose for photos and munch on fried *kabsay*, waiting for more guests. Eventually there is enough and the proceedings begin. An altar has been set up and everyone files past, placing a *kharta* in front of a picture of the Dalai Lama, then approach me and Choying, seated separately from all the other tables at the front of the room. Each person wraps a *kharta* around our necks and places presents or offering envelopes full of money in front of us. Tenzin Dorje goes first. Beaming, he steps forward with a large box of Coco Pops and places it gently before us. When everyone has finished and is seated, Kate kindly relieves us of the *kharta* burden and we begin to eat our beautifully prepared Thai dishes. By now the rain has abated and the room is full. The westerners wolf down the Thai curry and banana flower salad, the Tibetans approach the unfamiliar cuisine with trepidation.

One of the Amdo boys has wrestled control of the stereo and I realise the lyrics that are blaring out are absolutely obscene. Thankfully no one else notices and soon enough a beer bottle wrapped with a *kharta* is passed around and one by one the boys get up to sing mournful nomad songs, a tradition even at the happiest events. All have strong voices and take to the stage naturally. They sing facing Choying and me, swivelling around now and then to take in the audience. When Lobsang gets up I wonder what will come out of his mouth. He strides to the stage, throws off one arm of his jacket and then holds the beer bottle like a microphone up in the air, raising his face to the sky. His mouth opens and what comes out is '*Tsom Shay*', a mournful song from a common prisoner about taking the wrong path in life. It is singularly beautiful.

To counteract the sadness a group get up and sing at the top of their lungs a Tibetan folk song about the joys of gathering together. Some Australians, implored to sing a national song, manage to come up with 'Waltzing Matilda' once again. Eventually the bottle comes to our table. Choying and I stare at it. I silently implore Choying to do the honourable thing and sing on our behalf. He looks horrified but understands what is at stake. He rises and, shakily at first, then when everyone joins in raucously, belts out a nomad song. I am marrying the right man.

Song after song is sung until all the Tibetan ones have finished and the boys are left swooning Chinese soft pop. I decide to put on some disco and we all dance for hours until finally, at five o'clock, it is time to wrap it up. I leave the restaurant, a woman married to the man she loves.

The next day is the last day of the old year and McLeod Ganj is pulsating with the kind of energy usually seen at late-night shopping on Christmas Eve in the west. Everywhere women and men are cleaning their houses then painting the kitchen walls with flour solution and drawing images of the eight symbols of good fortune. Walking through the town most doorsteps are being covered with swastikas, the ancient sign of good luck and peace.

The roads are lined with stalls loaded down with large packets of sweets, young girls sit behind towers of *kabsay* while Indians sell *barfi* from the back of vans parked on the road. Tinsel decorations have replaced Buddhist postcards and the vegetable market is full of specially shipped in pomegranates and grapes.

The laneways are filled with people hauling great bags full of food trying to dodge people who have just emerged out of monasteries and are carefully cradling colourful *tormas* in the shape of animals that they will put on their altars. Every shop has a display of stacked wafers or cream biscuits or bags of Chinese imported sweets.

There are ten different rumours about whether the Dalai Lama will be at the Tsuglag Khang the next morning. Some say he will be at a *puja* there at 3 a.m., others say he is in retreat and won't be making an appearance. Just about everybody, though, is going to go down to the temple in the morning to check. That night the fireworks begin. Not the colourful spectacles of the west but loud bangs with no attendant visuals to brighten up the night. Choying warns me that whatever my mood the next morning, it is likely to signal the year ahead. It isn't until I notice Choying is bright and chatty the next morning that I remember to keep up my humour.

Losar dawns 'auspiciously' wet. We join the masses of people walking up and down Dalai Lama-Gi Road, heading to and from the Tsuglag Khang. We pass entire families rendered in blue, red, gold and green satin, covered by *chubas* lined with leopard-skin print and topped with heavily embroidered top hats with upturned fur peaks. Tiny children are dressed in knee-high felt boots and woollen *chubas* with tiger print linings and silk shirts. Hair is straightened and weaved; hands are covered with turquoise and coral rings; large oblong amber, turquoise and coral necklaces are heaped upon each other, and the best crystal *malas* are being fingered.

At the temple crowds of people are doing *kora* of the main *gompa*, ducking into prayer rooms to add ghee to already burning butter lamps encased in large silver candleholders. The throne where the Dalai Lama sits to give teachings is particularly revered with piles and piles of *khartas* gently placed on it and lines of people who are waiting to touch their heads to the seat. Old people are carefully pulling crumpled ten-rupees notes from the folds in their *chubas* and placing them reverently on the altar. At each stop are a bowl full of barley and *tsampa*; each person gently pinches a small heap between the fingers of their right hand and tosses it three times into the air as an offering to the Triple Gem— the Buddha, the Dharma and the *Sangha* or spiritual community.

Choying and I circle the *gompa* and come back out onto the balcony where hundreds of people are pushing the prayer wheels around and slowly circumambulating the building. A posse of old Tibetan men weave through the crowd carrying buckets ladling out sweet rice with sultanas into the palms of anyone who passes by. There is a ruckus in the corner of the balcony where a man is dispensing chai into polystyrene cups.

Choying and I make our way into the crowded main temple. Everyone has their shoes on and are in vague lines waiting to pass a large table on the stage spread with mounds of offerings; heaped Indian *barfi*, pots with newly sprouted grass, stacks of oranges and grapes and pomegranates, pyramids of peanut brittle layered with spun sugar, mounds of Ferrero Rocher chocolates and pineapple jubes and a huge stack of twisted honey-coloured *kabsay* four metres high.

A monk is taking the *khartas* flung at him and hanging them on the grate that protects a huge statue of Chenrezig. Old Tibetans are pushing with a new-found ferocity, making sure they touch all the sacred objects, elbowing in front to bow their heads below the silk-covered loose-leaf scripts encased in glass that hold the Buddha's entire teachings. They shuffle to the Dalai Lama's throne and touch their head to his seat, squirming away from the arms of the monks who try to pull them away.

We follow the winding crowds up to the Nechung Temple and repeat the same devotions. Outside more people are looking in wonder at larger-than-life *tormas* that have been erected—tall pointed garden stakes that are pressed with butter mixed with food colouring and sculptured into two dimensional stacks of rams' heads, vibrant flowers, suns, moons, lotuses and always topped with an *OM*.

Our time at the temple finished, Choying and I begin our round of visits. Everyone has hired televisions to watch the celebrations in Lhasa and turned up their heaters full blast to provide some semblance of comfort on this special day. Each house has a specially decorated altar with seven bowls usually filled with water or actual offerings to symbolise the seven libations of drinking water, washing water, flowers, incense, light, food and perfume, and topped with two crossed-over incense sticks. Each house has a table stacked with food, ready to fill any visitor. Once this is partaken of, the host leaves to cook a further meal. It is a celebration of gluttony and chang. People stay drunk for three days.

In Lhasa the show goes on with dancing and singing troupes. The Tibetans on the television are revelling in new fashions. One performer wears a *chuba* wrought in full white fur with one bare arm; another has shortened hers and paired it with furry knee-high snow boots and oversized hunks of earrings that dangle down to the navel. Now and then a crooner will emerge in traditional Khampa dress—a *chuba* over the top of wide white trousers tucked into upturned boots—with his long black hair sprayed solidly in a wave that curves at his forehead and heads straight down his back. In a culture where commenting on someone's fatness is the height of social civility, the man's lardy cheeks protrude with each line of love he sings to the assembled Chinese dignitaries and Tibetan government mandarins. My Tibetan women friends sigh at his attractiveness. Interspersed between the cultural performances is stand-up comedy of the slapstick variety which pokes fun at Tibetans' own penchant for finding short cuts to make merit or their historical disposition for ending disagreements with knives.

Having had our fill of cabaret, Choying and I head out into the rain up to Tushita Meditation Centre, which is hosting a *Losar* lunch. Everyone is greeting each other '*Tashi Delek La Losar*,' or 'Happy New Year', on the street, taking in each other's finery. Collecting people on our way, we next head to Tenzin's relatives' house at the Tibetan Children's Village. There we watch more television. Various friends drop in, join us on the bed, drink chai or have *momos* and, their duty done, quietly head off to the next place. Tibetans are a very social people but there is, I've noticed, no need for small talk. Just to visit and sit quietly is enough—

as long as you eat the host's food you've done the right thing. As night falls we all head back down to McLeod Ganj, to the sounds of trance music pulsating out from Rock'n'roll. New tourists wander around wondering why all the Tibetan shops are closed and asking where the celebrations are.

The next day we get up early and repeat the performance, trying to visit as many people as possible lest they get offended and remember our rudeness for the rest of the year. By the afternoon my mouth is ripped ragged from too much sugar and soft drinks and the baby is kicking as though I have fed it with a caffeine drip. We end up at a friend's house speechless with exhaustion, sitting around yet more piles of *kabsay* and meat. As the westerners lie against the cushions, the Tibetans put on some folk music and sing their hearts out, then roll a *kharta* around another beer bottle and pass it around, making everyone sing. Their strong resonant voices, alive with longing for Tibet, shame our half-hearted renditions of Elton John and the Bee Gees.

Lying in bed the next morning I feel like a sack of potatoes, bruised mentally and physically from the intense socialising. However, Lobsang and Choying are off in their best clothes on an important mission. The third day of *Losar* is *Sang Sol* and down on the *kora* hundreds of Tibetans have gathered in the dawn to hang new prayer flags and burn incense. By the time I emerge early in the afternoon McLeod Ganj is alive but shabby from all the celebrations. Drunk boys weave down the street in broad daylight: old couples hobble past quickly; people stop each other on the street to chastise their absent friends.

By Saturday the three-day celebrations have come to an end and the market is like a ghost town. We can almost feel the earth below us heave with the snores of people sleeping off inebriation and overindulgence.

Meanwhile the Indian and Tibetan landlords are rubbing their hands together with glee. *Losar* over, it is only twelve days to go until the Dalai Lama's teaching and the great floods of tourists and Buddhists who pour into McLeod Ganj. It is a time of mass eviction and overnight rent hikes. Lobsang, who has been renting a 3000-rupee per month room for 6 months, is asked to leave the next day. Two English girls have come looking for a room and are prepared to pay double the price. Landlords turn up, spy heaters on and demand an extra 300 rupees per month in the hope that tenants will move out.

I am to leave tomorrow and start to pull out my backpack, feeling infinitely sad I will be leaving Choying and taking our unborn child with me. I am going back to my family and my country but Choying will be left in McLeod Ganj. I feel like part of the great conspiracy of hurt that accompanies the Tibetan people. I hate to think of Choying being in McLeod Ganj waiting for his papers at the mercy of corrupt and lazy officials while missing out on the first precious months of our baby's life. Even after his IC is issued we have to apply for a visa for him to enter New Zealand. We will have to go through this torturous process apart. The weight of separation hangs over us. Every word feels poignant yet inadequate. Choying busies himself packing my things.

That night Choying and I are to leave for Delhi, where he will put me on a plane. When we leave our home, McLeod Ganj puts on a spectacular show. It hails as I lock our door and head up the stairs for the last time, followed by a bag-laden Choying, Lobsang and Tenzin Dorje. We meet our friends for one last dinner then head to the bus where everyone offers a *kharta* and says goodbye. I dislike crying, not because of its emotional intensity but because I'm one of the unfortunate who can't do it in a dignified manner with small tears streaking down my face. My entire face contorts, my throat constricts and my mouth quivers until I look really pained. Kate catches it, as do some of the other women, leaving our Tibetan husbands horrified. They are so stoic, at least in public, tending not to see partings as sad episodes but as just another of life's twists and turns. Choying and I get on the bus and chug down the hill. Once we have rounded some bends past Forsythe Ganj I look back to say goodbye to McLeod Ganj.

It sits under a deep blue rain cloud. The Tsuglag Khang looks luminous in the dusk with lights twinkling all around it. Further along the ridge the rise and fall of rooftops are slowly lighting up one by one. It occurs to me that this is the last time for years I will see this small thriving community where, despite their foibles, people are profoundly connected, where spirituality is still central to people's lives. It is also a lesson in impermanence. The McLeod Ganj that I know, the street boys, the *momo-las*, the discontented and the wise old lamas will fade into memory as my child grows.

I am leaving McLeod Ganj knowing that I cannot fulfil my goal of knowing Buddhism through its most devout people. Tibetans' dispositions are far too varied for me to come up with any conclusions. Instead I have been confronted with the full range of contradictions characteristic of all humanity. I have met saints and scammers, found an incredible fraternity amongst people while also discovering those who are willing to ruin other people's lives because of jealousy. I have found both a spiritual laziness and an intellectual agility. I have come to know people who mix superstition and rationalism in the same breath and who seem to make sense anyway.

I still don't know if Tibet truly was a land of mystical antiquity, where birds give birth to dogs, and plants turned into insects, or whether people believed in miracles solely because of the absence of science. Indeed, I have lost my appetite for drawing conclusions about the virtues of the Tibetan people in exile and am more interested in what made me want to discover their true nature in the first place. It is true what Kamtrul Rinpoche first said to me: that coming to McLeod Ganj and writing a book would be my practice of dharma, of finding the truth about me.

As the lights disappear from sight I say goodbye to that extraordinary person whom I didn't meet this time but who had a profound influence on my life in McLeod Ganj—the Dalai Lama. Through his presence and words he has proven himself— and his approach to life—to be truly worth following.

As I settle back into my seat Choying gently tells me that by the time I get on the plane Tenzin Dorje will have left India. He told Choying that he had decided to sneak back into Tibet to see the family he has been missing desperately since he escaped ten years ago. Despite Choying's fears his friend will be caught, Tenzin Dorje was determined to return.

On our last night together I tell Choying of the prayers I made one year ago in front of the Chenrezig statue at the Tsuglag Khang in the days following Kamtrul Rinpoche's divination about my future. I asked to meet a man to share my life with. I asked for someone with a good heart who would be resolute in what he understood to be important in life. I asked for someone who would be loyal and that, if our love were good, he would recognise that and treasure it. I wanted to be able to benefit this person somehow because my own life was so fortunate. I also asked that I could have a baby with this man. My prayers have been answered.

The last time I see Choying is outside the entrance to Delhi's Indira Gandhi International Airport. Only passengers are allowed inside so we must say our farewells in the full glare of the bustling public area outside the building. At the last minute I desperately want to cling to him. I don't care about all the careful decision-making; I don't think I can get on the plane. He kisses me and gently prises me away, telling me I must go home. It makes me feel worse when I realise his voice is faltering. Somehow, through a veil of tears, I turn and go inside.

Choying stands at the large window watching me go through to the checkout counter. As I reach the customs area that will take me from view, I turn around one last time. Standing there, among all the jostling people, he raises his hand and kisses his wedding ring.

EPILOGUE

At a hospital in New Zealand on a balmy night in May, a seven-pound five-ounce baby boy came into the world. While the umbilical cord was still being cut, Choying and I were on the phone laughing and crying and congratulating each other on the arrival of our son.

It was to be some time though before our little family could be reunited. Five months of daily phone calls to Delhi as Choying waited in a hotel room in Majnukatilla for his identity certificate to be issued, of begging officials in both New Zealand and India to speed up our application, of sharing the frustrations and joys of parenting through phone calls and emails, and of wondering if and when we would be together again.

Finally, in early October when our son was just over five months old, flight TG991 touched down at Auckland Airport, and out of the throng Choying emerged. To my western-adjusted eyes he looked exquisitely Tibetan, with his thick black hair, his dark skin, high cheekbones and long, fine eyes. Out on the forecourt Choying picked up our son for the first time and gave him a long-awaited cuddle, the one that he had been dreaming of for such a long time. For a moment our son's eyes slid toward me with a questioning look, wondering who this man was; but then he gave in, deciding it was all a great game, and let out a squeal of delight. Needless to say, it was fabulous to hold my husband again.

As I write this, we have been together for six weeks. Our son—a strong-minded boy who we all adore—sleeps in a cot overlooked by the Tara thangka that changed all our lives. The past month and a half has been hilarious and frustrating, and trying and heart-warming for all of us. I find myself explaining all the things I take for granted: why we pay taxes, how a welfare state looks after the disadvantaged, what the share market is and why we need road rules.

I now watch Choying as he comes to grips with being a wage earner. He likes the autonomy and responsibility of having a job but can't believe how the money seems to disappear on bills and necessities. He can't quite accept the fuss over things like safety requirements but is thrilled at getting paid for three weeks' holiday each year. Choying loves supermarkets, but is dumbfounded that everything—from clothes to furniture—seems to be manufactured in China.

Choying has had to learn quickly the art of parenting but our son now recognises his *pa-la* and Choying is treated to an especially wide grin when he walks in the door from his factory job. Just last week, when we were bathing our son, he stopped and said to me that he realised of all the lifestyles in the world monks had the easiest time. I think he was referring to the lack of complication and the freedom to contemplate while being provided for—a real luxury in the west.

We are happy together, and every Sunday Choying calls his mother to tell her that he is well and part of a loving extended family. She can't conceive of what country he is in so he has to make do by telling her he had to fly for a day and a night to get here. One day when Choying has New Zealand citizenship we plan to go to Tibet and stay with his family, as it is important to both of us that our son feels, and speaks, Tibetan and is aware of his special inheritance.

Sometimes I can hear Choying at night exclaiming '*Jo Wo Rin Po*' and I know he is on the phone to the friends left behind in McLeod Ganj, telling them about the strange idiosyncrasies of his new life. After one such phone call Choying gently woke me to share some good news. Tenzin Dorje, whom we hadn't heard from in such a long time, had finally reached the safety of Nepal, bringing with him thirteen other escapees from Tibet. He was on his way back to Sera Monastery in South India to resume his studies. Choying and I are so thankful he was looked after.

Kate and Tenzin had a baby girl soon after our son was born and are nicely settled in Melbourne, although Tenzin's dream of becoming an instant millionaire hasn't yet transpired. Instead, he has a job framing pictures. Kate tells me the atmosphere—of sitting and sawing and sanding while chatting with his co-workers and looking forward to the smoko—really suits him. Like me, Kate is in good health and loves being a mother. We often find ourselves chatting on the phone while simultaneously breastfeeding, wondering how our lives changed so fast.

Lobsang and Elizabeth are still together—despite many tears and a trial separation. They have had a rocky time establishing themselves in Sydney, with Elizabeth back working in the film industry and Lobsang adjusting to working life. He has had a couple of different jobs and now works with some other Tibetans in a factory. This Christmas we will be together in New Zealand for a few days so they can meet our son and we can catch up on our time apart.

To our eternal sadness, Tenzin Delek—a peaceful lama who only wants to benefit the world—remains incarcerated in a Chinese prison. And as I write this, the Chinese government has dealt another devastating blow to Tibetan dreams of autonomy by completing a railway line that links Lhasa to the northwestern province of Qinghai. The highest railway in the world, it will ship tens of thousands of Han Chinese into the country to swamp the Tibetan population. It will also make it easier to import Chinese culture into what was once one of the most unique and isolated countries in the world. I recently found that one of the railway's fiercest critics, Tenzin Tsundue—he of the agile mind and the faded sweatshirt and jeans—was featured in the fashion magazine *Elle* as one of the most stylish men in India.

Isn't life strange sometimes?

ACKNOWLEDGMENTS

To my friends, who have never ceased to offer their help and support, come what may. This includes Claire Harvey and Christine Hansen who both went through my first draft with a finetooth comb, kindly pointing out my penchant for cliches and strange grammar. Simon Mount, thank you.

Felicity Abbott, Tsundu Woser, Fiona Harrison, Samdup Gyatso, Helen Patrin and Kunchok Gyaltsen gave me their unwavering support and provided much of the inspiration for this story.

Tacia Strawbridge and Grant Whitehouse were endlessly generous in helping keep my life together while I was overseas, as was Wendy Tee, Harriette Cowan, Ruth Cowan, Lance Scott and Needeya Islam.

The *Australian*'s travel editor Susan Kurosawa accepted almost every story idea I pitched at her, keeping me in rupees—thank you. Fellow journalists at the *Australian*, especially Elisabeth Wynhausen and Jill Rowbothom, were always encouraging.

In McLeod Ganj, people graciously offered me their expertise, including Thupten Samphel, Jan Van Besten and Monica Joyce.

Thank you to all the people who kindly consented to be interviewed.

Staff at Allen & Unwin, including Jo Paul, Catherine Taylor and Julia Stiles, and my agent Jane Ogilvie and friend Amanda Sumner-Potts were fantastic from the beginning. Much appreciation also goes to Richard Walsh and Christine Wallace for getting the ball rolling. Amitabh Tripathi of the New Zealand Embassy in Delhi deserves my greatest appreciation.

And finally, a big thank you must go to my parents, Jackie and Thurlow Walker, who, after looking forward to a serene retirement, generously opened their home to their returned daughter and her new family. Words can't express how much I appreciate your help.

REFERENCES

Bernstorff, D & von Welck, H 2004, *Exile as Challenge: The Tibetan Diaspora*, Orient Longman, Delhi

Craig, M 1997, *Kundun: A Biography of the Family of the Dalai Lama*, Fount, London

Dalai Lama, Gyatso T 1991, *Freedom in Exile*, HarperPerennial, New York

Dalai Lama, Gyatso T 1983, *My Land and My People: Memoirs of the Dalai Lama of Tibet*, Potala Publications, New York

French, P 2003, *Tibet, Tibet*, Knopf, New York

French, P 1994, *Younghusband: The Last Great Imperial Adventurer*, HarperCollins, London

Gyatso, P 1998, *Fire Under the Snow*, The Harvill Press, London

Harrer, H 1970, *Seven Years in Tibet*, Pan Macmillan, London

Mackenzie V 1998, *Cave In the Snow*, Bloomsbury Paperback, London

Mullin, G H 2001, *The Fourteen Dalai Lamas: A Sacred Legacy of Reincarnation*, Clear Light Books, Santa Fe

Murphy, D 1969, *Tibetan Foothold*, Pan Macmillan, London

Pema, J 1998, *Tibet, My Story*, Element Books, Boston

Shakya, T 1999, *The Dragon in the Land of Snows: A History of Modern Tibet Since 1947*, Columbia University Press, New York

Snellgrove, D & Richardson H 1995, *A Cultural History of Tibet*, Shambhala Publications, Boston

Tsering, L 2003, *Tomorrow, and Other Poems*, Rupa & Co, Delhi

Tsundue, T 2003, *Kora: Stories and Poems*, Students for a Free Tibet, UK